Western Heritage

THE WESTERN LEGACIES SERIES
Published in Cooperation with the
National Cowboy & Western Heritage Museum

Western
HERITAGE

A Selection of Wrangler Award–Winning Articles

EDITED BY Paul Andrew Hutton

FOREWORD BY Charles P. Schroeder

University of Oklahoma Press : Norman

LIBRARY OF CONGRESS CATALOGING-IN-PUBLICATION DATA

Western heritage : a selection of Wrangler Award–winning articles / edited by
Paul Andrew Hutton ; foreword by Charles P. Schroeder.
    p. cm. — (Western legacies series ; 9)
  ISBN 978-0-8061-4206-7 (pbk. : alk. paper)
  1. West (U.S.)—Civilization. 2. West (U.S.)—History, Local—19th century.
3. Frontier and pioneer life—West (U.S.) 4. Indians of North America—West
(U.S.)—History—19th century. 5. West (U.S.)—In literature. I. Hutton, Paul
Andrew, 1949–
  F591.W4637 2011
  978'.02—dc22
                                        2010045773

Western Heritage: A Selection of Wrangler Award–Winning Articles is Volume 9
in the Western Legacies Series.

The paper in this book meets the guidelines for permanence and durability of
the Committee on Production Guidelines for Book Longevity of the Council on
Library Resources, Inc. ∞

Copyright © 2011 by the University of Oklahoma Press, Norman, Publishing
Division of the University. Manufactured in the U.S.A.

To Brian W. Dippie

Contents

Maps

Foreword

Everyone loves a good story. Beyond entertaining us, stories often define how we think about people and places. Much like the image of the open seas, that of the American West is swathed in colorful stories of its intriguing past and provides fodder for fertile imaginations. Whether true or fanciful, stories of the West characterize a culture that interests a worldwide audience.

The mission of the National Cowboy & Western Heritage Museum is to "preserve and interpret the evolving history and cultures of the American West." So we cannot be satisfied with just holding and displaying great collections of art, material culture, and archival material. We must always be seeking ways to convey the deep and complex heritage of the West in an understandable and even inspirational way. Writers featured in this anthology surely hit that mark.

The Museum appreciates talented writers who tell stories of the West skillfully and compellingly. Each year for a half century, we have bestowed the coveted Wrangler Awards on those who excel in that regard. This collection represents the fine work of several Wrangler Award winners.

Very often, stories of western folks describe a culture strongly bound by "the Code of the West." Things such as courage, respect, self-discipline, loyalty, integrity, and defense of principle show up regularly in storylines rooted in western life, whether fact or fiction. The renewed thirst for those principles apparent in contemporary society heightens our enthusiasm for sharing these accounts.

The West was indeed a crucible. Going back to the dime

novels and cinema matinees, as well as the factual accounts of memorable pioneers, the West has always been presented as a place where character was tested and exposed for its strengths and weaknesses. The tests came from the elements, the isolation, the clashes between cultures seeking to dominate the territory, and the conflicts between those with good and evil intentions. Few locales around the world have spawned so many tales centered on the variations in human nature, ranging from the heroic to the repugnant.

Works selected for this book allow us to see people of the West in three intersecting circles: "The Native West," "Cowboys and Cattle Country," and "Battles Lost and Won" (involving various conflicting parties). These articles tell of clashes over race, religion, ethnicity, and commerce, as well as challenges to the establishment of law and order. Through these conflicts, the West discovered its legendary spirit.

We are proud of our association with the University of Oklahoma Press, the outgrowth of which has been our Western Legacies Series, including this anthology. The quality of the Press's work is highly regarded throughout the publishing world, and always a pleasing complement to the material we provide. Likewise, Paul Andrew Hutton, the editor of this publication and one of its distinguished contributors, is tops in his field. Paul has been recognized by the Western Writers of America and has received his own Wrangler Awards from the National Cowboy & Western Heritage Museum for the excellence of his writings on the West.

We hope the reader enjoys these articles, and comes away with a renewed sense of the passions that defined the American West. They continue to provide its alluring mystique.

Charles P. Schroeder
President
National Cowboy & Western Heritage Museum

Introduction

Throughout the month of June 1965, a wagon train slowly made its way from the Texas Panhandle toward Oklahoma City, Oklahoma. On Saturday morning, June 26, 1965, the wagonmaster lined his rigs into a grand parade of Indian dance groups, school marching bands, western riding clubs, and an array of local politicians and dignitaries. They all fell in behind film star and western icon John Wayne in a colorful cavalcade that wound its way through the crowded streets of Oklahoma City to the site of the new National Cowboy Hall of Fame & Western Heritage Center atop Persimmon Hill.

The "Hall," as it came to be known affectionately, was the brainchild of Chester A. Reynolds, who dreamed of a world-class museum that would celebrate the exploits of the American cowboy and preserve the colorful history of the American West. Reynolds initiated an ambitious $6 million fund-raising campaign, and construction began on a thirty-seven-acre site in June 1959. Reynolds died in 1958 and this inhibited fund-raising, but others took up his cause, and the museum finally opened its doors to the public on Sunday, June 27, 1965. Over twelve thousand visitors jammed the facility in its first week of operation.

A handful of executive directors—Dean Krakel, B. Byron Price, Kenneth W. Townsend, and Charles P. Schroeder—have guided the Hall through good times and bad. They all held steadfastly to Chester Reynolds's vision, and with their talented curators and staffs, built the magnificent National Cowboy & Western Heritage Museum (a new name adopted in 2000 to better reflect the museum's mission) into the 200,000-square-foot, internationally known museum that stands today as a monument to our rich western heritage.

A series of galleries explores the story of the American frontier experience, interpreting the history while also celebrating the vital role played by the arts—literature, film, sculpture, and painting—in developing the modern image of the American West. The Donald and Elizabeth Dickinson Research Center at the museum has evolved into a major resource for the study of the content of the various galleries while also establishing its reputation as an important library for western history scholars. The museum's colorful official publication, *Persimmon Hill*, carries the story of the West to an even larger national audience.

A major component of the growth of the museum's reputation has been the Western Heritage Awards, first given in 1960, five years before the museum even opened. Over the past fifty years, this black-tie gala has evolved into the western version of the Oscars, celebrating outstanding achievements in literature, film, television, and song. For the first ten years, the award ceremony was held at Oklahoma City's historic Skirvin Hotel before moving to the museum's Founders Hall in 1970. Joel McCrea, the film star and western rancher who had long played a pivotal role in the museum's development, hosted the first ceremony at the museum. (In recognition of his vital board leadership, a magnificent statue of him based on his performance in the 1944 epic film *Buffalo Bill* now dominates Persimmon Hill—a perfect realization of the blending of the historical and cinematic West so richly celebrated by the museum and the Western Heritage Awards.) Celebrities from John Wayne (1960) to Tom Selleck (2010) have added glamour and star power to the ceremonies, assisting enormously with the fund-raising so essential to the achievement of the museum's mission.

The Western Heritage Award, or Wrangler, as it is called, is a bronze statue designed by artist John Free. Over the years, categories for the award have evolved to reflect changes in the world of western literature, television, film, and music. Winners are reflective of the talented, dynamic, and creative individuals who have shaped our collective vision of America's West over the past half century. A look at the initial winners in each category is instructive, from John Wayne for his epic film *The Alamo* (1960) to W. Bruce Bell for his article in *Kiwanis Magazine* on the Chisholm Trail (1961) to Alvin Josephy for his magnificent *American Heritage Book of Indians* (1962) to James Horan's 1961 novel, *The Shadow Catchers,* to Michael Martin Murphey's songs from his 1992 *Cowboy Christmas* album. The awards have served as a "who's who" of the preservation and creative expression of our western heritage and lifestyle.

This book presents a selection of Wrangler Award winners in the magazine article category. To pick a representative group from such a stellar list of Wrangler winners was no easy task. A complete list of Wrangler winners is appended to this volume. Selection was based on content, style, and length; the essays chosen reflect the widely varied approaches used in interpreting our frontier history. Our authors include distinguished academic historians, famous investigative reporters, two grand literary figures of both fiction and nonfiction, and even a celebrated Hollywood screenwriter. All of these authors bring a deft hand to historical analysis combined with a graceful literary style. This combination has always been the primary criterion for winning a Western Heritage Award.

These tales of the West are meant to entertain as well as to inform. The western story is rich in color and romance, but the selected articles do not shrink from the darker side of that story. With triumph for some came tragedy for others. From their sacrifice and their struggle—be they buffalo hunter or horse trader, patriot chief of the Sioux or Apache, cowboys riding for the brand in South Texas or on the Powder River, legendary Texas

Rangers or doomed wagon train emigrants, army regulars dying under the guidon of the Seventh Cavalry or volunteer Rough Riders—they represent some of the major episodes in creating a nation. The American West—a fluid meeting ground of stark contrast, of cruel tragedy and glorious triumph, of rugged individualism and democratic cooperation, of environmental determinism and bold adaptation—has become recognizable to all as the wellspring of American exceptionalism. The West defines America for Europe as well, with the cowboy emerging as the greatest of American icons around the world. Just as these themes have become central to our national consciousness and our international image, so too have they found expression in the galleries of the National Cowboy & Western Heritage Museum and in the collection of award-winning essays you now hold in your hands. This collection thus celebrates both the West and the fiftieth anniversary of the National Cowboy & Western Heritage Museum's prestigious Wrangler Award.

PART ONE
The Native West

When the Buffalo Roamed

DAN FLORES

Late in the nineteenth century, a member of the Piegan band of the Blackfeet—a people so synonymous with the northern plains that their identity is merged with the very topography of the country along the Rocky Mountain front of Montana—told writer George Bird Grinnell a story of the beginning of the Great Change. By historical standards, Wolf Calf's story was not an old one, for it came from memories extending back only 175 years at the most. Perhaps that was why it seemed so fresh, so resonant.

Many years before, a group of Piegans had been camped on the Belly River near a very ancient and important place the Blackfeet called Smash the Heads. As they and other people of the northern plains had done for at least seven thousand years, they were driving buffalo over the cliff—a practice that gave the place its name—and they had just made a successful drive. Many buffalo were already dead, killed by their fall from the rimrock (this trap for buffalo was called a *pishkun*); those only crippled were being slaughtered along the foot of the cliff.

Then something very strange happened. From over the backbone of the mountains to the west, apparitions appeared,

Originally published in *Wild West* (April 1997): 46–52, 84–86.
Reprinted by permission of Weider History Group.

moving rapidly down the foothills like birds in flight but trailed by clouds of dust. As details came into focus, some must have thought the apparitions were elk, but as they drew closer, they took on a human look, too. As Wolf Calf told the story, "All the Piegans were astonished and wondered what this could be. None of them had ever seen anything like it, and they were afraid. They thought it was something mysterious. The chief of the Piegans called out to his people, 'This is something very strange. I have heard of wonderful things that have happened from the earliest times until now, but I never heard of anything like this. This thing must have come from above [i.e., from the sun], or else it must have come out of the hill [i.e., from the earth].' . . . As it drew nearer, they could see that it was a man coming, and that he was on some strange animal."

The apparitions were Kutenai Indians from west of the Rockies—a man and his wife and children—and they were all mounted on horses, the first the Piegans had ever seen. They rode up with a matter-of-fact request: they had come to trade for meat from the drive. But of course the Piegans had eyes only for the strange, snorting, dancing animals. What of them? They were new animals from the country to the south, the Kutenai told the Piegans, but there were already plenty at hand beyond the mountains. The leader of the Piegan band that day was named Dog, Wolf Calf recalled, but the impression those mounted Kutenais made on him must have been powerful, because eventually he became known as Many Horses, one of the first Blackfeet headmen to lead his people into horse owning, riding, and buffalo hunting. This had happened only six generations before Wolf Calf's time, when he and other Blackfeet witnessed that whole world crashing down around them.

From any perspective, that world of sunlight and grass, bison, Indians, and horses seems cometlike, building to the historical brilliance that made it provocative and compelling, then winking out, apparently forever. Being born Native American was and is no prerequisite for mourning the loss of a world like that, a wilder life in nature. A similar sentiment fueled Henry David Thoreau's musings about the difference between the New England described by the Pilgrim Fathers and those same woods in the 1850s. Compared to the America the Pilgrims had found, Thoreau reflected, his experience in the forests was analogous to listening to a symphony played without most of the instruments. As he concluded in his famous essay "To Know an Entire Heaven and an Entire Earth," previous generations had acted like demigods and impoverished his world by, in effect, plucking from the heavens many of the brightest stars.

Looking out my windows at the American West from a Rocky Mountain valley in Montana on the eve of the twenty-first century, I can understand both Wolf Calf's pathos and Thoreau's lament. Outside my door is a classic western landscape that, at first glance, seems very little different from what the Salish and Kutenai buffalo hunters saw. The mountain valley and its sagebrush foothills haven't gone anywhere, and neither—in places—have the fescues and bluebunch wheatgrasses, the cottonwood and aspen groves along the river. But, in fact, I inhabit an impoverished nature. The bison herds that the early British traders described as frequenting this valley two centuries ago are entirely gone from here now.

In your mind's eye, picture the process of the erasure: Sizable herds right to the end, but more and more sporadic in their appearances until the last time or two it was almost magical and they seemed like echoes of a past world rather than tangible beasts of the present. Soon the foothills no longer smelled of them, and their tracks no longer appeared along the creeks. Two winters' worth of snow melted their droppings into the soil, and magpies eventually hauled off all the lingering tufts of hair still snagged on the sagebrush. Their wallows gradually filled in with vegetation and disappeared. Their trails, which through the centuries had significantly shaped the very topography of the West, were appropriated by cattle, were deepened into gullies, or drifted in and became unrecognizable. Today, the only physical evidence that the great animals were ever here is the infrequent skull or scapula eroding out of a stream bank. These bones and accounts, such as those of the Snake River brigades and the oral memories of the Native peoples, are about all that remain to testify that a century ago the Bitterroot Valley was at the western edge of a great buffalo continent.

Yet only an instant of time ago—and for more than ten thousand years before that—it was. Most people interested in the West probably assume that they have a working knowledge of the cause of this impoverishment. Certainly, the ultimate fate of the great bison herds that once were found throughout America is one of the most famous and stunning stories of modern environmental history. But unless you have kept up with recent work in bison paleontology, Native American studies, and environmental history, chances are, your knowledge is incomplete. In fact, what we thought we knew about how the buffalo country worked and what happened to the buffalo in the nineteenth century almost certainly is a gross historical simplification. Understanding the larger bison story requires a perspective on history that bites off chunks of time a lot larger than the ones we are used to dealing with, plus an acknowledgment of forces that traditional history has often been too myopic to see.

In an evolutionary sense, bison, like humans, are not true natives of North America. The giant species of bison from which our modern animal springs were Eurasian in origin and migrated to North America across the Bering land bridge when ocean levels dropped during the Pleistocene glaciation pulses of the past 2 million years. *Bison latifrons,* the great long-horned bison, adapted to the northern tundra but then declined when a gradually drying climate opened up the great western grasslands. By establishing an ecological beachhead—the beginnings of an eventual Great Bison Belt on the plains east of the American Rockies—another large, imposing herd of bison called *Bison antiquus* became an important, although by no means dominant, feature on the grasslands of 12,000–14,000 years ago. In a kind of American mirror of Africa, it shared those grasslands with elephants (mammoths), herds of equine grazers (several species of horses), antelopes (pronghorns), and dromedaries (one-humped camels). This American Serengeti had all the expected predators, too, including lions (on the Great Plains, both *Panthera*, the steppe lion, and sabertoothed cats) and canid pack predators (dire wolves and coyotes). Giant terratorns (Pleistocene birds of prey, now extinct) played the role of vultures.

Isolated from Eurasia since the breakup of the hypothetical supercontinent of Pangaea, the Americas had long lacked one significant species that Africa had—humans. By 11,200 years ago, if not before, that was no longer true; the people we know as the Clovis big-game hunters had followed the Asian herds into America.

America's large animals, having long evolved in the absence of human predators, seem to have been in no way prepared for that arrival. Within two thousand years of the first evidence of humans in North America, a great wave of large faunal extinctions swept the Americas, and the resemblance to Africa ended forever. Exactly why almost three-quarters of all the species of large mammals and birds (all the mammoths, mastodons, horses, camels, and sloths and all their predators and scavengers, along with the giant species of bison) became extinct in the North America of a hundred centuries ago is a hotly debated topic in paleontological circles. A warming, drying climate seems certain to have played a role, but the majority of respected biologists of recent years are convinced that the arrival of the Clovis people was critical. Possessed of a remarkable flint-tool kit, the Clovis hunters were big-game specialists whose concentration on female and juvenile animals probably pushed animals with long gestation periods and few defenses against human predation into a barrage of remarkable extinctions.

That great extinction crash of a hundred centuries ago set in motion ecological ripples that enormously affected later times. Nature's response to the stress of new hunting pressure and all those now-vacated grazing niches was to evolve a dwarfed species of bison (our modern animal) that possessed a much faster reproductive turnover time and other traits more adaptive to the new conditions. *Bison bison* appeared as a fully emerged species about five thousand years ago, and in the absence of any real grazing competition, it performed an ecologically normal but historically remarkable adaptation—it filled the vacuum, occupied the niches of dozens of now-dead competitors, and multiplied into the enormous herds that boggled the imagination of all those who saw them. In an evolutionary sense, the modern bison can best be understood, perhaps, as a "weed species" that proliferated in America as a result of a major ecological disturbance. Subsequent Indian societies that hunted bison thus were exploiting a situation that has had few parallels in world history, one that played out in American history as it did because of a very singular sequence of events.

That bison were still here when the Europeans arrived is fairly reasonable evidence that the 8,500-year-old ecology that emerged in the West after the Pleistocene extinctions ended had achieved some kind of dynamic equilibrium. Bison populations, grassland carrying capacity, and predation—including Indian populations and level of hunting stress—over more than eighty centuries evidently had settled into a sustainable balance. Certainly, there were ebbs and flows, periods when droughts on the plains pushed bison and Indians both eastward and westward to wetter areas and at least once shifted the entire Bison Belt north of present-day Colorado for many hundreds of years. Dozens of cultures came and went on the plains over the thousands of years between the Pleistocene extinctions and the arrival of Europeans, and some existed during periods when bison were regionally quite scarce. But the herds' adaptation to the Great Plains grasslands was such a remarkable fit that, even with relatively wasteful methods of harvest such as the buffalo jump, Indians never pressured them out of existence. In fact, the northern Great Plains were occupied by a succession of bison-hunting cultures that lived substantially the same life for more than eight thousand years, the longest sustained human lifeway in the history of the continent. A continuum such as this provoked a natural and entirely appropriate awe. Indians who were interviewed at the end of it all spoke of the spiritual significance that the bison plains held for their people. In many Indian religions, bison joined the winds and the stars as supernatural in origin. According to the mythologies of dozens of different plains tribes, including groups as disparate as the Kiowas, the Crows, the Comanches, and the Blackfeet, bison had their origins in the earth itself. Every spring, immense herds of new animals swarmed out of tribally significant places such as the Sweetgrass Hills or the canyons of the Llano Estacado, to overspread the plains once again. Like the stars, like the winds, bison could never be made to disappear. Of course, we know now that bison were almost entirely erased from the West in the nineteenth century. The question is how.

Among the things we know today that we didn't know when the near-extinction of the bison became a national scandal is the influence of weather on bison. About the time when Europeans were first becoming a presence in the Americas, a major climatic cycle set in across the Northern Hemisphere: the Little Ice Age.

For western buffalo hunters, it was a boon, setting the stage for the efflorescence that followed. The moister climate that began around AD 1500 benefited the western grasslands and gave rise to so many bison that they spilled over into the Rocky Mountain valleys and followed the meadows created by Indian burning practices all the way to the Atlantic shore.

Judged on grassland carrying capacity for modern livestock, the Great Plains never could have supported the numbers of bison—45–100 million—that our histories have often cited. Extrapolations from agricultural census data for the turn of the twentieth century indicate that, depending on weather cycles, the Great Plains had a carrying capacity for bison that fluctuated around 25 million, with perhaps another 5 million animals east and west of the plains. With the climate in a long, wet phase after 1500 or so, the bison herds were at peak size.

But changes resulting from contact between Europeans and Indians quickly began to shrink both the range and the number of bison. Although those changes had their origins in the arrival of Europeans, they were very much implemented by the Native peoples. Horses, which the Europeans reintroduced to the Americas after an absence of more than eight thousand years, became widely distributed through intertribal trade after the Pueblo Indians successfully revolted against Spanish rule in New Mexico in 1680. Feral horses reestablished themselves in their old grazing niche in a fraction of ecological time—by 1800, an estimated 2 million horses roamed wild below the Arkansas River. Indian horse herds, reckoned as a new form of wealth, were growing rapidly as well and drew many new groups to the source of supply on the plains, where the lives of Indians in the West would be altered dramatically. In addition, because horses and bison have an 80 percent dietary overlap, horses competed directly with the bison for grass. When almost three dozen Native tribes abandoned old ways of life and flocked to

the plains as mounted hunters, pressures on the bison populations increased considerably.

After 1700, a new ecological situation emerged. New arrivals
to the plains, such as the Comanches and Sioux, were not only
drawn to the core of the bison's range but also were engaging in
wars over hunting territories with Apaches, Crows, Blackfeet,
and others. At the same time, starting with the Taos trade fairs
around 1705 and in the horticultural villages on the Missouri and
Red rivers in the 1730s, the bison country was being opened to
trade with Europeans. Trade between Indian groups in the West
was old, but it had been conducted primarily as symbiotic gift
exchanges. But Euro-American agents of the big fur companies
began to probe the plains with the goods of the industrial world,
and their interests lay in acquiring large quantities of products
for the global market—furs, mostly, but also horses to supply the
advancing American frontier.

This was a new kind of trade, and fairly early on, the buffalo-
hunting tribes learned that there was yet another item the traders
found desirable. Indian women worked long hours to produce
beautifully tanned bison robes, different from later dried hides
in that they were softly pliable and finished with the hair on.
Traded at places such as Fort Benton, Fort Union, and the
Hudson's Bay posts in Canada, the robes created an insatiable
demand in the East and Europe. They became a major hunting
motive for Plains Indians at least as early as the 1820s, when
nearly 100,000 robes were shipped to New Orleans every year.
By the 1840s, another 85,000–100,000 Indian-produced bison
robes were arriving in St. Louis annually. The Hudson's Bay
trade eventually nearly rivaled the trade farther south, reaching
an annual peak of 73,278 robes between 1841 and 1845.

Built by evolution to be prolific, bison needed to be thinned
by almost 20 percent each year to keep them in equilibrium
with the grasslands. On the wilderness plains, natural mortality

took care of about half that 20 percent. Wolf predation seems to have accounted for another third. The remainder of the bison that needed to be thinned each year (about one-sixth of the 20 percent) had long been harvested for subsistence—food and all those domestic uses that Indians had for buffalo—by the tribes of the West. Recent, careful work indicates that these subsistence requirements were roughly six and one-half bison per person every year. But the robe trade quickly began to transform and skew the old ecology. The Southern Cheyennes, for example, by the 1840s were taking almost three times the number of animals they needed for subsistence alone to fill their agreements with traders at Bent's Fort, in what is now Colorado. Unlike wolves, which killed calves and sick and injured animals, Indian market-hunters focused on prime, breeding-age cows. It was the robe trade, more than anything else, that led observers including George Catlin, John Audubon, and Father Pierre-Jean De Smet to worry publicly before midcentury that bison were doomed. The persistent wooing of the traders, who resorted to offering alcohol when other goods were less desirable, and the steady movement of the tribes into market hunting later led agents for the Blackfeet to try to have the robe trade legally stopped.

Among the tribes that kept particularly good records (on painted buffalo robes) for this period, the Kiowas are justifiably famous. The Kiowa calendars tell us that beginning in the 1840s, buffalo were becoming increasingly scarce. In fact, the symbol for "many bison" appears only once in Kiowa history after 1841. We also know that in the 1840s, many Indian agents reported starvation conditions on the plains, that the Assiniboines were eating their horses, and that in Texas the Comanches were likewise reduced to consuming twenty thousand horses out of their own herds.

In the long history of the bison, what was happening was an unprecedented confluence of historical forces. Not only were bison having to compete with horses for grass and water, but they were further reduced by the onset of a drought that began in 1846 and is now known to have been the start of the endgame for the Little Ice Age. By then, the bison's ancient drought refuges on either side of the plains had been filled with homesteaders. Another threat arrived with the domestic cattle brought by American emigrants on the overland trails. Biologists still aren't sure how and when the bison herds contracted the exotic diseases brucellosis, tuberculosis, and anthrax, but they agree that virtually all the animals that survived in the 1890s were infected. Bizarre and inexplicable bison die-ups were occurring on the plains as early as the 1860s, though. Finally, hunting stress on the herds had escalated dramatically by 1840, after the U.S. government had relocated some 87,000 Eastern Indians to the border of the plains during removal.

What all this newly considered information means is that historians are now convinced that these factors had produced a stressed and seriously depleted bison herd in the West fully a quarter century before the white hide hunters arrived to deliver the coup de grâce in the 1860s and '70s. By the time Sitting Bull and George Armstrong Custer were circling one another in 1876, the white hide hunt was already over in Kansas and Texas; as best we can figure, it had produced no more than 5 million hides and perhaps as few as 3.5 million. Farther north, in the spring of 1879, Canadian Indians and Métis found no bison at all, and they surged into Montana, where a final hunt—this time in competition with white hide hunters—took place north of the Yellowstone. This last great western herd probably numbered about 1.5 million animals, from which the white hide hunters harvested some 320,000 hides. As for Wolf Calf's people, the Blackfeet had their last great hunts in 1881, taking some 100,000–150,000 animals. Two years later, in the spring of 1883, Blackfeet hunters searched everywhere for bison but killed only 6.

The animals that had for so many centuries appeared as constant as the stars and the winds were somehow gone, apparently returned to the earth.

In 1881, former Texas Indians exiled to Oklahoma held a sun dance on the North Fork of the Red River. Kiowa shaman Buffalo-Coming-Out had danced and made magic, calling on the herds once more to erupt out of the Llano Estacado canyons and overspread the plains. A century later, those of us—and I am one—who long for a return of wild bison to the West have faith that Buffalo-Coming-Out's magic worked. It's just taking awhile.

2

Tragedy at Red Cloud Agency
The Surrender, Confinement, and Death of Crazy Horse

JEFFREY V. PEARSON

The sun was high and bright in the morning sky on May 6, 1877, when Crazy Horse dismounted his pony on the plains of western Nebraska a few miles outside Red Cloud Agency.[1] For a moment, he stood there, surveying his people—the Oglala subchiefs and warriors dressed in the regalia of their warrior societies and singing their death songs, and behind them, the women and children and the elderly still making their way over the rolling sand hills. In front of Crazy Horse stood a modest assembly of military officers and enlisted Indian scouts from the agency. The contrast must have struck a chord in the war leader: behind him was his past, a defeated people on the brink of starvation; before him was his future, a people united in arms with their former enemy.

As the sun climbed toward its zenith, all eyes focused on Crazy Horse. To the uninformed spectator, it was a simple gesture: Crazy Horse loosened the knots in his horse's tail. For those familiar with Lakota customs, however, this action carried great significance. By untying the knots, Crazy Horse was giving notice that he was no longer at war.[2] The warrior who had fought "Three Stars" Crook at the Rosebud, "Long Hair" Custer

Originally published in *Montana The Magazine of Western History* 55, no. 2 (Summer 2005): 14–27. Reprinted by permission of *Montana The Magazine of Western History*.

at the Little Bighorn, and "Bear Coat" Miles at Wolf Mountains would fight no more.

Having declared his intentions, Crazy Horse walked to within a few yards of the officer the Lakotas called White Hat, Lieutenant Philo Clark, and sat down. Extending his left hand—according to Lakota custom, the heart is on the left side—Crazy Horse said, "I want to shake hands while seated, because that means our peace shall last." Clark seated himself across from Crazy Horse and took the proffered hand. With the ceremonies opened, the Oglala agency head chief Red Cloud, who had led the surrendering band to its rendezvous, joined the two men. The subchiefs of Crazy Horse's band and the other officer with Clark advanced and shook hands. After exchanging pleasantries, He Dog, one of Crazy Horse's subchiefs and an Oglala Shirt Wearer, said, "I have come to make peace to those I like and have confidence in." He removed his warbonnet and placed it on Clark's head. Next, he removed his shirt and placed it in the young lieutenant's lap. Finally, as a demonstration of trust, he placed his pipe in Clark's outstretched hands. Crazy Horse, looking to Clark as if to explain He Dog's gesture, stated, "I have given all I have to Red Cloud."[3]

Thus began the last chapter in the extraordinary life of Crazy Horse. Since coming of age in the late 1850s, he had fought to preserve the Lakotas' way of life. By spring 1877, however, he had accepted the painful realization that his people could no longer resist the invasion of their homeland.[4] Although surrender at Red Cloud Agency would mean the loss of their freedom, it would also mean food, clothing, and blankets from the agency's stores and rest without fear of attacking soldiers. Peace, however, would remain as elusive for Crazy Horse as it had been throughout his war-filled life.

With the surrender of Crazy Horse, American officials turned their attention to resolving the final issues required to establish peace on the northern plains. Nine months earlier, on August 15, 1876, Congress had passed legislation requiring the Lakotas to relinquish their claims to all land outside the Great Sioux Reservation. For the Oglalas at Red Cloud Agency and their Brulé neighbors at Spotted Tail Agency, the legislation meant that they would have to relocate their agencies to Dakota Territory. The question of where Crazy Horse and the nontreaty Lakotas—known at the two agencies as the "Northern Indians"—would have their agency had yet to be answered.[5]

For Crazy Horse, this issue was a critical one. Earlier in the spring, as the Oglalas debated their future, Brulé chief Spotted Tail had arrived at their village near the forks of the Powder River with new surrender terms from General George Crook: the Oglalas would be required to give up their arms and horses, but they would be permitted to select the site of their own agency.[6] This news immediately shifted the balance of power within Crazy Horse's council. Previously, a faction supporting the continuation of the war had held sway. Crook's promise convinced the council—and Crazy Horse—to accept surrender.[7]

When Red Cloud arrived in Crazy Horse's camp in April, he offered the same terms as Spotted Tail but with a proviso: Crazy Horse would have to accompany a delegation of agency leaders going to Washington, D.C., to personally make peace with the president. As an incentive to surrender, Crook offered to allow Crazy Horse and his band to go on a buffalo hunt once all "hostile" bands had arrived at the agencies. But by extending these promises, military authorities unwittingly planted the seeds of controversy. In the coming summer, Red Cloud Agency, which already possessed a well-deserved reputation for political intrigue, would become a hotbed of rumors and accusations swirling around Crazy Horse. Although military authorities mostly ignored such gossip, by August Crazy Horse's actions had made it difficult for military officials to maintain their faith in him.[8]

Summer, however, dawned with a promise of peace. On May 16, 1877, the *Cheyenne Daily Leader* reported that the "sullen, discontented look worn by the hostiles when they first came in, is fast disappearing now." It seemed, as a newspaper correspondent recorded, that Crazy Horse wished only to "get along straight and well." Military officials kept Crazy Horse's camp "filled [with] soldiers, in uniform or without," to report "each and every act taking place under their observation," but the Oglala leader readily cooperated with all requests. He received visitors with a hearty handshake and extended every courtesy. At the behest of Lieutenant Clark, he became an Indian scout, participating in parades with other uniformed Indians and executing drills at Camp Robinson, the military post a mile and a half from Red Cloud Agency. As interpreter William Garnett later stated, "We got along with Crazy Horse pretty good, just the same as any friendly Indian."9

Most important of all, Crazy Horse appeared willing to join the delegation to Washington. William Garnett thought Crazy Horse looked forward to the journey. When Crazy Horse learned that Garnett had accompanied an 1875 delegation, he asked many questions. Pleased by the interpreter's answers, Crazy Horse, according to Garnett, announced that he "would begin to learn the use of the fork at the table. He said he had got to do it."10

Furthermore, Crazy Horse knew where he wanted his new agency: a broad flat close to the headwaters of Beaver Creek near modern-day Gillette, Wyoming, a place with plenty of water and abundant game. Crazy Horse told Clark of this place on the day he surrendered, and on May 25, he repeated the description at an assembly of Indian leaders. According to He Dog, the placement of the proposed agency was important because it was "in the middle of Sioux territory, while the location by Fort Robinson was on the edge of it."11

The wheels of bureaucracy moved too slowly for Crazy Horse. By the end of July, the military's inaction on the matter of the agency and the promised buffalo hunt had made him restive. Complicating matters, as the summer progressed, Crazy Horse began to hear frightening rumors about the Washington trip. He Dog later said that Spotted Crow and "others" warned Crazy Horse it was merely a "decoy" to lure him away to a place where "they will have you in their power." Black Elk and his son-in-law John Provost also influenced Crazy Horse, telling him that the whites would not allow him to return from Washington. According to Provost, Crazy Horse "would be imprisoned; perhaps placed upon an island in the sea and indefinitely confined, or otherwise disposed of so that he would never return." Others simply told Crazy Horse that he would be killed.[12]

As the weeks passed, Crazy Horse became increasingly belligerent. At the end of July, he refused to draw his scout pay or endorse ration receipts and began making threatening "demonstrations." Red Cloud Agency's recently appointed Indian agent, James Irwin, complained to Commissioner of Indian Affairs John Q. Smith in early August that Crazy Horse "has all the time been silent, sullen, lordly and dictatorial." More ominous to officials were Crazy Horse's threats to leave the agency and lead his people to Beaver Creek.[13]

Displeasure with Crazy Horse was not limited to the new agent alone. As time passed, Red Cloud and other agency leaders grew jealous of him. Since Crazy Horse's arrival, these leaders had watched his celebrity increase. Reporters and military officers regularly visited his lodge and reportedly gave their host gifts and money. In addition, Camp Robinson officers seemed willing to grant Crazy Horse special privileges to secure his participation in the Washington delegation. Yet the most threatening aspect of Crazy Horse's presence, at least to Red Cloud, was his popularity with the warrior-aged men. Agency chiefs still maintained their authority through the support of the young men, and Crazy Horse's resistance to agency rules made him increasingly popular with them.[14]

As tensions mounted, a rumor spread that Crook planned to depose Red Cloud as the agency head chief and replace him with the younger Crazy Horse. Although the rumor's validity was dubious at best, Red Cloud could not ignore it. The previous year Crook had carried out a similar plan, appointing Spotted Tail as head chief when he suspected Red Cloud of diverting supplies to the hostile camps. At the time, Crook's actions meant little because Spotted Tail, a Brulé, would never be recognized by the Red Cloud Agency Oglalas. Crazy Horse, however, was an Oglala. By midsummer, he had come to represent a clear threat to the established Lakota power base.[15]

The agency rift remained concealed until July 26, when the Indian leadership assembled to hear General Crook's announcement that the much-anticipated buffalo hunt could begin as soon as arrangements could be made. Special Agent Benjamin Shapp, visiting the agency to check Irwin's progress, reported that the news met with quiet approval from all present. When officials suggested a celebratory feast at Crazy Horse's camp, however, "Red Cloud and one or two others left the room." Unsure of what the departures meant, Shapp paid them no mind. Later that night, around ten o'clock, Indians representing Red Cloud's people and "several other bands" appeared at the agent's door and told him that such a feast might appear as an attempt to appease the Oglala. Yet their greatest concerns focused on what they thought would happen if Crazy Horse participated in the hunt. According to Shapp, Red Cloud and the other agency leaders regarded Crazy Horse as an "unreconstructed Indian" who "seemed to be chafing under restraint; and in their opinion was only waiting for a favorable opportunity to leave the agency and never return." They warned Irwin that Crazy Horse was "tricky and unfaithful to others, and very selfish as to the personal interests of his own tribe." If allowed to leave the agency, "at least 240 braves, well armed and equipped, would go on the warpath and cause the government infinite trouble and disaster. . . . The ammunition that would be furnished to them would be used for the destruction of the whites, against which they seemed to entertain the utmost animosity."[16]

Irwin agreed with Red Cloud's representatives, concluding that the events of summer "had disturbed and excited the Indians" to a dangerous degree. The agent did not believe that Crazy Horse possessed sufficient influence to lead a large-scale breakout, but he and Shapp felt that the commissioner of Indian affairs should "take such *prompt* and *effective measures to secure* the protection of the government as the emergency might require." The agent, however, felt helpless to act because the army still maintained faith in Crazy Horse. When Irwin reported Crazy Horse's behavior to Camp Robinson commander Lieutenant Colonel Luther P. Bradley, Bradley dismissed the accusations as hardly credible.[17]

Like Irwin, Special Agent Shapp believed that the hunt would provide Crazy Horse the opportunity to execute some plot. At the time he penned his dispatch, Shapp had learned that one of the agency Indians had traded four ponies for "an ordinary rifle." He felt the implications of this transaction were ominous: "They seemed determined to secure arms at all hazards, and will exchange property of great value for them."[18]

Moreover, the claims voiced by Red Cloud's representatives were not groundless. Earlier that summer, perhaps in late June, Crazy Horse's people had hosted a sun dance. When preparations reached the stage at which a mock battle was to be held, the Lakotas chose to reenact the battle of the Little Bighorn, with Crazy Horse's people representing the warriors who defeated Custer and agency Lakotas representing Custer's troopers. "When the fight was on," Garnett reported, "instead of striking the Custer party lightly as was usual, some of the others struck their opponents with clubs and war clubs [with] hard blows." In a short time, the mock battle spiraled into brutal beatings. This unexpected violence forced Garnett and the other "Custer soldiers" to pull their pistols and fire warning shots at Crazy Horse's warriors.[19]

The turmoil that seemed to surround Crazy Horse enveloped his own band. By mid-August, several of his subchiefs had relocated to the camps of agency band leaders to ensure that their families received their biweekly rations. Notable among these were He Dog and Little Big Man, who supposedly left following a dispute over a woman. According to Chips, Crazy Horse's medicine man, Crazy Horse and Little Big Man "got in a fight over it [a woman] and were never friends again." He Dog, however, claimed that there was no animosity between himself and Crazy Horse. A Bad Face Oglala, He Dog elected to move near Red Cloud's village to be closer to relatives. When he asked Crazy Horse if they would become enemies as a result, Crazy Horse responded, laughing, "I am no white man. . . . Camp where you please."[20]

Although Crazy Horse's intentions will forever remain a mystery, it was clear that he felt increasingly frustrated. His suspicions grew until he openly refused to make the trip to Washington unless the army established the Beaver Creek agency beforehand. On one occasion, Crazy Horse angrily proclaimed, "I am not going there. I wanted to go, but you have changed my mind. Still deep in my heart I hold that place on Beaver Creek where I want my agency. You have my horses and my guns. I have only my tent and my will. You got me to come here and you can keep me here by force if you choose, but you cannot make me go anywhere that I refuse to go."[21]

Military officials appeared willing to dismiss Crazy Horse's bad behavior and even organized a small hunt for him. Forced to return earlier than expected, however, Crazy Horse grew angry. He thought the hunt had been cut short in order to resume talks over the Washington trip. When asked by Clark to join the delegation on August 18, Crazy Horse again refused. Instead, he listed the names of men he wanted to go in his place and demanded that Red Cloud, Spotted Tail, and the other established agency chiefs be tossed aside. Given his spy network, Clark no doubt knew of the rumor mongering, and he seemed to appreciate the Oglala's apprehension, but he was equally aware of the rumors circulating about Crazy Horse's intentions to revolt. Crazy Horse's defiance tested Clark's patience. "Force is the only thing that will work out a good condition in this man's mind," Clark concluded. "Kindness he only attributes to weakness." That Crazy Horse's headmen were "dead set against him in this matter" only made matters worse, in the lieutenant's opinion.[22]

On the last day of August, the agency Indian leadership declared their opposition to Crazy Horse with an ominous promise. At a council with Agent Irwin, American Horse, speaking on behalf of Red Cloud, Little Wound, Young Man Afraid of His Horses, No Flesh, and Yellow Bear, stated that over eight hundred Oglala men had gathered during the previous twelve days to discuss their views. They were united in their desire to see their new agency established on the White River and to begin learning the agricultural skills that would free them from having "the Great Father always feeding us." When Irwin inquired about Crazy Horse, though, the agent received a disheartening reply: American Horse told Irwin that they had repeatedly worked "to quiet Crazy Horse and bring him into a better state of feeling," but he had refused to attend the council and there was nothing more they could do with him. The only assurance they could provide was that "they would see that Crazy Horse did nothing about the agency that would hurt [Irwin's] feelings."[23]

Time was working against the maintenance of peace at the Red Cloud Agency. In the midst of attempts to settle the question of the membership of the Washington delegation, General Crook ordered officials at Camp Robinson and Camp Sheridan, the military post attached to Spotted Tail Agency, to seek Indian scouts to help stop the Nez Perce exodus then taking place in the Pacific Northwest. Clark, who commanded the posts' scout units, immediately directed several of his mixed-blood scouts to recruit warriors for the mission, and on August 30 he summoned Crazy Horse and the other leaders to a council at Camp Robinson.[24] Through interpreters Frank Grouard and Louis Bordeaux, Clark asked the men if they would be willing to fight against the Nez Perces. All refused. Clark began to pressure them, and the meeting quickly broke down.[25] Finally, and for unknown reasons, the Indian leaders changed their minds. Crazy Horse said that he had promised not to make war anymore and was surprised that "the same men who had desired to have this pledge from him were urging him to go killing men again," but he would take his warriors north and "camp beside the soldiers and fight with them until all the Nez Perces were killed."[26]

Grouard, however, mistranslated Crazy Horse's statement as "we will go north and fight until not a white man is left." Bordeaux attempted to correct Grouard's mistake, but curiously, Clark, renowned for his signing ability, at first accepted the translation. Infuriated, Bordeaux stormed out. The Indians could clearly see Clark's discomfiture. Amid shouts and accusations, the meeting degenerated into chaos. Clark ordered Grouard to find William Garnett.[27]

Unaware of the events, Garnett when he arrived saw only that Crazy Horse "was not right." Clark immediately directed the interpreter to ask the Oglala leader if he would lead some of his warriors against the Nez Perces. Crazy Horse replied with a stern "No," and the exchange turned into a shouting match.

Crazy Horse told Clark that he was "soft" and did not know how to fight, then informed the officer that he and his people would resume the hunt that had been cut short. Clark replied that Crazy Horse could not take his people anywhere without permission. The only way he and his men could leave was as army scouts. Crazy Horse turned to the other Indian leaders, saying, "These people can't fight; what do they want to go out there for; let's go home; this is enough of this."[28]

The next morning Crazy Horse returned to Camp Robinson with a large group of warriors. Speaking to Clark through Garnett, Crazy Horse told the lieutenant that he would fight the Nez Perces, but he would not wait for the soldiers. He and his entire village were leaving immediately on a hunt. Once the soldiers caught up, they would join the campaign.[29] Clark repeated that Crazy Horse and his people could not leave the agency. By this time, it was apparent that the Oglala war leader was searching for an excuse to take flight.

Word of the acrimonious exchange greatly alarmed Camp Robinson's commanding officer. The following morning Bradley sent a telegram to Fort Laramie to requisition additional cavalry troops. These troops would bring Camp Robinson's garrison to over seven hundred soldiers and three hundred enlisted Indian scouts. The commanding officer also wired General Crook at Fort Laramie, stating that "Crazy Horse is behaving badly. . . . Every Influence that kindness could suggest has been exhausted on him." Finally, Bradley telegrammed General Philip Sheridan, commander of the Division of the Missouri, to warn him of the potential emergency. Sheridan directed Crook to proceed immediately to Red Cloud Agency.[30]

Crook arrived at Camp Robinson on September 2 and received a briefing on events, including Grouard's translation error. Hoping that his presence might soothe Crazy Horse's disposition, Crook directed Clark to organize a council for the following

day. Clark sent word to the various Indian leaders to gather on
White Clay Creek. As a special measure to secure Crazy Horse's
presence, the lieutenant enlisted He Dog's aid to host a small
feast to honor Crazy Horse and issued gifts and two oxen. Crazy
Horse declined the invitation, sending an apology to He Dog:
"Tell my friend that I thank him and am grateful, but some
people over there have said too much. I don't want to talk to them
any more, no good would come of it." Aware of the rumors, He
Dog pleaded with his friend: "These people have been telling you
not to go to Washington because the army will kill you. It's not
true, whatever they tell you. Don't believe them. They lie. They are
jealous of you. I'm telling you that you should go with me." He
Dog believed that his friend had refused to attend the feast because two visitors, Colonel Bradley and D. H. Russell, had made
him feel uncomfortable earlier that day by shaking hands and
speaking with Crazy Horse in a way that made him suspicious.
They had given him a knife as a gift—an omen of trouble, Crazy
Horse believed.[31]

The next morning Garnett and a scout named Baptiste "Bat"
Pourier were waiting to escort the general to the council when an
Indian scout named Woman's Dress, Red Cloud's nephew, ventured by and inquired what the two were doing. Upon hearing
their reply, Woman's Dress "unraveled a tale which brought the
most important affair of the day to a sudden pause." Woman's
Dress warned, "Don't you go there with General Crook[.] When
you hold this council at White Clay, Crazy Horse is going t[o]
come in there with sixty Indians, and catch General Crook by
the hand, like he is going to shake hands, and he is going to
hold on to him, and those sixty Indians are going to kill Crook
and whoever he has with him." Stunned, Garnett demanded to
know where Woman's Dress learned of this plot. Woman's Dress
said that two other Indian scouts, Little Wolf and Lone Bear,
had listened outside of Crazy Horse's lodge the previous night.

Amazed, Garnett and Pourier brought Woman's Dress before the general to repeat the tale. Pourier, related to Woman's Dress by marriage, attested to the scout's trustworthiness and warned the general not to attend the council. The general seemed torn until Clark spoke up. "General," the lieutenant said, "it is no use to go. . . . We have lost a man just like you, and we lost General Custer. . . . There is no use for you to start in there when you have no protection."[32]

Clark ordered Garnett to bring several of Red Cloud's loyal followers to Camp Robinson for a private council. When Garnett arrived at the council, he noticed that "Crazy Horse was not there and none of his followers were there either." Approximately an hour later, Red Cloud, Little Wound, Red Dog, Young Man Afraid of His Horses, No Flesh, Yellow Bear, High Wolf, Slow Bull, Black Bear, American Horse, Three Bears, Blue Horse, and No Water learned of the assassination plot from Clark, news that was as surprising to them as it had been to Crook. Crook informed the men that Crazy Horse must be arrested. They agreed and "proposed killing him; but General Crook told them it must not be done as it would be murder."[33]

Denied permission to kill Crazy Horse outright, Red Cloud and the others agreed that they would select their two best warriors and that once assured of support, these men would make the arrest. Crook instructed that Crazy Horse not be attacked without an attempt to secure his peaceful surrender. If, however, Crazy Horse resisted, the agency leaders had permission to take him by force, killing him if necessary. The general directed Clark to issue arms and ammunition back at the post. Before the Indians left, Clark added that he would give the man who arrested Crazy Horse a bounty of two hundred dollars and a fine racing pony.[34] Believing himself no longer needed, Crook turned control of the operation over to his trusted lieutenant and departed Fort Robinson.

The operation's secrecy did not last long. As Garnett awaited Red Cloud's return, an orderly directed the interpreter to go immediately to Bradley's office. Standing in the room with Bradley were Agent James Irwin, interpreter Leon Pallady, and He Dog, who had learned of the plan after being summoned to Red Cloud's camp. Garnett immediately judged that He Dog must have divulged the plan. "It was too bad to go after a man of the standing of Crazy Horse in this manner in the night-time without his knowing anything about it," chided Bradley after Garnett confirmed He Dog's story. "They ought to do this in broad daylight." To Bradley, the plan seemed to be little more than vigilante justice, and he felt certain that it could only end with the death of Crazy Horse and many of his followers. Moreover, Bradley was aware that another group of Northern Indians was on its way to Camp Sheridan to surrender. Should the arrest go wrong, it could signal a rebirth of the war. Staring at Garnett, the post commander announced, "The life of Crazy Horse is just as dear to him as my life is to me," then he turned and dismissed Garnett and summoned Clark. Crazy Horse's arrest would be postponed until dawn. Furthermore, eight companies of cavalry would accompany Red Cloud and his warriors in hopes of surrounding the village by a force so overwhelming that Crazy Horse would recognize the folly of resisting.[35]

On the morning of September 4, 1877, nearly one thousand cavalry troopers, Indian scouts, and warriors streamed toward Crazy Horse's village six miles beyond Camp Robinson. Upon striking the White River, the force turned to the northeast and divided into two columns, the Indian scouts under Clark taking the north bank and Lieutenant Colonel J. W. Mason's Third Cavalry, complete with field artillery and Gatling guns, on the south bank. There was great excitement in the ranks as scouts raced ahead. When the columns came within a mile of the village, however, a scout returned with the news that Crazy Horse's villagers were scattering and that he had already fled. He could be seen in the distance riding toward Spotted Tail Agency.

Clark immediately dispatched a group of Indian scouts to pursue Crazy Horse, reminding them of the bounty before they left.[36] The balance of the strike force returned to Camp Robinson, where it would be needed to preserve order once the frightened Lakotas were brought in.

Clark's scouts managed to keep the war chief in sight but never got within rifle range. Throughout the afternoon, Crazy Horse and his companions used the terrain to their advantage, preserving their lead and their horses' strength. The chase ended shortly before 4:00 P.M when Crazy Horse entered the Miniconjou village of Touch the Clouds a few miles outside Spotted Tail Agency. Realizing that his warriors were outmatched, No Flesh led the scouts to nearby Camp Sheridan to notify officials of Crazy Horse's presence.[37]

Crazy Horse's arrival set off a whirlwind of activities. In the Miniconjou village, women disassembled their lodges and prepared for flight as the nearly three hundred warriors readied themselves for battle. Years later Jesse M. Lee, a young lieutenant serving as the Brulé agent, remembered the anger of the Indians who heard Crazy Horse's tale: "The bold warrior, the venerated hero of the braves, who had often led them to victory, was in the midst of his devoted friends, and to them he was a hunted victim of rank injustice and cruel persecution." For the officers of the tiny garrison stationed at Camp Sheridan, the situation was akin to sitting on a powder keg. In the face of the danger, Lee ironically recalled the words that Clark had said to him on his last trip to Camp Robinson: "Lee, don't you worry. . . . Crazy Horse can't make a move without my knowing it, and I can have him whenever I want him."[38]

In hopes of calming the Miniconjous, Camp Sheridan commanding officer Major Daniel Burke dispatched a few

Brulé scouts along with Joe Merival and Charlie Tackett to the Miniconjou village. Merival and Tackett soon returned and informed Burke that Crazy Horse, Touch the Clouds, and several hundred warriors had prevented the village from taking flight and were on their way to the post. The scouts warned the officers to exercise every precaution to avoid a clash. Touch the Clouds's warriors were eager to vent their anger.

Major Burke planned a demonstration of his own to show that the military meant no harm and to convince Crazy Horse to return to Camp Sheridan. Together with Lee, Louis Bordeaux, and post surgeon Dr. Egon A. Koerper, Burke would go out to meet the warriors. Otherwise, thought Lee, Crazy Horse would lead Touch the Clouds's people from the agency and inaugurate another Indian war with a "merciless slaughter of unsuspecting and innocent whites."[39]

A mile and a half from the post, the officers met the advancing war party. Crazy Horse and Touch the Clouds rode beside one another in the center of what one officer described as a "line of battle." On the opposite side of Crazy Horse and to his rear, Lee observed White Thunder and Black Crow, Brulé scouts. The scouts held their weapons at the ready in order to shoot Crazy Horse if he attempted to do harm. To everyone's surprise, when the two parties came together, Crazy Horse rode ahead and extended his hand in friendship.

With the men from Camp Sheridan in tow, Touch the Clouds and his warriors escorted Crazy Horse to the post, their mutual fears of both groups eased. Still, the news of Crazy Horse's presence prompted others to take action. As Crazy Horse's party entered the parade ground, a force of Brulés loyal to Spotted Tail stood their ground as the Miniconjous rode to within eight feet of them. Defiantly, Spotted Tail, Crazy Horse's maternal uncle and agency head chief, took up a position immediately in front of Crazy Horse and began berating his nephew: "We never have trouble here! The sky is clear; the air is still and free from dust. You have come here and you must listen to me and my people! *I am chief here!* We keep the peace! We, the Brulés, do this! They obey ME! Every Indian who comes *here*, must obey me! You say you want to come to this Agency to live peaceably. If you stay here, you must listen to me! That is all!"[40] Without responding, Crazy Horse dismounted and accompanied the officers into the adjutant's office. Spotted Tail, Touch the Clouds, and a few other headmen followed. Inside, Crazy Horse remained silent as the officers questioned him. The strain of the day's events clearly showed on his face. Lee remembered years later that "Crazy Horse seemed to realize his helplessness" and appeared like a "frightened, trembling wild animal brought to bay, hoping for confidence one moment and fearing treachery the next." Finally, Crazy Horse explained that he left Red Cloud Agency after seeing soldiers approaching his camp. He came to Spotted Tail Agency to protect his sick wife, but now he wanted to stay and he wanted his people transferred to Spotted Tail as well. Here, Crazy Horse thought, his people could live in peace.[41]

Surprised by this announcement, Burke and Lee explained to Crazy Horse that he would have to return to Camp Robinson and speak with officials there first. Although they pledged to use their influence to arrange his transfer, the two officers could promise him only that no harm would come to him if he returned. Lieutenant Lee added that he would personally escort Crazy Horse to Camp Robinson and arrange a meeting with Bradley. These assurances seemed to lighten the Oglala's spirits. Turning to Bordeaux, Crazy Horse told the interpreter that he had sworn to the Great Spirit before he surrendered that he would never make war again; he wanted only to live in peace. He told Clark that he did not want to fight the Nez Perces. These words had angered Clark, and Crazy Horse did not understand.[42] As a demonstration of his faith, Burke allowed the fugitive to spend the night at Touch the Clouds's camp. The towering Miniconjou leader gave his word that he would have his guest back at the post the following morning.

Crazy Horse arrived at Camp Sheridan at the appointed hour on September 5, 1877, but the night had robbed him of his confidence. When he met Burke and Lee, Crazy Horse told them that he no longer wished to return to his agency because he was "afraid something would happen." The two officers replied that it would be impossible to settle matters if Crazy Horse did not return and repeated their promise that no harm would come to him. Crazy Horse at last relented when the officers agreed to his terms: neither Lee nor Crazy Horse would carry any weapons; the lieutenant would make arrangements for Crazy Horse to explain to Bradley why he fled; and Lee would confirm that he and Spotted Tail agreed to host Crazy Horse if the transfer was approved.[43]

After making a brief stop at Touch the Clouds's camp to eat breakfast and find a saddle for Crazy Horse, the journey began. Lee permitted Crazy Horse to ride with seven unnamed friends "in the interests of fair play" and to impress on Crazy Horse that he was returning to Red Cloud Agency of his own free will. Touch the Clouds and High Bear rode with Lee in his ambulance. Small groups of scouts sent by Major Burke rode alongside.[44]

When the party was within fifteen miles of Camp Robinson, Lee and Clark exchanged messages.[45] Clark stated that Colonel Bradley had left orders for the prisoner to be taken directly to the adjutant's office. From Clark's curt response, Lee deduced that his prisoner would not be allowed an audience with Bradley. Worse yet, Lee suspected that Crazy Horse would be placed under arrest and confined to the guardhouse, because the adjutant's office lay adjacent to the jail. This realization, combined with the lieutenant's expectation that Crazy Horse's return might lead to violence, prompted Lee to direct the Indian scouts to form ranks on each side of his ambulance with their weapons drawn. Crazy Horse and his seven friends already rode behind the wagon.

Surrounded by his escort, Crazy Horse entered Camp Robinson and proceeded directly to the adjutant's office. Bradley watched the procession from his porch. Mounted soldiers stood beside the barracks on the eastern edge of the parade field with their rifles in hand, and anxious warriors loyal to Red Cloud filled the open area at the center of the parade ground. Outside the adjutant's office, He Dog waited with a concerned look on his face. As Crazy Horse neared the adjutant's office, he understood the reason for He Dog's concern: Red Cloud and another large group of armed warriors packed the space between the barracks as well as the area on the other side of the adjutant's office.[46] Crazy Horse remained on his horse as a group of soldiers exited the adjutant's office and approached Lee. The Oglala did not understand the words that passed between the soldiers, but an interpreter told him that Lee was pleading with the officer of the day to allow Crazy Horse a council with Colonel Bradley. The officer, Captain James Kennington, refused to grant Lee's request.

Realizing that Kennington intended to follow his orders to the letter, Lee turned to Crazy Horse and told him to go into the adjutant's office to await his return. When the Oglala leader climbed out of his saddle, Little Big Man took hold of Crazy Horse's arm. Little Big Man informed his prisoner that he and the other Red Cloud Indians would do whatever "White Hat" Clark directed.[47] Lee stood outside the office to ensure that Little Big Man, Touch the Clouds, and the other Spotted Tail Indians passed into the building unmolested. He then requested that Crazy Horse not be disturbed until Bradley could be consulted. Lee hoped that once the officer learned of Crazy Horse's reasons for fleeing and his cooperation at Camp Sheridan, a meeting could take place.

The lieutenant crossed the parade ground to Bradley's home, where he made his request to the lieutenant colonel in "earnest and respectful language." "T'was no use," Bradley regretfully announced; "it was too late to talk." According to Lee, "the orders were peremptory; . . . he [Bradley] could not change them; General Crook himself could not change them, nothing further need be said, and the sooner Crazy Horse was turned over, the better." The following morning, Crazy Horse would be taken to Wyoming Territory to be put on a train for the military prison at Dry Tortugas, Florida.[48]

Disheartened, Lee returned to the adjutant's office and called for Bordeaux. The lieutenant told his interpreter that there was nothing more they could do. The lieutenant attempted to hide the harsh reality of the situation by informing Crazy Horse and his friends that it was too late in the day to meet with Bradley. A meeting would be held the following morning. Crazy Horse, Touch the Clouds, High Bear, and the others seemed satisfied. In fact, the Oglala chieftain seemed delighted by the delay. Lee, not knowing how Crazy Horse would react to being locked in the guardhouse, repeated his promise that "not a hair on his head" would be harmed if Crazy Horse did as he was told; Lee directed him to accompany Kennington. Crazy Horse rose to his feet, walked across the small room, and took Kennington by the hand. As the two stepped toward the door, Little Big Man walked up behind Crazy Horse and grabbed his left hand. All seemed well. Still, the lieutenant staunched his feeling of desperation only with difficulty and, sensing the same from his interpreter, warned Bordeaux "not to get into any trouble on account of Crazy Horse."[49]

As Lee led Crazy Horse through the doorway, he noticed that Red Cloud and a growing crowd had positioned themselves immediately in front of the office door with their weapons held menacingly; their attitude suggested that they were there to cut off any escape attempt. Two other Lakotas wearing soldier's uniforms fell into formation ahead of and behind Crazy Horse as the group approached the building next door, where a soldier carrying a bayonet-capped rifle paced back and forth in front of the entrance.

As the party walked to the guardhouse, Little Big Man repeated his intent to remain with Crazy Horse wherever he went. At the entryway, Kennington released Crazy Horse's hand, opened the door, and walked into the poorly lit room. Without losing sight of the officer, Crazy Horse stepped inside, followed by Little Big Man and the two uniformed Indians. When the door closed, it revealed a cell with the prisoners inside shackled to heavy metal balls resting on the wooden floor. Stunned, Crazy Horse shouted, "I won't go in there. It is the place where prisoners are kept."[50]

In desperation, Crazy Horse jerked his hand away from Little Big Man and lunged at his guards, knocking them into the wall. Startled by the commotion, Kennington turned and saw his prisoner reach into his belt and pull out a well-concealed trader's knife. Swinging the blade wildly, Crazy Horse leapt for the passageway outside, while Little Big Man recovered his arm and attempted to pull him back into the center of the room. Seeing the two men grappling, Kennington drew his sword and advanced, but Crazy Horse sliced through the air with his knife, halting Kennington in his tracks. As the struggle continued, the two Lakota guards flung the door open and dashed out, shouting, "It's [the] guardhouse! It's [the] guardhouse!"[51] Within seconds, Crazy Horse exited the building, dragging Little Big Man, who still held onto his left arm.

The disturbance attracted the attention of everyone on the parade ground. When he saw the struggling figure emerging from the door, Red Cloud shouted for his warriors to "shoot to kill." Crazy Horse continued jerking and twisting violently, screaming, "Let me go! Let me go! Let me go!" When Little Big Man did not release his grip, Crazy Horse spun around and brought his blade down. Reflexively, Little Big Man let go and grabbed his bleeding arm.[52]

Crazy Horse's freedom was brief. Immediately, a sentinel standing guard near the jail confronted him. As the fleeing warrior lunged at the soldier, he was tackled by Swift Bear, Black Crow, and Fast Thunder, three of the Brulé scouts who had ridden with him from Camp Sheridan. At that moment, Kennington emerged from the guardhouse and shouted at a stunned private standing a few feet away, "Stab the son-of-a-bitch!" The private, William Gentles, inched toward the struggling figures and lowered his bayonet. When the Oglala's twisting form revealed itself, the private thrust his bayonet into Crazy Horse's back. Crazy Horse screamed with agony, "They have stabbed me." Gentles impaled him again.[53]

The crowd stood in stunned silence as Crazy Horse fell to the ground. Then, as if by unheard command, it separated itself into Red Cloud and Crazy Horse supporters. When Swift Bear realized that Crazy Horse was hurt, he told the injured man, "We told you to behave yourself." Hesitatingly, He Dog made his way through the crowd. Seeing his friend gasping for breath, He Dog cut the blanket he was wearing in half and covered Crazy Horse. Moments later another Lakota, Closed Cloud, spread over Crazy Horse the blanket he had dropped during his escape attempt. Regaining consciousness for a moment, Crazy Horse grabbed Closed Cloud by the hair and shouted, "You all coaxed me over here and then you left me!"[54]

Dr. Valentine McGillycuddy, Camp Robinson's contract surgeon, made his way through the crowd to examine Crazy Horse. After kneeling to inspect the wounds, he announced to

Kennington that Crazy Horse was dying. Kennington shouted orders to four guards: "Pick that Indian up and carry him to the guardroom!" As the guards stepped forward, warriors sprang forward and leveled the rifles they had concealed. Bat Pourier, standing beside Kennington, frantically shouted, "For God's sakes, Captain—stop, or we are all dead men!" In the pause that followed, the interpreter assured the warriors that the soldiers were trying to take Crazy Horse to a place where he could be given medical aid.[55]

Fearing what might happen if Kennington attempted to forcibly remove Crazy Horse to the guardhouse, McGillycuddy sprinted across the parade ground to Bradley's quarters to suggest an alternative. Bradley, perhaps not realizing the seriousness of the situation, initially directed that Crazy Horse be placed in the post prison. McGillycuddy protested that with "ten thousand Indians around us, . . . it would mean death to a good many people. . . . I suggested that we effect a compromise and put Crazy Horse in the Adjutant's office, where I could care for him until he died."[56] Bradley reluctantly agreed.

It was nearly 5:00 P.M when Crazy Horse's warriors carried him into the adjutant's office. At his request, they placed him on the wooden floor, and McGillycuddy immediately administered morphine to ease the dying man's pain. Soon Crazy Horse's father, Worm, arrived, and he, Touch the Clouds, McGillycuddy, and Pourier stayed with Crazy Horse. Eased by the morphine, Crazy Horse remained unconscious most of the evening. Dr. McGillycuddy later remembered that Worm bitterly denounced those whom he felt were responsible for his son's condition: "We were not agency Indians; we preferred the buffalo to the white man's beef, but the Gray Fox [Crook] kept sending his messengers to us in the north saying come in, come in." "Well," Worm reflected, "we came in, and now they have killed my boy." The old man's anger grew as the evening passed. "Red Cloud was jealous of my boy. He was afraid the Gray Fox would make him head chief; our enemies here at the agency were trying to force us away, so probably we would have been driven soon back to our hunting grounds in the north." Outside, Crazy Horse's people fired their rifles in displays of anger; Red Cloud's people moved a short distance to Clark's residence.[57]

Around 10:00 P.M, Crazy Horse seemed to rally. He spoke briefly with his father, saying, "Father, it is no use to depend upon me; I am going to die." He also asked to speak with Jesse Lee. To the officer, Crazy Horse said, "My friend, I do not blame you for this. Had I listened to you, this trouble would not have happened to me. No white man is to blame for this; I don't blame any white man; but I blame the Indians." Shortly thereafter Crazy Horse fell unconscious again. Bordeaux, who remained in the adjutant's office as Lee's interpreter, observed that the war chief's body was "growing cold." Crazy Horse never regained consciousness.[58]

An hour and a half later, at approximately 11:40 P.M., Crazy Horse stopped breathing. When the scout broke the news to Worm, the old man cried, "My son is dead without revenging himself!" Touch the Clouds crossed the room. Kneeling down, the Miniconjou covered his friend with a blanket, put his hands on Crazy Horse's chest, and announced, "It is good; he has looked for death, and it has come."[59]

Angeline Johnson, the wife of an officer posted at Camp Robinson, wrote to her sister of Crazy Horse's death: "They feared an attempt would be made to rescue him in the night, so the soldiers were kept ready for instant action all night, pickets out in every direction and everything warlike but no attempt was made." Mrs. Johnson also informed her sister that none of the agency Indians had approved of Crazy Horse's actions during the previous summer. With the exception of his own band, they all thought that the war chief had brought his death upon himself.[60]

Most military officials shared this opinion. Both Bradley and

Clark reported that Red Cloud Agency was again quiet within a few days of Crazy Horse's death. Bradley said that the leading men of Crazy Horse's band were on friendly terms, adding that they were "satisfied that his death [was] the resolve of his own folly." Clark was more direct. On September 9, he wrote to General Crook, "Crazy Horse's death is considered by most of the Indians as a right good thing for all concerned."[61]

Since Crazy Horse's death, controversy has surrounded the notion that he was the victim of a conspiracy fomented by the agency leadership. In considering that possibility, William Garnett should be allowed a final comment. Some ten years after Crazy Horse's death, Little Wolf asked Garnett, "What do you suppose caused Crazy Horse to be killed?" "You killed Crazy Horse!" Garnett quickly replied. When asked what he meant, Garnett told Little Wolf of the assassination plot that he had supposedly overheard outside of Crazy Horse's lodge and then repeated to Woman's Dress. Little Wolf denied ever having heard of the plot.[62]

Not long thereafter, happenstance brought Garnett together with Woman's Dress. When Garnett repeated Little Wolf's comments, Woman's Dress called Garnett a liar and denied "that he had ever stated that Little Wolf and Lone Bear had acted such parts." Woman's Dress insisted "it was he himself who overheard the secret utterances of Crazy Horse—that he had sat behind him, enveloped in his blanket when the chief was unbosoming himself, supposedly in secret." While Garnett was engaged in this argument, Bat Pourier was listening to Woman's Dress outside his line of sight. Pourier, recognizing the substantial differences in the stories, shouted, "Woman's Dress, you are a liar!"[63]

Years later, Judge Ricker tallied the sad results of the plot fabricated by Woman's Dress: "Woman's Dress had caused to be spread among the officers of the post a falsehood against

Crazy Horse, imputing him to the basest criminal purpose. It precipitated the immediate marshalling of force against him—his flight; his pursuit; his voluntary return; the deception to get him into the guard house and close the doors on him before he should suspect he was a prisoner—his discovery of the betrayal at the last instant; his revolt; the fierce struggle; his mortal wound; his death."[64]

Notes

1. *New York Herald*, May 7, 1877, in *The Surrender and Death of Crazy Horse: A Source Book about a Tragic Episode in Lakota History*, ed. Richard G. Hardorff (Spokane, Wash.: Arthur H. Clark, 1998), 212. The first Red Cloud Agency was located near modern-day Crawford, Nebraska. The agency was established in 1873 and abandoned in 1878.

2. H. L. Scott and James McLaughlin, "Report of William Garnett, Interpreter to General H. L. Scott and James McLaughlin," p. 1, copy in Burgess Memorial Collection, Holland Library, Washington State University, Pullman.

3. *New York Herald*, May 7, 1877; Scott and McLaughlin, "Report of William Garnett," 1; *Chicago Times*, May 7, 1877, in Hardorff, *Surrender and Death*, 201.

4. Thomas R. Buecker and R. Eli Paul, eds., *The Crazy Horse Surrender Ledger* (Lincoln: Nebraska State Historical Society, 1994), 14. According to a May 8, 1877, entry, Crazy Horse's band consisted of 899 men, women, and children. They surrendered 2,200 ponies, horses, and mules along with forty-six breechloaders, thirty-five muzzleloaders, and thirty-three revolvers.

5. George E. Hyde, *Red Cloud's Folk: A History of the Oglala Sioux Indians* (Norman: University of Oklahoma Press, 1937), 280; James C. Olson, *Red Cloud and the Sioux Problem* (Lincoln: University of Nebraska Press, 1965), 224–25; Robert W. Larson, *Red Cloud: Warrior-Statesman*

of the Lakota Sioux (Norman: University of Oklahoma Press, 1997), 205–206; Thomas R. Buecker, *Fort Robinson and the American West, 1874–1899* (Lincoln: Nebraska State Historical Society, 1998), 88.

6. Oliver Knight, "War or Peace: The Anxious Wait for Crazy Horse," *Nebraska History* 54 (Winter 1973): 526, 531. See also Harry H. Anderson, "Indian Peace-Talkers and the Conclusion of the Sioux War of 1876," *Nebraska History* 44 (December 1963): 244. There is some debate about what General Crook actually promised the Lakotas. The August 15, 1876, legislation that seized the Black Hills also required that the Red Cloud and Spotted Tail agencies be moved to the banks of the Missouri River. Knowing that the Lakotas did not want to relocate to the Missouri, Crook became a proponent for establishing the new agencies in their former hunting ranges south of the Yellowstone River. It is doubtful that Crook guaranteed that Crazy Horse would be allowed to select the site for his own agency.

7. Both He Dog and Red Feather told Eleanor Hinman that they thought they were only visiting Red Cloud Agency. See Paul D. Riley, "Oglala Sources on the Life of Crazy Horse: Interviews Given to Eleanor H. Hinman," *Nebraska History* 57 (Spring 1976): 19–20, 25–26. In another interview, He Dog indicated that he knew Crazy Horse was surrendering. See Robert A. Clark, "He Dog's History of Crazy Horse," in *The Killing of Chief Crazy Horse*, ed. Robert A. Clark (Glendale, Calif.: Arthur H. Clark, 1976), 51–60.

8. Clark, "He Dog's History," 59; E. A. Brininstool, "Chief Crazy Horse: His Career and Death," *Nebraska History* 12 (January–March 1929): 7.

9. *Cheyenne (Wyo. Territory) Daily Leader*, May 16, 1877, in Hardorff, *Surrender and Death*, 214; John G. Bourke, *On the Border with Crook* (New York: C. Scribner's Sons, 1892), 418; Scott and McLaughlin, "Report of William Garnett," 1.

10. "William Garnett Interview," in Hardorff, *Surrender and Death*, 28. This interview also appears on pp. 79–100, reel 1, tablet 2, Eli S. Ricker Collection, Nebraska State Historical Society, microfilm copy at Center for Southwestern Research, University of New Mexico, Albuquerque (hereafter cited as CSR).

11. Riley, "Oglala Sources," 20.

12. Ibid., 25; Hardorff, "William Garnett Interview," 29. Although attributed to Garnett, the wording of this passage and others obtained from

Eli Ricker's interview are most likely the judge's interpretation of what Garnett told him. Black Elk was the father of the holy man immortalized by John G. Neihardt.

13. "Billy Hunter Statement," in Hardorff, *Surrender and Death*, 60–61; John Irwin to J. Q. Smith, August 4, 1877, ibid., 167. Billy Hunter and William Garnett are the same man. Garnett used the surname of his stepfather, John Hunter, until 1885, then took the name of his natural father, Richard Garnett. William's mother was a Lakota woman named Looks at Him whom Richard Garnett met while serving at Fort Laramie before the Civil War.

14. Buecker, *Fort Robinson*, 105, 88–89.

15. Riley, "Oglala Sources," 47; Hyde, *Red Cloud's Folk*, 278, 284–87; Olson, *Red Cloud*, 231–38; Larson, *Red Cloud*, 206–209; Buecker, *Fort Robinson*. See also "Surround of Red Cloud and Red Leaf Camps," *Nebraska History* 15 (October–December 1934), 277–95.

16. Benjamin Shapp to J. Q. Smith, August 15, 1877, in Hardorff, *Surrender and Death*, 168–70.

17. Ibid.; Irwin to Smith, August 4, 1877.

18. Shapp to Smith, August 15, 1877.

19. Catherine Price, *The Oglala People, 1841–1879: A Political History* (Lincoln: University of Nebraska Press, 1996), 205.

20. Ibid., 161; "The Second Chips Interview," in Hardorff, *Surrender and Death*, 86; Riley, "Oglala Sources," 24.

21. Riley, "Oglala Sources," 25.

22. Hardorff, "Billy Hunter Statement," 61; Lieutenant W. P. Clark to General George Crook, August 18, 1877, in John G. Bourke diary, 1878, vol. 78, pp. 72–76, United States Military Academy Library, copy at CSR.

23. John Irwin to J. Q. Smith, September 1, 1877, in Hardorff, *Surrender and Death*, 174–75.

24. Crazy Horse had already refused to join the campaign. In the letter to the commissioner of Indian affairs, Irwin stated that Crazy Horse "object[ed] to the Indian enlisted men going out to [the] Big Horn [country] to meet Joseph's band." Irwin to Smith, August 4, 1877.

25. Many band leaders, Crazy Horse among them, believed they were actually being recruited to capture Sitting Bull, who had led his followers to Canada the previous winter. See Olson, *Red Cloud*, 242–43; Larson, *Red Cloud*, 213; and Buecker, *Fort Robinson*, 106.

26. "Louis Bordeaux Interview," in Hardorff, *Surrender and Death*, 104.

27. Brininstool, "Chief Crazy Horse," 38; Charles M. Robinson III, *A Good Year to Die: The Story of the Great Sioux War* (New York: Random House, 1995), 338. There are discrepancies in the various accounts of this meeting. According to Jesse Lee, Grouard mistranslated Touch the Clouds's words. In his account, Lee stated, "It soon became evident that Frank Grouard had (through honest mistake, no doubt) misinterpreted Touch-the-Clouds (perhaps Crazy Horse, too)." Dr. McGillycuddy reported that the statement made by Crazy Horse and the mistranslation were told to him by "a reliable check interpreter." Brininstool, "Chief Crazy Horse," 15, 36–38.

28. Hardorff, "William Garnett Interview," 31–32. Because of Crazy Horse's threats, Camp Robinson officials did not send their scouts to join the Nez Perce campaign on August 31 as planned. See Philip Sheridan to George Crook, September 1, 1877, in Hardorff, *Surrender and Death*, 175–76.

29. Hardorff, "Billy Hunter Statement," 61.

30. Luther P. Bradley to adjutant general, Department of the Platte, August 31, 1877, roll 282, Letters Received by the Office of the Adjutant General, 1871–1880, microfilm M666, copy at Fort Robinson Museum Archives, Crawford, Nebraska; Philip Sheridan to George Crook, September 1, 1877, in Hardorff, *Surrender and Death*, 175.

31. Clark, "He Dog's History," 60; Riley, "Oglala Sources," 22–24.

32. Scott and McLaughlin, "Report of William Garnett," 2. See also "William Garnett's Account," in Clark, *Killing of Chief Crazy Horse*, 77–78. The man to whom Clark was referring was General E. R. S. Canby, who was killed during the Modoc wars in 1873.

33. Scott and McLaughlin, "Report of William Garnett," 3; Hardorff, "Billy Hunter Statement," 62. See also Clark, "William Garnett's Account," 78. He Dog told Hinman that Crazy Horse was not at this council meeting and that he attended the council that night at Clark's office. Riley, "Oglala Sources," 20.

34. Scott and McLaughlin, "Report of William Garnett," 3. See also Clark, "William Garnett's Account," 79.

35. Hardorff, "Billy Hunter Statement," 41–42; Luther P. Bradley to adjutant general, Department of the Platte, September 7, 1877, in Hardorff, *Surrender and Death,* 183–84; Clark, "He Dog's History," 61.

36. John G. Bourke diary, vol. 78, pp. 59–60. See also Hardorff, "William Garnett Interview," 43–46. No Flesh, a war leader who had ridden into the Custer battle with Crazy Horse, led the scouting party of approximately twenty-five warriors. In a letter to General Crook, however, Clark put the party's number at ten. Hardorff, "William Garnett Interview," 43–46.

37. Hardorff, "William Garnett Interview," 46–48; Brininstool, "Chief Crazy Horse," 19.

38. Brininstool, "Chief Crazy Horse," 18, 19; Hardorff, "Louis Bordeaux Interview," 97.

39. Brininstool, "Chief Crazy Horse," 19.

40. Ibid., 20, 23. See also Hardorff, "Louis Bordeaux Interview," 106.

41. Brininstool, "Chief Crazy Horse," 22, 23. See also Hardorff, "Louis Bordeaux Interview," 106.

42. Brininstool, "Chief Crazy Horse," 22–23. See also Hardorff, "Louis Bordeaux Interview," 105–106.

43. Brininstool, "Chief Crazy Horse," 23.

44. At one point, Lee and Bordeaux both fell asleep in the ambulance for a short time, which allowed Crazy Horse to ride ahead of the main party. He returned without protest, stating that he had only left to water his horse. During this absence, Lee believed, Crazy Horse secured the knife that he later used to escape from Camp Robinson's guardhouse. Brininstool, "Chief Crazy Horse," 24; Hardorff, "Louis Bordeaux Interview," 108.

45. The two posts were forty-three miles apart.

46. Riley, "Oglala Sources," 21.

47. Hardorff, "William Garnett Interview," 52; Hardorff, "Louis Bordeaux Interview," 109. See also Brininstool, "Chief Crazy Horse," 23.

48. Brininstool, "Chief Crazy Horse," 24–25; "General Allison's Remarks," in *Crazy Horse: The Invincible Oglalla Sioux Chief,* ed. E. A. Brininstool

(Los Angeles: Wetzel, 1949), 41; "Dr. V.T. McGillycuddy's Recollections of the Death of Crazy Horse," in ibid., 48; "Major H . R. Lemly's Account of the Murder of Chief Crazy Horse, as an Eye-witness," in ibid., 50.

49. Hardorff, "Louis Bordeaux Interview," 109.

50. Hardorff, "William Garnett Interview," 52; Hardorff, "Billy Hunter Statement," 63.

51. John G. Bourke diary, vol. 78, p. 83. See also Hardorff, "Billy Hunter Statement," 63; and Scott and McLaughlin, "Report of William Garnett," 7.

52. Riley, "Oglala Sources," 21; Hardorff, "William Garnett Interview," 54. Also see Scott and McLaughlin, "Report of William Garnett," 7.

53. Hardorff, "Louis Bordeaux Interview," 110. See also Brininstool, "Chief Crazy Horse," 27. Determining the actual words that Crazy Horse uttered is impossible. The quotation used here is from Hinman's interview with He Dog in Riley, "Oglala Sources," 21.

54. Scott and McLaughlin, "Report of William Garnett," 7; Riley, "Oglala Sources," 21, 29. He Dog claimed that Crazy Horse asked where he had been wounded, then said, "I can feel the blood flowing." Red Feather supplied Hinman with the information about Closed Cloud. He Dog stated in an interview that Standing Buffalo and "another Indian" also gave blankets to Crazy Horse.

55. Brininstool, "Dr. V. T. McGillycuddy's Recollections," 45; Brininstool, "Major H. R. Lemly's Account," 57–58.

56. Brininstool, "Dr. V .T. McGillycuddy's Recollections," 45–46.

57. Ibid., 40.

58. Hardorff, "Louis Bordeaux Interview," 111, 112. See also "Gen. Jesse M. Lee's Account of the Killing of Chief Crazy Horse at Fort Robinson, Nebr.," in Brininstool, Crazy Horse, 34.

59. Luther P. Bradley to assistant adjutant general, Department of the Platte, September 10, 1877, in Hardorff, Surrender and Death, 185; Baptiste Pourier interview, March 6, 1907, pp. 19–25, reel 3, tablet 13, Eli S. Ricker Collection, Nebraska State Historical Society, Lincoln. Also see Hardorff, "Louis Bordeaux Interview," 92.

60. Phillip G. Twitchell, "Camp Robinson Letters of Angeline Johnson, 1876–1879," *Nebraska History* 77 (Summer 1996): 93, 94.

61. Bradley to assistant adjutant general, Department of the Platte, September 7, 1877, in John G. Bourke diary, vol. 78, p. 70; Philo Clark to George Crook, September 9, 1877, ibid., p. 71.

62. Hardorff, "William Garnett Interview," 36.

63. Ibid., 36–37.

64. Ibid.

3

The Remodeling of Geronimo

C. L. SONNICHSEN

He was born in the cool, pine-clad mountains of eastern Arizona somewhere near the headwaters of the Gila River, and he must have been a sleepy youngster, since his Apache name was Goy-ah-kla, "The Yawner." (Charles Fletcher Lummis spelled it Goy-ath-lay in his poem "Man-Who-Yawns.") According to his own account, he grew up to be an aggressive and successful young warrior and was married early to the slim and beautiful Alope, only to lose her and their three children to Mexican troops who slaughtered the women and babes while the men were trading and probably drinking in a small Chihuahua town. After that great loss, he said, "my heart would ache for revenge against Mexico," and he became a swift and deadly raider, on both sides of the boundary, with a new name—Geronimo. There is no agreement about how or when he got it, but it became a cry of fear in the mouths of his victims and a battle slogan for his fighting men.

Not a hereditary chief, he was nevertheless a forceful leader, especially of the disgruntled and discontented, and he had an impressive record among the Apaches as a shaman or medicine man who could call on his Power to help him cure certain illnesses and—more important—enable him to predict

Originally published in *Arizona Highways* 62, no. 9 (September 1986): 2–11. Reprinted by permission of *Arizona Highways* Magazine.

future events, tell what was happening in places far away, and interfere, with startling results, with the normal course of nature. An old man, a member of the band, told anthropologist Morris Edward Opler fifty years after the event that once when they were crossing open ground at night and shelter was still far away, Geronimo invoked his Power to postpone daybreak. "So he sang, and the night remained for two or three hours longer. I saw this myself." So far as is known, nothing like this had happened since the sun stood still for Joshua while the children of Israel finished off the Amorites in Old Testament times.

The Apaches knew he was a man of power even before the American Civil War, but he was not well known among the white people until the great chiefs Victorio, Mangas Colorado (also known as Mangas Coloradas), and Cochise were out of the picture. By 1880, however, he had established himself as a leader of malcontents and rebels, a red-handed raider who hated restraint, brooded over his wrongs, and talked loud and long about his grievances. Charles Lummis, who went to Fort Bowie, Arizona, in 1886 to report the end of the Apache campaigns for his Los Angeles newspaper, called Geronimo "a talker from Jawville." Lummis had a poor opinion of all Apaches at that time ("born butchers and hereditary slayers"), but thirty years later his views had changed, and he gave Geronimo his due, and maybe a little more, in his 1928 volume *A Bronco Pegasus*. The Man Who Yawns, he said, could do something besides talk.

> The most consummate warrior
>   since warfare first began,
> The deadliest Fighting Handful
>   In the calendar of Man.

Yes, he was taken prisoner once—and only once—by white men. Agent John P. Clum of the San Carlos Indian Reservation and his Indian police surrounded Geronimo and took him by surprise at Ojo Caliente in New Mexico in 1877. They took him in chains to San Carlos, but they never caught him again. Thereafter when he came in, as he did three times, he came on his own terms and in his own good time.

San Carlos was not a good place for mountain Apaches to live. Most of it was a parched desert (biographer Angie Debo calls it "a pestilential flat"). The water was bad, and it was over-populated by Apache standards with other tribesmen, some of whom were not friendly with the Ojo Caliente group.

In 1878, Geronimo and a band of sympathizers left the reservation and headed for Mexico, raiding and killing as they went; he stayed out until 1879, when he returned to San Carlos. He stayed about a year, then again escaped to Mexico, where he made his headquarters until 1883, when he once again returned to San Carlos. When he went back, Geronimo found that his circumstances had not improved. Military supervision was hard to bear. Rations were in short supply, and the Apaches were forbidden to brew and drink *tiswin,* their corn liquor. Another edict said they could not discipline their wives in traditional fashion—beating them for small infractions, cutting off their noses for unfaithfulness. The Apaches also suspected that the agent was making off with their food supply.

Said the Agent to Geronimo
   "Your ration is too fat!
I got a load of weeviled flour—
   We'll tone you down on that!
And meat just makes you ugly—
   I'll let the beef herd go—
I see some pretty money."
   "Ahnh" said Geronimo.

A small band led by Geronimo escaped the San Carlos reservation for the third and last time in 1885. With him went

ninety-two women and children, eight boys, and thirty-three
men. Five thousand soldiers could not catch him.

> They never saw a hair of him,
>   But ever and oft they felt—
> Each rock and cactus spitting lead
>   From an Apache belt.

Not until General George Crook enlisted two hundred
Apache scouts did the troops come close. "We're fighters and
we're stayers," Lummis said, but "we couldn't fight Apaches till
we Hessianized their blood!"

Even then it took many months—until September 1886—
and much blood and treasure to wear Geronimo down and
induce him to surrender. Meanwhile, every rancher in southern
Arizona and New Mexico feared for his life, and with good
reason. The Apaches moved fast and spared none who got in
their way.

Regional newspapers screamed for protection and blamed
the bumbling generals for their troubles. Eastern periodicals
picked up the chant, and Geronimo became, for several million
Americans, the personification of bloody and merciless savagery,
"the worst Indian who ever lived." General Crook, the best
military friend the Apaches ever had, called him "a human tiger."
John Clum, the only man who ever captured him, thought the
Apache troubles would be over if Geronimo could be brought in,
tried, and hanged. The man in the street in Tucson was convinced
that all the Apaches should be destroyed or at least moved out
of Arizona.

To the pioneer settlers of Arizona and New Mexico,
Geronimo was a bloody-handed murderer, and this image of
Geronimo the Wicked endured until the third quarter of the
twentieth century. It was kept alive by a variety of writers, beginning with the leaders of the Indian-fighting U.S. Army, all of

whom wrote memoirs "at the request of friends and family." To them, the Apaches were "the hostiles"—not freedom fighters and hardly human beings. They had to admit that Geronimo was a formidable opponent, a "wily savage," but that meant he was treacherous, slippery, and without honor.

White historians went along. Frank C. Lockwood in 1938 called Geronimo "a cruel, perfidious rascal, hated and distrusted by Apaches and white men alike." Dan Thrapp in his definitive *Conquest of Apacheria* (1967) aimed at objectivity but was not about to make a hero out of this "doughty recalcitrant" whose influence was "baleful."

It was for the novelists, however, that Geronimo and his warriors provided a priceless opportunity. They needed villains for their white heroes to overcome, and the Apaches seemed ideally suited for the role. Edward S. Ellis in *On the Trail of Geronimo* (1901) tells a silly story about a young West Pointer assigned to Arizona who overcomes a band of "dusky fiends" led by Geronimo. Captain Charles King, a better writer, published *An Apache Princess* in 1903. A chief's daughter falls in love with the handsome lieutenant, shows her ferocious nature by stabbing his enemies, and leaves him "with the spring of a tigress" when he reveals his love for a white girl. Popular novels from then on treat the Apache as a benighted heathen. The paperback westerns of the 1940s and 1950s give him very little credit. "In his free-running state," says James Warner Bellah, a retired colonel from the East, he is "only a step from the beast. He is lecherous and without honor or mercy, filthy in his ideas and speech, and inconceivably dirty in person and manners" (*A Thunder of Drums*, 1961).

Between 150 and 200 of these popular novels dealing with the Apache wars appeared before 1980, and Geronimo is the evil influence in many of them. Even when the Apache leader is called something else—Chingo the Butcher, Diablo, Diablito,

Satanio—he looks like the 1884 photograph of Geronimo at San Carlos, the best-known of his many likenesses. "The face was one that might look from a smoky window of hell, a beaked nose, a thin slit of lipless mouth" (Gordon D. Shireffs, *The Valiant Eagles,* 1962); "in the unyielding slitted mouth one saw determination, in the eyes and mouth and bone of his face was ruthlessness, a cruelty ages old" (George Garland, *Apache Warpath,* 1961).

As late as 1972, "the wily old butcher" took a leading role in Lewis B. Patten's *Hands of Geronimo,* and in the unspeakably violent novels of the seventies and eighties, notably the Cuchillo Oro series by Englishman Terry Harknett (under the pen name William James), the cover blurb points out that the books "are inspired by such notorious Indian warriors as Cochise and Geronimo."

Thus, Geronimo the Wicked has gone marching on down through the years; but Geronimo the Good was there all the time, getting ready to equal and eventually surpass him.

The first signs of change were visible when the Yawner was in full career. The entering wedge was the consciousness that all the Indians had been abused and betrayed by whites and the U.S. government. People talked about the "Tucson Ring," which put rocks in flour sacks and stole the Indians' beef. Whether such a ring ever existed is doubtful, but General Crook believed it did, and so did Lummis (citing "fraud and villainy constantly practiced in open violation of laws and in defiance of public justice"). People back east were quick to point the finger. After the black people of the South were emancipated, the reformers attacked the army and the Indian Service. "I only know the names of three savages upon the plains," said Wendell Phillips in 1870—"Colonel Baker, General Custer, and at the head of [them] all, General Sherman."

It took some time, however, to begin to convince the country that the Apache was a human being. One of the first in the field to do so was novelist Harold Bell Wright, with *The Mind with the Iron Door* (1923). He introduces an Apache named Natachee, educated in the white man's schools but unable to find a place in either of his two worlds. The white man, Wright says through Natachee, has ruined the Apaches through his lust for gold. Natachee's only comfort is his perception that "by this gold shall the destroyers, in their turn, be destroyed." Lummis came into the picture in 1928 with *A Bronco Pegasus,* celebrating Geronimo's dedication and endurance, and in 1927 Edgar Rice Burroughs (of Tarzan fame) published the first of two novels in which Geronimo, old and wise, comments sadly on the perfidy of the white man. "Some day," he hopes, "the Pindah-lick-oyee will keep the words of the treaties they have made with the Shishinday—the treaties they have always been the first to break."

Several first-rate novels appeared in the 1930s, all taking the side of the Apache, but the climax was reached in 1947 with Elliott Arnold's *Blood Brother,* a best-seller and the basis for the popular motion picture *Broken Arrow.* By this time, the white man had become the murderous savage, and the Apache was the truly civilized human being. "There is no private hoarding," says Tom Jeffords, the central character, a blood brother of Cochise and husband of the beautiful Son-see-ahray, "no cheating. Whatever they have is divided equally. There is no caste system. . . . I wonder by what standards we have arrogated to ourselves the right to call Indians savages. . . . Who are we to come along and try to make them over our way?"

In the novels that follow *Blood Brother,* the white man goes down as the Indian goes up. "Have you ever stopped to realize," asks a character in Hunter Ingram's *Fort Apache* (1985), "that the Caucasian race is the scourge of the earth? The Apache kills on an individual basis. . . . They plan to wipe out whole cul-

tures at once." Lummis agrees and applies a little whitewash to
Geronimo:

> He spared nor child nor womankind
>   but Pagans never knew
> how Christians wholesale—like Cevennes,
>   or St. Bartholomew

Behind it all are the white man's guilt feelings and his urge
to make restitution. The Wheeler-Howard Act of 1933 began
to restore the Indians' land, culture, and religion. Millions of
dollars have gone to the tribes to compensate them for the
loss of their homelands, and the Apaches have had their share.
Sentimentalists have written books celebrating the Indians'
kinship with nature. Serious historians have documented the
white man's crimes. Motion pictures have got on the Indian
bandwagon and preached the same sermon. Dee Brown's *Bury
My Heart at Wounded Knee* was a best-seller, and almost nobody
doubts now that the white man was the great villain and the
Indian was the innocent victim.

Geronimo could not escape being transformed with the
rest, and he assisted materially—though unintentionally—in his
own transformation. He allowed a white school superintendent
named S. M. Barrett to record and publish his life story—a
development that had far-reaching consequences. For the first
time, an Apache described his boyhood and growing up. Making
an appealing juvenile out of him was quite possible, and in at
least seven fictional works by English and American authors,
Geronimo emerges as a model for American youth—a sort of
Apache Boy Scout.

Anthropologists and Indianists of various complexions
pushed Geronimo's remodeling a little further by explaining
Apache social organization and religion. Geronimo as a shaman
came into the picture frequently. And all the while, somewhere

out of sight, Geronimo was being sanctified as a symbol of heroic resistance to entrenched injustice.

In California, where many young people seceded from the middle-class world and tried to become wild and free, like the Indians, an emancipated group moved onto a vacant area owned by the University of California at Berkeley and named it the Power to the People Park. When university authorities tried to move them out, a printed broadside appeared on the street with a picture of Geronimo on it and the words "Your land is covered with blood. Your people ripped off this land from the Indians. If you want it back now, you will have to fight for it."

There was not an Indian among these indignant people, and there was no major battle, but the point had been made. Geronimo, like Lincoln, "belonged to the ages" and was available as a symbol to anyone who had a use for him. Among those who found a use were the people of the Paris underground, who called themselves *les apaches,* and paratroopers in World War II, who invoked the name of Geronimo as they leaped from their airplanes into space.

It remained for Forrest Carter in his 1978 novel, *Watch for Me on the Mountain,* to raise Geronimo to the level of Moses and George Washington and even higher. He fights to keep his people free, leads some of them to a Promised Land deep in the Mexican mountains, and is in constant communion with the Higher Powers. We see what his possibilities are when Chokole, a warrior woman, is dying, staked out on an anthill by Mexican soldiers, and a great eagle comes to her. He "stretched out taloned feet, and braked against the air, landing close to Chokole. She saw him turn his head, looking at her. . . . Chokole blinked her eyes. It was Geronimo." Neither Moses nor George Washington could equal that. Geronimo is the Apache Messiah.

We have arrived at the place where the old rule applies: if you can't lick 'em, join 'em! We have made Geronimo our own.

"The spirit of the Apaches," says biographer Alexander B. Adams, "lives wherever men and women are struggling against overwhelming odds for freedom and justice. We, as Americans, should be proud that the Apaches' story is part of our country's heritage."

It would have been better if Geronimo had died fighting the bluecoats in Mexico. It is sad to read that he spent his last years raising watermelons on a patch of land at Fort Sill, Oklahoma; that he traveled to fairs and conventions to show himself to curious crowds; that he sold the buttons off his shirt for a quarter apiece and carried a supply of replacements; that he died of pneumonia after getting drunk in Lawton. He had left the Christian church and gone back to the old religion, but Charles Lummis told it the way it should have been:

> But Goy-ath-lay, whose breechclout score
>   two nations mocked at will—
> Serenely yawned himself to death
>   in Sunday school at Sill.

4

Charlie's Hidden Agenda

Realism and Nostalgia in
C. M. Russell's Stories about Indians

RAPHAEL CRISTY

betwine the pen and the brush there is little differnce
but I believe the man that makes word pictures is the greater.

—C. M. Russell

Known as "The Cowboy Artist," Charles M. Russell (1864–1926) depicted late nineteenth-century life in Montana and, by extension, America's trans-Mississippi West in art that attracted international acclaim. In addition to his paintings, sketches, and sculptures, Russell also wrote and published several dozen stories that demonstrate his adept way with words. Most of his writings appeared first in Montana newspapers and several books distributed regionally. Since his death in 1926, a few published volumes of his illustrated letters have expanded public appreciation for his personality and wit. Both the published stories and the letters reflect Russell's exceptional skills as a humorist and raconteur, and Russell's published stories especially embody a personal and perceptive view of the American West. Yet these writings have been largely overlooked as sources for serious study by most literary and

Originally published in *Montana The Magazine of Western History* 43, no. 3 (Summer 1993): 2–15. Reprinted by permission of the author.

historical commentators in the decades since they first appeared in print.[1]

The narrative form of Russell's published works may have deterred serious consideration of their substance. At face value, his writings are unsophisticated and charming, written in seemingly uneducated rural prose with droll humor. On reconsideration, however, many of Russell's stories, which depict episodes from the West of the 1820s through the 1920s, show a keen awareness of a place undergoing rapid transformation as it emerged from the nineteenth century into the twentieth century. Russell's works reflect a subtle yet firm grasp of the magnitude of that change as he witnessed it during his lifetime.

Russell's casual writing style grew directly from his oral delivery. Numerous firsthand accounts testify to the memorable impact of Russell's storytelling in cow camps, saloons, bunkhouses, and ranch parlors. More than a decade after Russell's death, a fellow cowboy recalled, "At camp and elsewhere Charlie Russel was always the center of attraction. . . . Russel always had a meal time story and the boys circled around him as close as possible, eating with legs crossed, plate on knees."[2] Russell's own letters as well as what others said about him suggest that he used this same vernacular style when he spoke informally. When the mood suited him, Russell seemed to create amusing tales spontaneously, and he apparently told many more stories than he ever published.[3]

In 1903 Russell and his wife, Nancy, began annual excursions outside Montana to sell his art. At social gatherings in New York, Los Angeles, and other cities, he impressed celebrities and high-society urbanites with his yarn-spinning. Will Rogers noted in the introduction he wrote for *Trails Plowed Under*, the posthumous anthology of Russell's stories, "Why you never heard me open my mouth when you was around, and you never knew any of our friends that would let me open it as long as there was a chance to get you to tell another one. I always did say that you could tell a story better than any man that ever lived."[4]

Russell's enthusiasm for storytelling carried considerable momentum when the right circumstances prevailed. Fergus Mead, Russell's second cousin, remembered that Charlie "never stopped talking—spinning yarns. Lots of 'em are in Trails Plowed Under and in his letters. . . . He was an articulate sun-of-a-gun."[5] Yet Russell told stories only if someone could get him to talk. When Russell did not sense a mutual understanding and appreciation for his western story subjects, he was reluctant to perform.

As shy as he sometimes was to tell stories, Russell also struggled to write, once complaining to actor William S. Hart that he was "average on talk," but if handed a pen and paper, "Im deaf an dum."[6] Nevertheless, after years of telling his stories aloud, Russell committed some of them to paper in the colloquial slang and informal style he had known and used throughout his life in Montana. In 1906 Russell contributed a story titled "A Savage Santa Claus" to a special Christmas section of the *Great Falls Tribune*. Then, in 1907, 1908, and 1909, *Outing Magazine* published five of his more serious stories, and between 1916 and 1921 Russell wrote twenty stories for the newly formed Montana Newspaper Association (MNA).[7] Founded by W. W. Cheeley, H. Percy Raban, and O. F. Wadsworth, the MNA published editorial and advertising newspaper supplements in Great Falls from 1916 through 1942. In the 1920s, some two-thirds of Montana's more than 170 daily and weekly newspapers carried the supplements, which offered special emphasis on Montana historical subjects. Although the MNA received twenty contributions from Russell, getting the cowboy artist to write anything, it was said, was "like pulling teeth."[8]

From 1921 until his death in 1926, Charlie Russell gathered thirty-six stories and essays, including most of the twenty already published by the MNA, into two books: *Rawhide Rawlins Stories* (1921) and *More Rawhides* (1925). When the first *Rawhide Rawlins* book appeared, in 1921, Montana was experiencing a severe economic depression and drought, which prompted Russell to tell a Great Falls newspaper reporter, "These are hard times for a lot of folks.... If this book is going to give anybody a laugh and make him forget his troubles for a while, I want the price low enough so that people to whom a dollar means a dollar will feel that they're getting their money's worth."[9]

At a time when Nancy Russell first demanded and received $10,000 for one of her husband's larger oil paintings, *Salute to the Robe Trade* (1920), Charlie purposely priced the *Rawhide* books at one dollar. Russell seemed to want "a lot of folks" in Montana to be able to read his stories. The year after he died, Nancy reissued all but one of her husband's *Rawhide* stories and nine other Russell tales in *Trails Plowed Under*.[10]

Russell showed no sign of having a national audience in mind when he constructed humorous stories to embarrass certain Montana friends. "An old trickster," according to writer William Kittredge, Russell recorded both amusing and serious local legends about unusual events happening to specific people. In the process, he dramatized regional history and supplied cultural vitality to the national perspective of the American West.[11]

Particularly rich in social commentary are Russell's Indian stories. While most of his stories on other topics emphasize humor, Russell's tales about Indians, while not devoid of humor, tend to maintain a more serious tone. They also deliver significant historical information, and unlike the supposedly humorous *Wolfville* stories by Alfred Henry Lewis and writings by other westerners such as Bill Nye and Mark Twain, Russell never seems to have purposely demeaned Native Americans. In fact, Russell carefully challenged the racist assumptions of his Montana audiences. Even among his contemporaries, only

E. C. "Teddy Blue" Abbott, Frank Bird Linderman, and a few
others shared his outspoken, positive views of Indian people.
Russell could even add blunt social commentary that he knew
Montanans would read while holding much different attitudes
toward Indians.[12]

Russell's writings about Indians, then, would seem to merit
especially close attention because they provide the clearest expression of his sense of the negative impact of whites on the
transformation of the northern West in the late nineteenth century. One Russell historian has observed that Charlie's paintings
evolved over his lifetime "away from documentary realism to
what might be called romantic realism grounded in nostalgia.
His portrayal of the Indian is a case in point."[13] While some
Russell enthusiasts debate the degrees of romance and nostalgia
in Russell's work, the observation does provide a reasonable con-
struct for considering Russell's approach to Indians. Once, when
informally illustrating George Bird Grinnell's history of the
Cheyenne Indians, *The Fighting Cheyennes,* for example, Russell
wrote, "The Red man was the true American   They have almost gon but will never be forgotten   The history of how they
fought for their country is written in blood   a stain that time
cannot grinde out   their God was the sun   their church was
all out doors   their only book was nature   and they knew all
its pages[.]"[14]

Russell's strong sense of admiration for the Cheyennes and
other Indian peoples began with his own family. His great-uncles,
William, Charles, George, and Robert Bent, who, along with
Ceran St. Vrain, founded Bent's Fort in southeastern Colorado
in 1834, "were the fairest manipulators of Indians in the history
of the mountain trade and maintained an elsewhere unheard-of
standard of honor in dealing with them." William Bent married
the daughter of a Cheyenne chief, and George Bent, their son,
provided information for Grinnell's Cheyenne books.[15]

Like most Americans of his time, Russell believed that Indian tribal and racial identities soon would disappear through subjugation, starvation, or assimilation. Unlike many of his contemporaries, he believed that such a fate was unjust. "We stole every inch of land we got from the Injun," he wrote, "but we didn't get it without a fight, and Uncle Sam will remember him a long time."[16]

Two of Russell's letters expressed his dismay with the changes forced on the Indians by misguided government paternalism. He told fellow cowboy, Kalispell taxidermist, and Montana Fish and Game Commissioner Harry Stanford, "the only real American . . . dances under the flag that made a farmer out of him   once nature gave him everything he wanted.   now the agent gives him bib overalls hookes his hands around plow handles and tells him its a good thing   push it along   maby it is but thair having a hell of a time prooving it. . . .   nature was not always kind to these people but she never lied to them."[17] In a letter to U.S. Senator Paris Gibson, Russell used his dry wit to make a case against assimilation: "Speaking of Indians. I understand there is a man back in your camp Jones by name who has sent out orders to cut all the Indians hair   if Jones is stuck to have this barber work done he'd better tackle it himself as no one out here is longing for the job   the Indians say whoever starts to cut thair hair will get an Injun hair cut and you know that calls for a sertean amount of hide."[18]

Charlie Russell's opposition to federal Indian policies was out of step with prevailing white attitudes in Montana. In *The Rocky Mountain Husbandman,* published in White Sulphur Springs near the Judith Basin, where Russell worked as a cowboy in the 1880s and 1890s, Robert Sutherlin expressed editorial views toward Indians that constitute one local example. Sutherlin preached that Indians must be assimilated and their tribal structure and way of life destroyed.[19] An especially rabid editorial, titled "The Red Devils" (appearing in the *Mineral Argus*, another Judith-region newspaper), read in part,

> During the past summer small lodges of Bloods, Piegans and Crows have been prowling around the Musselshell, Judith and Missouri valleys, killing stock and stealing horses . . . the property and belongings of white settlers. . . . There is to be no further favoritism shown thieving red devils by the military authorities. . . . The "Noble (?) Red Man" will speedily realize that, if he desires to exist on this sphere, he must remain on the grounds set aside for his exclusive occupation. This is as it should be, yet the big-hearted, philanthropical, goggle-eyed, heathen converter and Indian civilizer of Yankeedom cannot understand it and will probably protest.[20]

Wyoming newspaperman Bill Nye, in sarcastic editorials, took journalistic racism to another level of anti-Indian rhetoric, especially when he wrote in 1879,

> As usual, the regular fall wail of the eastern press on the Indian question, charging that the Indians never commit any depredations unless grossly abused, has arrived. . . . Every man who knows enough to feed himself . . . knows that the Indian is treacherous, dishonest, diabolical, and devilish in the extreme. . . . He will wear pants and comb his hair and pray and be a class leader at the Agency for 59 years, if he knows that in the summer of the 60th year he can murder a few Colorado settlers and beat out the brains of the industrious farmers.[21]

In contrast with these prevailing white attitudes, Russell gently confronted local racism, as shown in his letter to Senator Gibson: "the subject of conversation was the Indian question the dealer Kicking George was an old time sport who

spoke of cards as an industry . . . the kicker alloued an Injun had
no more right in this country than a Cyote   I told him what he
said might be right but there were folks coming to the country
on the new rail road that thaught the same way about gamblers
an he wouldent winter maney times till hed find the wild Indian
would go but would onley brake the trail for the gambler[.]"²²

Racial dislike in early twentieth-century Montana focused with
special intensity on small wandering bands of Chippewa and
Cree Indians who collected in squalid camps on the outskirts
of Helena, Great Falls, and other towns. To aid the destitute
Indians who were suffering during an especially severe winter,
Russell helped launch a local relief fund by making a candidly
impromptu announcement for the *Great Falls Tribune:*

> It doesn't look very good for the people of Montana if
> they will sit still and see a lot of women and children
> starve to death in this kind of weather. . . . Lots of people
> seem to think that Indians are not human beings at all
> and have no feelings. These kind of people would be the
> first to yell for help if their grub pile was running short
> and they didn't have enough clothes to keep out the cold,
> and yet because Rocky Boy and his bunch are Indians,
> they are perfectly willing to let them die of hunger and
> cold without lifting a hand. I know that the majority of
> people of the state are not that way, however, and if they
> are called upon they will be glad to help the Indians out.²³

Russell's public participation in the relief effort was unchar-
acteristic. Despite the extroverted and comic storytelling side
of Russell's personality, he lived a relatively private life, seldom
expressing political or religious attitudes outside his household.
Charlie's statement in the *Tribune* and his public gesture of
dropping the first money into the hat reflected a special intensity

of concern for the landless Indians. On this occasion, Russell felt sufficiently moved to take a public stand and then write privately to U.S. Senator Henry L. Myers urging support for the establishment of the Rocky Boy's Reservation near Havre.

> A friend of mine Frank Linderman has been trying to get a bill passed for a strip of land for the Chippaway and Cree indians. These people have been on the verge of starvation for years and I think it no more than square for Uncle Sam, who has opened the West for all foreigners, to give these real Americans enough to live on. . . . I understand that Senator Dixon is fighting the indian bill. Mr Dixon has the earmarks of a man that was never hungry in his life. I would like to lead the Senator to the Chippaway camp right now with the temperature ranging from 10 to 30 degrees below zero and show him what real starvation meant. And if he has anything under his hide like a heart he would change his talk.[24]

Russell also supported Linderman in his political and bureaucratic struggle against Washington inertia and Havre real-estate boosters. With a note of encouragement to his friend and a copy of the letter to Senator Myers, Russell included his own political cartoon of an obese capitalist "Land Hog" preventing an Indian family from crossing into the United States from Canada: "Frank   its hard work this letter writing for me so I am sending this sketch to show how I feel about the Indians question   of course I apologise to the whole hog family . . . but the land hog dont come in the same class[.]"[25]

Charlie Russell's infrequent and typically private efforts on behalf of Indian welfare reflected neither a lack of concern for Indians nor some protective reflex for his public image and art sales. Adverse public opinion in Montana would have made no significant dent in Russell's artistic stature, and his pro-Indian

sentiments were already well known locally. By 1913, exhibits of
Russell's art arranged by Nancy in New York and other major
cities had boosted the price of his paintings well beyond the
means of most Montana people who might be offended by pro-
Indian political efforts. Russell simply led a life of artistic tunnel
vision. His actions on behalf of Indians in his time reflected less
an indifferent cynic purging his own "social guilt," as one art
critic has speculated, and more a compassionate yet preoccupied
artist responding impulsively to immediate human suffering.[26]

Charlie Russell's actions supporting the Crees and Chippewas
demonstrated his belief that Indians needed to adapt to white
American society. Nevertheless, his Indian stories consistently
expressed admiration for the least assimilated Indian—the traditional warrior—who was forced to live within a reservation but
cooperated in few other ways with white authorities. Such appreciation did express a form of nostalgia. Nevertheless, Russell's
vision of Indians was not too idealistic or "goggle-eyed." He
showed a serious awareness of the lethal violence often associated with old nomadic tribal ways. In his story "The War Scars
of Medicine-Whip," Russell started a narrative about a deadly
clash between Blackfoot and Sioux warriors with a description
of the battle's instigator: "That old savage is the real article, an'
can spin yarns of killin's and scalpin's that would make your hair
set up like the roach on a buck antelope."[27]

Although he used racist language common at the time,
Russell loaded a negative term such as "savage" with an ironic
sense of cautious respect. The story's cowboy narrator acknowl-
edges that, in certain circumstances, this old warrior would be
his mortal enemy. Russell's use of "savage" in "The War Scars of
Medicine-Whip" and other stories suggests an inverse meaning,
much the way he used "gentlemen" when referring to the hunters
who annihilated the wild buffalo.[28] Charlie Russell could respect
the unassimilated warrior's independence and loyalty to his na-

tive culture while not necessarily wanting to be his best friend. "I admire this red-handed killer," he wrote in the "War Scars" tale:

> The Whites have killed his meat an' taken his country, but they've made no change in him. He's as much Injun as his ancestors that packed their quivers loaded with flint-pointed arrows, an' built fires by rubbin' sticks together. He laughs at priests an' preachers. Outside his lodge on a tripod hangs a bullhide shield an' medicine bag to keep away the ghosts. He's got a religion of his own, an' it tells him that the buffalo are comin' back. He lights his pipe, an' smokes with the sun the same as his folks did a thousand winters behind him. When he cashes in, his shadow goes prancin' off on a shadow pony, joinin' those that have gone before, to run shadow buffalo. He's seen enough of white men, an' don't want to throw in with 'em in no other world.[29]

Most Americans believed that "it was necessary to obliterate all vestiges of native cultures" and make Indians into an imitation of white people.[30] Even the more compassionate Indian sympathizers advocated the sacrifice of Native American cultures and religions, believing that Christianity alone could save Indians from total destruction. For Charlie Russell, forcing Indians into an alien way of life was a futile exercise that would destroy a valuable culture. In his dry-eyed brand of nostalgia, Russell's writings expressed appreciation for anyone who resisted or fell victim to the unstoppable momentum of the transitional frontier.

Through periodic contacts with Indians, Russell accumulated information that appeared in his art as well as his stories. His use of this information showed an understanding of the complex and conservative Indian social relationships that did not readily embrace outsiders. Russell generally spoke with cautious modesty of his own direct experiences with Indians. "My Indian study came from observation and by living with the Blackfeet in Alberta for about six months. I don't know much about them even now; they are hard people to savvy." Russell's narrator for the essay "Injuns," known only as Murphy, warned, "if I told only what I know about Injuns, I'd be through right now."[31]

Russell's portrayal of Medicine-Whip's situation on the reservation, for example, was not an attempt to write documented history. Nevertheless, the details of characterization, setting, and narrative style are consistently authentic and could represent Blackfoot oral history despite the absence of any Medicine-Whip (or other Indian names associated with Russell stories) among registered (American) Blackfoot or (Canadian) Blood tribal name records. "Whether or not Medicine-Whip ever existed," Canadian historian Hugh Dempsey has noted, "the adventure Russell recounted could easily have been told to him, as he said, while he was in camp along the Bow River."[32]

In another mixture of fact and fiction, Russell's narrative "The Trail of the Reel Foot," which first appeared in 1916, was based on accounts of a Fort Pierre, South Dakota, half-blood Indian named Clubfoot George Boyd. Boyd's two frostbite-damaged feet had been amputated from instep to toes and left moccasin tracks in the snow that confused Gros Ventre warriors during the winter of 1864–65.[33] In Russell's innovative version of the story, the encounter between white and Indian cultures is complicated by the fur trapper's completely reversed clubfoot. "His right foot's straight ahead, natural; the left, p'intin' back in his trail." Russell crafted a humorous scenario out of the irony of Indian confusion with unusual footprints in the snow.

At first the humor seems to be based on a patronizing attitude toward Indian superstition, which attributes the opposing footprints to "two one-legged men travelin' in opposite directions."[34] Later, when Sioux warriors see Reel Foot's actual physical defect, they respect his condition as an honorable wound, suffered probably in battle or torture, and abstain from killing him. Russell showed how the Sioux cultural attitude respecting human disfigurement differed from the ridicule and disgust typically found in the author's audience. Russell's narrator, Dad Lane, articulates that unsympathetic attitude in a joke: "I never do look at him without wonderin' which way he's goin' to start off."[35] In contrast, Sioux values about disfigurement spare Reel Foot's life. Russell's presentation of the humanistic nature of dangerous Indian warriors in a humorous context contradicted the white stereotype of bloodthirsty Indian "braves" and exposed one of the differences between Indian and white cultures.

Interracial marriage between white men and Indian women also generated considerable controversy in proper white society of both the nineteenth and the twentieth century but provided Russell with yet another means of defending Native cultural differences. Many white men in interracial marriages experienced diminished stature in white culture from the earliest years of the fur trade well into the twentieth century. Mountain men who took Indian wives, according to one historian, were the ones "the settlers hated the most, alleging against them every villainy that should be alleged against Indians." In 1937 a Montana woman gossiped in a letter to a Russell researcher, "I think I told you I saw James Willard Schultz in Great Falls at the Rainbow [Hotel]. . . . He impressed me as the sort of man who would love his Indian wife the best because he would like the servility."[36]

As a young man, Russell was not above lighthearted racial ridicule combined with self-deprecation. In 1888 Charlie and his pal Phil Weinard won first prize in a Helena costume party with Weinard dressed as an Indian man and Russell decked-out as his "squaw." Three years later, while still working as a cowboy, Russell wrote to a friend concerning an earlier opportunity to marry an Indian woman: "I had a chance to marry Young [L]ouse's daughter   he is blackfoot Chief   It was the only chance

I ever had to marry into good famley but I did not like the way my intended cooked dog and we broke of[f] our engagement[.]" In this private letter, Charlie joked about romance with an Indian woman by referring to cooking dog meat, knowing that the Blackfeet religiously avoided eating dog. Apparently, he assumed that his friend would appreciate the absurd lie.[37]

Russell dealt more directly with the sensitive topic of interracial marriage in his story "How Lindsay Turned Indian." In his opening words, narrator Dad Lane disagrees with the social stigma on interracial marriages: "Most folks don't bank much on squaw-men, but I've seen some mighty good ones doubled up with she-Injuns."[38] By the end of this lengthy yarn, Lindsay's adventures among the Blackfeet raised his stature beyond the negativity commonly associated with the "squaw-man" label.

Russell also used humor to make his audience more receptive to perceiving the harsh conditions under which Indian people lived. He reflected on the famine suffered by many Northern Plains Indian communities in the final quarter of the nineteenth century. In "Finger-That-Kills Wins His Squaw," for example, the story's main character appears when some cowboys, including the narrator, deliver a herd of government cattle for distribution to the Blackfeet. "There's an old Injun comes visitin' our camp, an' after he feeds once you can bet on him showin' up 'bout noon every day. If there's a place where an Injun makes a hand, it's helpin' a neighbor hide grub, an' they ain't particular about quality—it's quantity they want. Uncle Sam's Injuns average about one good meal a week; nobody's got to graze this way long till a tin plate loaded with beans looks like a Christmas dinner."[39] Here Russell accommodated the typical racist assumption that Indians were helpful or willing to work only when the time came to put away food. Then he presented the blunt verbal picture of people suffering starvation at the whim of the government.

More troubling than food shortages, "Curley's Friend" tells of an attempted massacre. In 1924, a grim narrative appeared in MNA weekly newspaper inserts about some cowboys on horse- and cattle-reprisal raids against local Bannack Indians on Montana's southwestern ranges in 1878. Occasionally the cowboys killed their opponents—men, women, and children—and dropped their bodies down an abandoned mine shaft to hide the grisly evidence. The journalist revealed a flippant attitude about the murdered Indians by stating, "The cowboys returned the fire with the result that all of the Indians including the squaws, were soon in shape to be 'snaked' [roped and dragged behind a horse] to the graveyard." Since that day, the writer said, "the old shaft [has been] the sepulchre of a dozen or more Bannack braves, as well as a few squaws and pappooses."[40] A year later, "Curley's Friend" appeared in Russell's *More Rawhides*. Curley tells of how he happened to interrupt forcibly a fellow cowboy's systematic shooting of a peaceful group of Bannack men and women. Disturbed by his companion's cold-blooded killing of Indian women who were begging for their lives, Curley forces the other cowboy to stop shooting, confiscates his gun, and earns himself a mortal enemy. Rather than bragging, Russell's narrator tells his story to explain why his life was spared at a later time by a Bannack war party. Apparently, the leading warrior recognized Curley and let him go free in the midst of lethal raids and skirmishes that left four other whites dead.

Russell's challenge was to deliver this story, in person or in print, to Montana audiences who may have sympathized more with the murderer than with Curley. To gain their trust and attention, Russell's narrator/hero could not be too compassionate for the Indian victims for fear of being rejected as a "big-hearted, philanthropical, goggle-eyed, heathen converter." So Russell had Curley disclaim, "I ain't no Injun lover, . . . but I'm willin' to give any man a square shake." By the end of his tale, Russell was ready for Curley to negate a basic tenet of frontier bigotry: "I heard that all good Injuns were dead ones. If that's true, I'm damn glad the one I met that day was still a bad one."[41]

Through storytelling, Russell manipulated popular assumptions and attitudes about Indians to place his divergent ideas subtly in the minds of his audience. Despite being the least polished of his stories, "Curley's Friend" raised the issue of genocide and provided a model for the individual initiative required to stop it. Curley's erratic story sequence, similar to the inconsistent flow of events in an impromptu oral narrative, and the complete absence of references to the bodies from multiple killings hidden in the old well suggest that Russell did not rely on the newspaper account for his story. Whether "Curley's Friend" came directly from Russell's imagination as a response to atrocities in the Bannack outbreak of 1877–78 or, more likely, originated from the actual storyteller/protagonist, Russell purposely brought his audiences face-to-face with the unpleasant dark side of transforming the frontier into "civilized" society.

Russell used characters who bridged Native and white cultures in yet other stories. One example is "Dad Lane's Buffalo Yarn," a story that also exposes the grossly unromantic side of buffalo hunting. The story has two narrators—Long Wilson and Dad Lane. Russell's first narrator, Long Wilson, describes how the professional buffalo hunters did their bloody killing, slaughtering dozens of animals at a time: "Whenever one tries to break out of the mill, there's a ball goes bustin' through its lungs, causin' it to belch blood, an' strangle, an' it ain't long till they quit tryin' to get away an' stand an' take their medicine. Then this cold-blooded proposition in the waller settles down to business, droppin' one at a time an' easin' up now an' agin to cool his gun, . . . These hide hunters 're the gentlemen that cleaned up the buffalo."[42]

Following Long Wilson's description of buffalo destruction,

Dad Lane tells of his survival with an Indian partner who has a dual identity. Raised with white people, the Indian uses the anglicized name of Joe Burke. Just under the surface of his white man's clothes and language, however, resides his Indian identity, Bad Meat. Burke, or Bad Meat, proves to be a good partner. When he and Dad Lane must fight for their lives with a war party, Bad Meat sheds his white clothes. "When it's light I'm surprised at Bad Meat's appearance," Dad Lane says: "Up till now he's wearin' white man's clothes, but this morning' he's back to the clout, skin leggin's, an' shirt. . . . He notices my surprise an' tells me it ain't good medicine for an Indian to die with white men's clothes [on]."[43]

Bad Meat helps Dad Lane survive both the battle and near-starvation on a burned-over range. Russell shows that Indian companionship and know-how have the highest value in life-or-death situations. In "Dad Lane's Buffalo Yarn," Russell emphasized the brutal destruction of the buffalo as well as the value of Native cultural persistence in the face of compulsory assimilation.

The ultimate cultural bridge between the Indian and white worlds in Charlie Russell's stories is not a human but rather a horse. Russell's story "The Ghost Horse" directly connects the days of the Indians' buffalo range and the whites' cattle business. The tale of this animal hero, an actual horse ridden by Russell throughout his eleven years as a cowboy and pampered for thirteen years after that, was written for the 1919 Great Falls High School yearbook, *Roundup Annual.* The writing style lacks all of the rural "cow camp" slang that Russell expressed in other stories. Rather, he wrote in "contemporary" English, possibly to communicate more directly with his younger audience. The story follows the life of a horse raised by Crow Indians to be a buffalo runner, stolen by the Piegan Blackfeet, and sold to a young cowboy. The narrative dwells on the horse's Indian days, but when the horse finally becomes the cowboy's property, Paint, as he is then called, encounters cattle herds and a raucous new town. Near the story's end, Russell shifts the narration to reflect Paint's viewpoint entirely. Tied outside a saloon, the horse witnesses a fatal gunfight. "Paint knew then," the story says, "that the white man was no different from the red. They both kill their own kind."[44]

In another story, titled "Finger-That-Kills Wins His Squaw," Russell simply used the harsh racism expressed by some of his narrators to set up his white audience for his version of human equality. "That story that Dad Lane tells the other night 'bout his compadre getting killed off," Russell has narrator "Squaw" Owens explain in his tale,

> sure shows the Injun up, . . . Injuns is born bushwackers; they believe in killin' off their enemy an' ain't particular how it's done, but prefer gettin' him from cover, an' I notice some of their white brothers play the same way. You watch these old gun-fighters an' you'll see most of 'em likes a shade the start in a draw; there's many a man that's fell under the smoke of a forty-five—drawn from a sneak—that ain't lookin' when he got it.
>
> I've had plenty of experience amongst Indians an' all the affection I got for 'em wouldn't make no love story, but with all their tricks an' treachery I call them a game people.[45]

"Squaw" Owens, like the hero in "The Ghost Horse," helps Russell cultivate the attention of his white Montana audience with a wary attitude toward a supposedly inferior and devious race. Nevertheless, his comparisons actually describe a ground-level sense of racial equality. Disguised in the racist language of his narrators, Russell's Indian stories provided entertaining propaganda that celebrated the validity of the endangered cultural life of American Plains Indians.

Russell's celebration of Indian cultures grew from an impulse that is easily categorized as nostalgic, a wish to return to a former home or a sentimental wish for a time gone by. He began one story, titled "Dunc McDonald," for example, with the nostalgic statement "Like all things that happen that's worth while, it's a long time ago."[46] In contrast with the spontaneous emotion in his letters to Harry Stanford and others, Russell's stories frequently reflect a more disciplined consideration of earlier times. Russell's Indian stories are not mere wishes for an idealized past and a vanishing race but instead use nostalgia with a purpose. His tales carefully contradicted the prevailing attitudes of his fellow westerners, who responded to Indians with disgust or condescension more often than with sympathy. The "romantic realism" that some historians perceive in Russell's paintings appears in the artist's Indian yarns less as nostalgic regret than as a depiction of harsh realities within which Russell may provide a moral of racial and cultural tolerance.

Interpreting the imagery in Charlie Russell's art has been a popular sport since he created his paintings. A recent Smithsonian exhibition and catalog have attracted controversy with strong interpretations of the political content of works by western artists, including Charles M. Russell. One historian argued that Russell purposely chose "to portray warring Indians as ruthless, bloodthirsty mobs" in works that "suited Russell's need to show the 'animal' quality of Indians in combat." A routine reading of Russell's story "Trail of the Reel Foot" might have softened this exaggeration of Russell's views toward Indians. The association of Russell with anti-Indian and pro-western expansionist attitudes, moreover, is simply incorrect.[47] Russell's own voice clearly states his sympathy and respect for Native peoples.

Charlie Russell's tales about Indians radiate his concern for the human impact of social changes in the transitional nineteenth-century West. While he lacked the political temperament of a Frank Linderman, Russell effectively used his artistic talent and ingenuity to create mildly subversive literature about local people and events. Russell's stories argue implicitly for tolerance of intermarriage between Indians and whites, for respect for cultural distinctiveness, and for appreciation of mixed-blood people. The stories also portray the loss of buffalo-based Indian societies and the cultural damage caused by government-mandated assimilation. While attempting to entertain with his stories, Russell did not avoid the unpleasant issues of Native American suffering because of land theft, starvation, and murderous violence. Without indulging in emotional hand-wringing over the injustice of the Indian peoples' circumstances, Russell provided subsequent generations with an honest perspective, on an individual level, of some of the consequences of accelerated social change in the American West.

Notes

Epigraph: Charles M. Russell to Sgt. Ralph Kendall, undated, in Charles M. Russell, *Good Medicine: Memories of the Real West*, ed. Nancy C. Russell (Garden City, N.Y.: Garden City Publishing, 1929), 77. Charles Russell and many of his quotable contemporaries routinely made spelling, punctuation, and grammar errors in their informal correspondence. Except for the occasional editorial clarification within brackets, each quotation is cited as originally written.

1. An exception is Robert L. Gale, *Charles Marion Russell*, Boise State University Western Writers Series 38 (Boise, Idaho: Boise State University, 1979).

2. Al P. Andrews to James B. Rankin, [May 3,1938], folder 1, box 1, MC 162, James Brownlee Rankin Research Collection: Charles M. Russell, 1910–1962 (hereafter cited as Rankin Papers), Montana Historical Society Archives, Helena.

3. A few versions of Russell's unpublished stories also survive in published accounts of other people. See, for example, "Tales Charley Told," in Frank Bird Linderman, *Recollections of Charley Russell*, ed. H. G. Merriam (Norman: University of Oklahoma Press, 1963), 18–28; Con Price, *Memories of Old Montana* (Hollywood, Calif.: Highland Press, 1945), 137–50; and Con Price, *Trails I Rode* (Pasadena, Calif.: Trails End Publishing, 1947), 89–102. See also Fergus Mead to James B. Rankin, May 10, 1938, folder 24, box 2, Rankin Papers.

4. Will Rogers, introduction to *Trails Plowed Under*, by Charlie M. Russell (Garden City, N.Y.: Doubleday, Page, 1927), xiv.

5. Fergus Mead to James B. Rankin, May 10, 1938, folder 2, box 2, Rankin Papers.

6. Russell to William S. Hart, June 29, 1902, in *Good Medicine*, 30.

7. Charles M. Russell wrote the following articles for *Outing Magazine:* "Mormon Murphy's Misplaced Confidence," 50 (August 1907): 550; "How Lindsay Turned Indian," 51 (December 1907): 337; "Dad Lane's Buffalo Yarn," 51 (February 1908): 514; "Finger-That-Kills Wins His Squaw," 52 (April 1908): 32; and "Longrope's Last Guard," 52 (May 1908): 176.

8. Austin Russell, *C.M.R., Charles M. Russell: Cowboy Artist* (New York: Twayne, 1957), 198. Original editions and microfilm copies of many Montana Newspaper Association supplements are on file at the Montana Historical Society Library, Helena.

9. Michael P. Malone and Richard B. Roeder, *Montana: A History of Two Centuries* (Seattle: University of Washington Press, 1984), 216, 217; "New Book by C. M. Russell Filled with Humor," Montana Newspaper Association (hereafter MNA), distributed October 31, 1921.

10. Seventeen stories with a foreword are collected in C. M. Russell, *Rawhide Rawlins Stories* (Great Falls: Montana Newspaper Association, 1921). Nineteen stories and essays with a preface are collected in *More Rawhides* (Great Falls: Montana Newspaper Association, 1925). Three stories published in MNA inserts were not reprinted in either of these two books. The *Rawhides* story "Johnny Sees the Big Show" was omitted from *Trails Plowed Under*.

11. William Kittredge, "Desire and Pursuit of the Whole: The Politics of Storytelling," *Montana The Magazine of Western History* 42 (Winter 1992): 11.

12. Alfred H. Lewis's books include *Wolfville* (New York: Stokes, 1897),
     Wolfville Days (New York: Stokes, 1902), *Wolfville Nights* (New York:
     Stokes, 1902), and *Wolfville Folks* (New York: Appleton, 1908). E. C.
     "Teddy Blue" Abbott and Helena Huntington Smith, *We Pointed Them
     North: Recollections of a Cowpuncher* (1939; repr., Norman: University
     of Oklahoma Press, 1989). Frank B. Linderman's books include *Indian
     Why Stories* (New York: Charles Scribner's Sons, 1915), *Pretty-Shield:
     Medicine Woman of the Crows* (1932; repr., Lincoln: University of
     Nebraska Press, 1972), and *Plenty-Coups: Chief of the Crows* (1930; repr.,
     Lincoln: University of Nebraska Press, 1962).

13. Brian W. Dippie, *Looking at Russell* (Fort Worth, Texas: Amon Carter
     Museum, 1987), 62.

14. Russell, written on illustration, in *Good Medicine*, 127.

15. A. Russell, *C.M.R.*, 19, 20; David Lavender, *Bent's Fort* (1954; repr.,
     Lincoln: University of Nebraska Press, 1972), 396n4; Bernard DeVoto,
     Across the Wide Missouri (Boston: Houghton Mifflin, 1947), 373; George
     E. Hyde, *A Life of George Bent: Written from His Letters* (Norman:
     University of Oklahoma Press, 1968), viii.

16. Russell, "Injuns," in *Trails Plowed Under*, 28.

17. Russell to Harry Stanford, May 8, 1925, in *Good Medicine*, 53.

18. Russell to Paris Gibson, February 4, 1902, in *Good Medicine*, 71.

19. Frank R. Grant, "Embattled Voice for the Montana Farmers—Robert
     Sutherlin's Rocky Mountain Husbandman" (Ph.D. diss., University of
     Montana, 1982), 132.

20. "The Red Devils," *Mineral Argus* (Maiden, Mont.), September 10, 1885,
     p. 2.

21. Bill Nye, "The Annual Wail," in *Bill Nye's Western Humor*, ed. T. A.
     Larson (Lincoln: University of Nebraska Press, 1968), 11, 12.

22. Russell to Paris Gibson, February 4, 1902, in *Good Medicine*, 70, 71.

23. Vern Dusenberry, "Montana's Displaced Persons: The Rocky Boy
     Indians," *Montana The Magazine of Western History* 4 (Winter 1954): 1;
     Great Falls Tribune, January 10, 1909, p. 12; Celeste River, "A Mountain
     in His Memory: Frank Bird Linderman; His Role in Acquiring the
     Rocky Boy Indian Reservation for the Montana Chippewa and Cree
     ..." (M.A. thesis, University of Montana, 1990), 146, 207.

24. Russell to Henry L. Myers, C. M. Russell folder, box 1, file 25, Linderman Collection, Museum of the Plains Indian, Browning, Montana.

25. Russell to Frank B. Linderman, file 5, box 4, Linderman Collection, Mansfield Library, University of Montana, Missoula.

26. Peter H. Hassrick, *Charles M. Russell* (New York: Harry N. Abrams/ Smithsonian Institution, 1989), 130.

27. Russell, "The War Scars of Medicine-Whip," in *Trails Plowed Under*, 177, 178.

28. Russell, "Dad Lane's Buffalo Yarn," in ibid., 42.

29. Russell, "The War Scars of Medicine-Whip," in ibid., 180.

30. Robert H. Keller, Jr., *American Protestantism and United States Indian Policy, 1869–82* (Lincoln: University of Nebraska Press, 1983), 3, 150, 151.

31. A. J. Noyes (Ajax), *In The Land of Chinook, or The Story of Blaine County* (Helena, Mont.: State Publishing Company, 1917), 121; Russell, "Injuns," in *Trails Plowed Under*, 25.

32. Hugh Dempsey, "Tracking C. M. Russell in Canada, 1888–1889," *Montana The Magazine of Western History* 39 (Summer 1989): 6, 14. The American Blackfoot and Canadian Blood tribes share a language and much culture. Russell used both terms when referring to the Indians he visited near High River, Alberta, in 1888.

33. Russell, "The Trail of the Reel Foot," in *Trails Plowed Under*, 17. See also "When the Gros Ventre Indians Trailed A 'Bad Medicine' Track . . . ," MNA, distributed December 24, 1924, and "Clubfoot Trail Puzzled Indians," MNA, distributed February 21, 1938. For Clubfoot George Boyd's version of the incident, see "General Nelson A. Miles' Pursuit of Sitting Bull during Winter of 1876 . . . ," by "Mon Tana Lou" Grille, MNA, distributed May 9, 1935.

34. Russell, "The Trail of the Reel Foot," in *Trails Plowed Under*, 18, 20.

35. Ibid., 18.

36. DeVoto, *Across the Wide Missouri*, 376; Cassandra O. Phelps to James B. Rankin, February 5, 1939, folder 5, box 3, Rankin Papers.

37. Phil Weinard to James Rankin, January 4, 1938, folder 13, box 4, Rankin Papers; Russell to "Friend Charly," May 10, 1991, in *Paper Talk: Charlie Russell's American West*, ed. Brian W. Dippie (New York: Alfred A.

Knopf, 1979), 20; Russell, "The War Scars of Medicine-Whip," in *Trails Plowed Under*, 185.

38. Russell, "How Lindsay Turned Indian," in *Trails Plowed Under*, 133.

39. Russell, "Finger-That-Kills Wins His Squaw," in *Trails Plowed Under*, 121, 122. See Helen B. West, "Starvation Winter of the Blackfeet," *Montana The Magazine of Western History* 9 (Winter 1959): 2.

40. Russell, "Curley's Friend," in *Trails Plowed Under*, 57; "'Horse Prairie Cowboys' Private Cemetery," MNA, distributed December 22, 1924, and a later version on March 14, 1938. The 1938 version was rewritten to reflect a less mirthful attitude toward Indian victims.

41. "Red Devils," *Mineral Argus*, 2; Russell, "Curley's Friend," in *Trails Plowed Under*, 57, 64.

42. Russell, "Dad Lane's Buffalo Yarn," in *Trails Plowed Under*, 41, 42. See also James A. Dolph and C. Ivar Dolph, "The American Bison: His Annihilation and Preservation," *Montana The Magazine of Western History* 25 (Summer 1975): 15.

43. Russell, "Dad Lane's Buffalo Yarn," in *Trails Plowed Under*, 47.

44. Russell, "The Ghost Horse," in *Trails Plowed Under*, 91, 99; Karl Yost and Frederic G. Renner, comps., *A Bibliography of the Published Works of Charles M. Russell* (Lincoln: University of Nebraska Press, 1971), 21, item 41. See also "The Pinto," MNA, distributed June 30, 1919, and June 3, 1922.

45. Russell, "Finger-That-Kills Wins His Squaw," in *Trails Plowed Under*, 121.

46. Russell, "Dunc McDonald," in ibid., 15.

47. Alex Nemerov, "Doing the 'Old America': The Image of the American West, 1880–1920," in *The West as America: Reinterpreting Images of the Frontier, 1820–1920*, ed. William Truettner (Washington, D.C.: Smithsonian Institution Press, 1991), 299–300.

PART TWO

Cowboys and Cattle Country

5

Bringing Home All the Pretty Horses
The Horse Trade and the
Early American West, 1775–1825

DAN FLORES

In the summer of 1834, just two years after having visited and painted the tribes of the Missouri River and northern plains country, western artist George Catlin got his first opportunity to observe and paint that counterpoint world, hundreds of miles to the south, on the plains of what is now western Oklahoma. Accompanying an American military expedition that sought to treat with peoples such as the Comanches and the Kiowas, Catlin had a singular chance to see firsthand the similarities and differences between these two regions of the early-nineteenth-century American West.

On the Missouri, Catlin had traveled and lived with fur traders from one of the big companies engaged in competition for wealth skinned from the backs of beavers, river otters, muskrats, and bison. The artist had painted (and mourned) the great destruction then under way there. In the different ecology of the southern plains, however, Catlin saw only a small-scale facsimile of the great economic engines that were stripping the northern landscapes of valuable animals, and on these southern prairies an altogether different animal caught his attention. "The tract

---

Originally published in *Montana The Magazine of Western History* 58, no. 2 (Summer 2008): 3–21. Reprinted by permission of *Montana The Magazine of Western History*.

of country over which we passed, between the False Washita and this place," he wrote while traveling in the vicinity of the Wichita Mountains that summer of 1834, "is stocked, not only with buffaloes, but with numerous bands of wild horses, many of which we saw every day." He went on, with obvious admiration: "The wild horse of these regions is a small, but very powerful animal; with an exceedingly prominent eye, sharp nose, high nostril, small feet and delicate leg; and undoubtedly, . . . [has] sprung from a stock introduced by the Spaniards."[1]

No other denizen of the plains was "so wild and so sagacious as the horse," Catlin wrote. "So remarkably keen is their eye, that they will generally run 'at the sight,' when they are a mile distant . . . and when in motion, will seldom stop short of three or four miles." Like many other observers, the artist was struck with the sheer beauty of the horse in its wild state: "Some were milk white, some jet black—others were sorrel, and bay, and cream colour—many were an iron grey; and others were pied, containing a variety of colours on the same animal. Their manes were very profuse, and hanging in the wildest confusion over their necks and faces—and their long tails swept the ground."

At roughly the same point in time that Catlin expressed his admiration for the wild horses of the southern plains, back in the horse country of Kentucky, John James Audubon, Catlin's fellow painter (and, in private, a thorn in his side), wrote that he had become acquainted with a man who had just returned from "the country in the neighbourhood of the head waters of the Arkansas River," where he had obtained from the Osages a recently captured, four-year-old wild horse named Barro. Although the little horse was "by no means handsome" and had cost only thirty-five dollars in trade goods, Audubon was intrigued enough to try him out. The horse proved a delight. He had a sweet gait that covered forty miles a day. He leapt over woodland logs "as lightly as an elk," was duly cautious yet a quick study in new situations, and was strong and fearless when coaxed to swim the Ohio River. He was steady when birds flushed and Audubon shot them from the saddle. And he left a "superb" horse valued at three hundred dollars in the dust. Audubon quickly bought Barro for fifty dollars silver and, gloating over his discovery, concluded that "the importation of horses of this kind from the Western Prairies might improve our breeds generally."[2]

What is most intriguing, historically, about Catlin's and Audubon's wild horse epiphanies is that they came so late. In fact, nearly simultaneously with the evolution of the fur trade on the northern plains, the remarkable wild horse herds of the southern plains had generated an economy of capture and trade (and often, theft) that, from the 1780s to the 1820s, had fairly dominated the region. Wild horses from herds like those Catlin saw in Oklahoma had been driven up the Natchez Trace to the horse markets in New Orleans and Kentucky at least as early as the 1790s, half a century before Audubon's test ride on Barro. That neither man seemed aware of this in the 1830s is fairly strong evidence for the underground nature of the early horse trade in the West—which is why historians, as well as Catlin and Audubon, have missed it.

Yet on the sweeping plains south of the Arkansas River, during the period when Americans were becoming such a presence in the West, this was the fur trade's equivalent, if on a smaller scale. The wild horse trade schooled many diverse Indian peoples in the nuances of the market economy, provided Spanish Texas a revenue base, intrigued a famous American president, and drew itinerant American mustangers who quite literally carried the flag with them into vast, horizontal yellow landscapes whose ownership seemed up for grabs.

The wild horse trade of the West had first come to the official attention of the United States in the period and in the same flurry of motion that would eventually add the Louisiana Purchase to the early republic. At the turn of the nineteenth century, bands of western wild horses were still primarily confined to the deserts, plains, and prairies of the Southwest. They first stirred interest from the wider world during the years when Thomas Jefferson, as vice president in the John Adams administration, was already contemplating various schemes for understanding and ultimately exploring the West, especially its southern reaches.

As early as 1798, in conversations about the West with informants such as General James Wilkinson, Jefferson began to hear stories about an intriguing individual known as "the Mexican traveller." His real name was Philip Nolan, and he was an Irish American adventurer who, Jefferson discovered, had made a series of journeys far into the unknown Southwest, returning time and again driving herds of captured wild horses to New Orleans or up the Natchez Trace to the horse markets of Kentucky. Wilkinson had raised Nolan in his own household, where the young man had no doubt absorbed dinner-table talk of revolution and westward expansion. That may have given Jefferson pause. He asked for other opinions about Nolan.[3]

The image that emerges of this shadowy and rather legendary figure is of a literate, athletic, and adventurous young man who was confident enough in his wide-ranging abilities to attempt things about which other men only speculated. William Dunbar, the Mississippi scientist who became Jefferson's primary associate in assembling information on the southwestern reaches of the Louisiana Purchase, knew Nolan and told Jefferson that he thought the man lacked sufficient education and was flawed by eccentricities "many and great." Nevertheless, Dunbar wrote, Nolan "was not destitute of romantic principles of honor united to the highest personal courage." Another Jeffersonian who knew Nolan, Daniel Clark, Jr., of New Orleans, told Jefferson that he thought Nolan "an extraordinary Character," one "whom Nature seems to have formed for Enterprises of which the rest of Mankind are incapable."[4]

What Jefferson learned from these informants was that, as early as 1790–91, when Nolan was barely twenty years old, he had embarked on a two-year journey into the Southwest, carrying a passport from Esteban Miró, the Spanish governor of Louisiana. He ultimately met and traveled with Wichita and Comanche Indians, providing them with an initial, apparently very favorable, impression of Anglo-Americans. Judging from what seem today very precise descriptions of a part of the continent then almost unknown to anyone except tribal people, Nolan got all the way to New Mexico, along the way learning that the numerous Indian tribes of the southern plains were dissatisfied with Spanish trade and very desirous of replacing their former trading partners, the French, with a new source of guns and European goods. The Osages, enemies of many of the groups farther west, were well armed themselves and made every effort to block traders from St. Louis from establishing relations with the tribes of the deep plains. Apparently, Nolan intended to address that opening.[5]

But—and this was what caught Jefferson's attention—the vice president learned that Nolan had not returned from the southern plains with the usual northern plains trader's packs of Indian-processed furs. Instead, it was horses he had brought back from these forays, some of them wild ones that he and his associates had captured, others traded from the Indians.

Although he had found "the savage life . . . less pleasing in practice than speculation" (he could not "Indianfy [his] heart," as he put it), Nolan had gone on a second expedition into the southern plains in 1794, and a third one in 1796. He had brought back only 50 horses in 1794, but the number had jumped to 250 in 1796; several of these, he had decided to take to Frankfort,

Kentucky, to sell. This had brought him and his horses to the attention of important people who clamored for more of his product. In 1797, packing seven thousand dollars' worth of trade goods, "twelve good rifles, and . . . but one coward," and a sextant and a timepiece, "instruments to enable [him] to make a more correct map" (which grabbed the attention of suspicious Spanish officials), Nolan launched a fourth expedition. When he returned in 1798, he was driving a herd variously estimated at between 1,300 and 2,500 western horses. In the Kentucky horse markets, these animals reportedly would have brought between $50 (for ordinary animals) and $150 (for truly outstanding horseflesh).[6]

When Philip Nolan returned from this fourth expedition, a letter, written in a fine, clear hand, awaited him. Vice President Jefferson began: "It was some time since I have understood that there are large herds of horses in a wild state in the country West of the Mississippi." Nolan, Jefferson averred, was in a privileged position, for "the present then is probably the only moment in the age of the world and the herds mentioned above the only subjects, of which we can avail ourselves to obtain what has never yet been recorded and never can be again in all probability." Although he pleaded with Nolan to send along any natural history particulars about the horse "in its wild state," what Jefferson really desired was an interview with a man who had seen a world he himself could only wonder at. Eventually, Jefferson hatched a plan to effect such an interview, writing Natchez scientist William Dunbar in a follow-up letter that he was most desirous of purchasing one of Nolan's animals, which he had heard were "remarkable for the singularity & beauty of their colours and forms."[7]

Most western historians who know a bit about Philip Nolan have long assumed that Jefferson's letter produced the expected response. According to both Wilkinson and Daniel Clark, Nolan and an "Inhabitant of the western Country" who was a master of Indian hand signs (this was probably Joseph Talapoon, a Louisiana mixed-blood) departed for Virginia in May 1800 with a fine paint stallion for Jefferson. However, neither Nolan nor the paint horse ever got to Monticello. For reasons that are not clear, Nolan got no farther than Kentucky, then turned back. In other words, "the Mexican traveller" stood up the Virginian who was about to be elected the country's third president.[8]

By October 1800, Nolan was making the final preparations for a fifth and, as it would prove, final expedition to the western plains. He told a confidant before he left Natchez that he had two dozen good men, armed to the teeth, and was taking a large quantity of trade goods. This time he did not have a passport from Spanish officials, who had grown increasingly alarmed at his contacts among the expansionist Americans. Since the 1780s, Spain had sought to control and regulate the western horse trade for its own purposes, so the lack of a passport meant that any horses Nolan captured would be illegal contraband. To his contact, Nolan enigmatically added, "Everyone thinks that I go to catch wild horses, but you know that I have long been tired of wild horses."[9]

By December, the party had traveled deep into the southern plains beyond the Trinity River. Following a visit to a Comanche village on one of the branches of the Red River, the Americans returned to what seems to have been Nolan's favorite mustanging country south of present-day Fort Worth. There they built corrals and began running horses on the windswept prairies. In March 1801, Indian scouts operating for a Spanish force that had been sent out to arrest Nolan located the Americans' camp. When Nolan refused to surrender, the Spaniards attacked. In the ensuing melee, the Spanish force killed Nolan and captured more than a dozen of his men, although seven of his party slipped away into the plains. Philip Nolan's intriguing adventures were over.[10]

Thomas Jefferson, who assumed the presidency at almost the same moment that Nolan was dying among his wild horses,

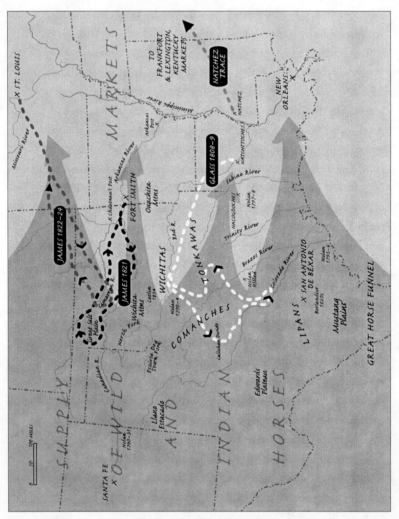

The early horse trade in the West.

would continue to be intrigued for years to come by the knowledge that horses had reverted to the wild in the West. Following
Nolan's death, Jefferson's hopes for understanding the natural
history of wild horses, and his growing sense that in the southern
West the horse trade might play an economic, diplomatic, and
geopolitical role similar to the one played by the fur trade in the
northern West, were embedded in his plans to send a Lewis and
Clark–type expedition into the Southwest. With Peter Custis,
the young University of Pennsylvania naturalist he attached to
his 1806 "Grand Expedition," Jefferson no doubt thought to put
a scientific observer among those herds. But during the same
summer that Lewis and Clark were returning from the Pacific,
Jefferson's second major expedition into the West encountered a
Spanish army four times its size and turned back. Peter Custis
would never get to be Thomas Jefferson's eyes among those
teeming wild horse herds. Nonetheless, Jefferson's dreams for the
West and wild horses would remain linked for years to come."

Jefferson never got to know what history can now reconstruct,
however imperfectly, about the wild horses of the nineteenth-
century West. Deep-time horse history commences with an
irony. Euro-Americans such as Jefferson understood that their
predecessors had brought the horse to the Americas and that,
after overcoming an initial fear of the animal, many indigenous
peoples in both North and South America had adopted the
horse. That simple act had revolutionized their cultures. But back
in the depths of time lay a surprising story that Jeffersonians
never suspected. Unlike many of the iconic animals of the West,
including even the bison, which had come to the Americas
after an evolutionary start in Asia, the horse was actually a true
American native. The ancestors of the horses Philip Nolan sold
in Kentucky had evolved 57 million years earlier as American
animals. If anything, the irony was even more profound than

that. Ten thousand years ago, after millions of years of evolution and after their spread to Asia, Africa, and Europe, horses unaccountably became extinct in the Americas. Equally perplexing, the horses that had migrated out of America to other parts of the world survived the Pleistocene extinctions. So thousands of years later, the Barb horses that danced and nickered beneath the Spaniards in their first entradas into the American West were in a real sense returning to their evolutionary homeland.[12]

That history is why horses were so phenomenally successful in going wild in the American West. From their primary seventeenth- and eighteenth-century distribution centers in the Spanish settlements of northern New Mexico, Texas, and California, feral horses escaped into the very landscapes that had shaped their ancestors' hooves, teeth, and behavioral patterns millennia earlier. When the Pueblo Indian Revolt of 1680 drove the Spaniards out of New Mexico for more than a decade, liberated livestock and horse culture famously got traded to tribes northward up the Rockies, passing from Puebloans to Utes, from Utes to Shoshones and Salish and Nez Perce, and, within half a century, to Blackfeet, Crows, and Crees.[13]

But in the chaos of the Pueblo Revolt, many animals also escaped to the plains. Similarly, when Spain abandoned its initial attempt to establish missions in Texas in the 1690s, the retreating Spaniards simply turned their mission livestock loose. Spaniards commonly did not geld stallions, and when they returned to Texas in 1715, they found that the stock they had left had increased to thousands. In some places, the countryside was blanketed with animals. A century later, a similar phenomenon was well under way in California.

By Jefferson's day, across the southern latitudes of the West, wild horse herds had become enormous in size. In Texas, Spanish bishop Marin de Porras wrote in 1805 that everywhere he traveled there were "great herds of horses and mares found close to the roads in herds of four to six thousand head." The California missions and presidios—having commenced with virtually no horses in the 1770s—found themselves surrounded by such growing bands of feral animals twenty years later that, beginning in 1806 in San Jose, then in Santa Barbara in 1808 and 1814, in Monterrey in 1812 and 1820, and generally throughout the California settlements by 1827, ranchers and colonists slaughtered large numbers of horses as nuisances and as threats to grass and water needed for domestic stock.[14]

With a century's natural increase, wild horses on the southern plains had become a sensory phenomenon, one observer noting that "the prairie near the horizon seemed to be moving, with long undulations, like the waves of the ocean. . . . [T]he whole prairie towards the horizon was alive with mustangs." Another observed, "[A]s far as the eye could extend, nothing over the dead level prairie was visible except a dense mass of horses, and the trampling of their hooves sounded like the roar of the surf on a rocky coast." A third wrote, "Wandering herds of wild horses are so numerous that the land is covered with paths, making it appear the most populated place in the world."[15]

It is fascinating to imagine a Great Plains ecology that integrated horses with bison herds, bands of pronghorns and deer and elk, wolves, cougars, and grizzlies. How large a component of that ecology they were is difficult to judge, because we have little beyond anecdotal accounts for estimating their populations. No one has been able to suggest horse numbers in the way we have worked out bison estimates. The writer J. Frank Dobie speculated that there were never more than 2 million wild horses in the West. He thought that well over a million of them ranged south of the Arkansas River, but he made no effort to track wild horse expansion over time or to calculate the effect of climate change on their numbers. Yet wet decades and droughts no doubt affected them, and from seed herds—not just on the southern plains but in places such as California, the Columbia Plateau, and Wyoming's Red Desert—wild herds were spreading out across the West.[16]

In the early period before 1825, however, the best hunting grounds for wild horses were clearly still the southern plains and the "mustang prairie" of South Texas—especially the former because it was the part of the West that possessed both wild horses and bison. Like favorite bison ranges, the concentrations of huge herds of horses in particular ecoregions produced profound cultural and ecological effects. The southern plains herds drew Indian peoples from all over the West, bringing Utes, Shoshones, Crows, Lakotas, Arapahos, Blackfeet, and many others into the southern prairies. And as wild and Indian horse herds steadily increased over the decades, their numbers cut into the carrying capacity of the plains for bison and other grazers.

As with bison and beavers and other furbearers farther north, useful animals in such enormous numbers as found among wild horses filled the human mind with thoughts of acquisition, wealth, and power—in other words, with thoughts of a potential economy.

The "great horse funnel" of the early nineteenth century took in tens of thousands of horses from its flared end on the southern plains and channeled them to trade marts including St. Louis, Natchitoches, Natchez, and New Orleans. Its historical origins are found in a simple equation. There was the supply—the horses, begetting generations of wild offspring across the immense, horizontal yellow plains of the Southwest. And there was the demand—the desire for wealth and status on the part of newly emergent Plains people such as the Comanches and the desire for revenue on the part of Euro-American colonial officials. There was also the desire for profits on the part of ambitious American traders and the desire for the product (animal-powered energy) by Americans pushing westward between the Appalachians and the Mississippi. The trick, eventually, would be to get the horses from the high plains of the West to the farms of the American frontier. With a couple of exceptions, the details of how it would all work are entirely familiar because it was so similar to the functioning of the fur trade. The big exception, which is the reason not much is known about this particular western economy, is the presence of corporate involvement in the fur trade and its absence in the horse trade.[17]

A fundamental characteristic of the American fur trade, regardless of geography, was the role that Indian people played as procurers of the resource. With the creation of trapping brigades by the Hudson's Bay Company and with the Rocky Mountain Fur Company's reliance on free trappers and the rendezvous system, the fur trade eventually produced a group of non-Native company employees who acted as procurers of furs. But Indians began as, and remained, major players in the nineteenth-century fur trade system. In good part that was because the Euro-American stage of the fur trade was based on a preexisting Native economy involving intertribal exchange of animal pelts and related trade items.[18]

Precisely the same pattern evolved in the western horse trade. Virtually from the start, horses became such revolutionary cultural agents, and so important to tribal ethnogenesis in the postcontact age, that barter exchanges of the animals became a central feature of western Indian life. Annual trade fairs in places such as the Black Hills and at fixed villages such as those of the Mandans-Hidatsas on the Missouri funneled horses in huge numbers from the Southwest to the northern plains. Even middleman groups emerged. The horse trade, for example, contributed to the segmentation of the previously agricultural Cheyennes into two geographic divisions, northern and southern, when the southern bands became central players in distributing horses northward up the plains.[19]

The various bands of the Comanches, another people newly drawn to the eighteenth-century southern plains because of horses, quite literally reconceived themselves in the context of horses and trade. They raided other tribes and Spanish colonists both for more horses and for captive children, training the latter as herders in an economy that became more pastoral by the decade. The Cheyennes and Comanches not only became famous catchers of wild horses but also, like the Nez Perces, became horse breeders, selecting animals for conformation, speed, and markings. From the heart of the southern plains, they marketed their animals northward to the horse-poor tribes of the northern plains and westward to New Mexicans via trade fairs in places such as Pecos, Picuris, and Taos—and eventually eastward to the Americans.[20]

No one duped these Native peoples into participating in the market economy. Indeed, to a significant degree, they created the western horse trade, built their own internal status systems around it, and for a century used it to manipulate the geopolitical designs of competing Euro-Americans anxious for profits and alliances with them. Of course, for Native people, the nineteenth-century western market economy came with many decided downsides. As with the fur trade, acquiring access to ever more animal resources meant that the horse trade would ultimately produce intertribal raids, wars, and territorial expansion. Eventually, the tribes of the southern plains would raid hundreds of miles southward, liberating new supplies of horses from Mexican ranches. And because northern winters were so hard on horses, raids for replenishment of tribal stock rippled from north to south every spring. As was always the case, when American traders entered these kinds of situations, things could get dicey.[21]

One result was that, soon after American horse traders such as

Philip Nolan entered the economy, initially procuring their horses from Native peoples by a trade carefully regulated and managed by the headmen of Indian bands, a point came when Americans took the same step the fur men had: with millions of wild horses running free on the plains, they turned to procuring the resource themselves. Just who originated the technique for catching wild horses in trade-sufficient numbers is difficult to ascertain. It may well have begun as an Iberian or North African equine art. By the time Americans entered the horse economy, many different peoples on the southern plains seem to have mastered it. The Wichita Indians taught Anthony Glass how to build pens and run wild horses; Nolan and others appear to have learned such skills from the French and Spanish settlers of western Louisiana towns such as Bayou Pierre and Natchitoches. Although George Catlin, the artist, provides us with accounts of Plains Indians capturing individual horses, the best descriptions we have of trade-volume mustanging strategies come from a third group involved in the horse trade: the Hispanic residents of Texas.[22]

As the wild horse herds of the southern plains grew into the hundreds of thousands across the seventeenth and eighteenth centuries, private horse hunters began to capture more and more of them to drive to Louisiana and Missouri to supply the emerging American market. Spain acted to declare the animals *mesteños*, which meant that they became the king's property. In a move that neither the United States nor Canada ever effected with bison, Spain proclaimed the vast wild herds of horses national property *(real camara y fisco de su magesta)*, subject to government regulation. This interesting development was part of the famous Bourbon Reforms, designed to strengthen the economies of Spain's colonies. The edict of 1778 required Spanish officials of the northern provinces (Provincias Internas) to place a tax of six reales on every wild horse captured from Spanish domains, thus creating the famous "Mustang Fund." Because captured wild horses were worth only three reales at the time, the initial tax was something of a miscalculation. In 1779, officials reduced the tax to two reales—a mere 67 percent rate. Spain required a license for citizens, plus a passport for noncitizens, who sought to catch or trade for its horses. Without the license or the passport, the trade was illegal and contraband.[23]

Enforcing this law proved impossible for a small Spanish population in an enormous setting. Yet, given how lucrative the mustang trade was, Spain needed to be able to enforce it. In the first six years of the tax, by January 1787, mustangers had paid taxes on seventeen thousand captured wild horses, some of which became colonial remounts but most of which appear to have ended up east of the Mississippi River, carrying American farmers and merchants and serving as mounts for southeastern Indians such the Chickasaws. As one San Antonio official put the matter in 1785, "The number of mustangs in all these environs is so countless that if anyone were capable of taming them and caring for them, he could acquire a supply sufficient to furnish an army. But this multitude is causing us such grave damage that it is often necessary to shoot them."[24]

Catching wild horses in this kind of volume required the same understanding of the animals' natural history that trapping did. It also required organization and carefully honed skills. Like trapping, it became a kind of wilderness art form, with its own material culture and its own internal terminology, but one that differed from trapping by aiming at *live* animal capture. Fortunately, a French scientist named Jean-Louis Berlandier left an account that describes the process by which mustangers captured wild horses in volume in the 1820s. What Berlandier recounted shows similarities to Indian techniques for impounding bison and pronghorns—and, in some particulars, even to the bison jump. But wild horse capture had clearly developed some nuances all its own.

Once mustangers were on the plains, among the herds and stallion bands, the first step was understanding the landscape sufficiently to know how to site what Berlandier called the *corrale*. "These are immense enclosures situated close to some pond," he wrote. Commonly they were built of mesquite posts lashed together with rawhide and were large enough that once inside, a herd could be swept into a circling, milling confusion in its center. "The entrance," Berlandier observed, "is placed in such a way that it forms a long corridor, and at the end there is a kind of exit." That corridor often consisted of brush wings that fanned out a half mile or more from the capture pen itself, usually oriented toward the south so that prevailing southwesterly winds would envelop an approaching herd in its own dust cloud, blinding it.[25]

To start the action, Berlandier's account relates, mustangers divided themselves into three groups, each group having a different role to play. After locating a likely herd, one group of well-mounted riders, the *adventadores,* had the task of startling the herd into flight and pushing it toward the brush funnel leading to the pen. Once the herd was in motion and a direction established, the animals would find themselves squeezed into a flight path by a second group of mustangers, the *puestos,* who were the most skilled riders and whose role consisted "of conducting that dreadful mass of living beings by riding full gallop along the flanks and gathering there, in the midst of suffocating dust, the partial herds which sometimes unite at the sound of the terror of a large herd." Finally, at the moment of truth, as the white-eyed, terrified horses were sweeping at breakneck speed into the trap, a third group of mustangers, the *encerradores,* were charged with closing the gate, sometimes dashing in to open it for an instant to allow stallions and older horses to escape.

What followed were scenes of such emotional impact that mustangers had a specialized vocabulary to describe them.

Captured wild horses "squeal[ed] terribly and rage[d] like lions."
They also died. Hispanic horse-catching jargon was rife with
the language of death—horses died from *sentimiento* (bróken-
heartedness) or from *despecho* (nervous rage). Then there was
the term *hediondo* (stinking), which designated a corral ruined
for further use by the aftereffects of having been jammed with
panicked and dying animals.[26]

Berlandier's description continues: "When these animals
find themselves enclosed, the first to enter fruitlessly search for
exits and those in the rear . . . trample over the first. It is rare
that in one of these chases a large part of the horses thus trapped
do not kill one another in their efforts to escape. . . . It has happened that the *mesteñeros* have trapped at one swoop more than
one thousand horses, of which not a fifth remained."

Exhausted by their efforts to escape, surviving horses were
roped one by one. "After some hours of ill treatment," Berlandier
concluded, "these *mesteñeros* have the ability to render them
half-tame a short while after depriving them of their liberty."[27]

The rhythmic creaking of saddle leather, the rustling and tin-
kling of swaying packs of trade goods, and the snick of hooves on
the cobbled plains surface must have ceased for a few moments
on the southern plains in early August 1808. After a five-week
outward journey, Anthony Glass and his party of ten traders,
driving sixteen packhorses that carried more than two thousand
dollars in goods and a riding remuda of thirty-two animals, had
finally come in sight of the thatched-roof village complex on the
Red River. Inhabited by peoples that the American horse traders
and their government knew as the "Panis," this complex was the
equivalent of the Mandan-Hidatsa towns on the Missouri. The
trio of villages was occupied by people who called themselves
Taovayas and Iscanis; today they are known, collectively, as the
Wichitas. In 1808, their acknowledged headman was Awahakei,

or Great Bear. And he had been expecting these Americans.[28]

Whether they built corrals and ran wild horses or traded for them with the tribes of the southern plains, American horse traders such as Philip Nolan had preceded the Louisiana Purchase in getting Americans into the horse trade economy. But in the aftermath of Jefferson's failed 1806 Grand Expedition, horse traders such as Anthony Glass—who rode down into the Wichita villages this August morning wearing the uniform of a U.S. military captain, his party of a dozen men traveling under an American flag—became private but overt agents of Jeffersonian geopolitical designs on the West. In the northern Rockies, of course, the trading posts and trapping parties of the American, Missouri, and Rocky Mountain Fur Companies consciously advanced U.S. claims for territory and tribal alliances in sharp competition with the posts and brigades of the Northwest and Hudson's Bay Companies, agents of the British Empire. On the southern plains and in the Southwest, however, the task of advancing America's empire fell to itinerant horse traders such as Glass. Indeed, in the decades following the Jefferson administration's clash with Spain over territory and boundaries, a whole series of American horse-trading expeditions worked as a kind of economic-diplomatic wedge to assert the interests of the new republic against a Spanish Empire distracted and overwhelmed by colonial revolutions across the Americas.

How successful the strategy was of allowing private economic interests to advance state geopolitical design is open to question (although one could argue that it has remained a fundamental of American foreign policy for two centuries now). On the southern plains between 1806 and 1821, it may have worked fairly well. In the aftermath of the events of that summer of 1806, with a Spanish army turning back an official American exploring expedition, and the ensuing escalation that, in the fall, would put an American force of twelve hundred troops eyeball to eyeball with a Spanish army of seven hundred, Spain seemed to blink. In 1807, it instructed frontier officials in its northern provinces to avoid any more "noisy disturbances" involving the Americans and to direct their efforts in stemming the contraband horse trade toward participating tribes rather than American traders. Hence, when Jefferson's Indian agent, Dr. John Sibley of Natchitoches, authorized and helped plan the Glass expedition, the captain's coat and U.S. flag (which Glass was to present to Awahakei to fly over the villages) reflected a Jeffersonian's musings about how to turn the horse trade to state advantage. As Sibley would remark, sagely, "[W]hoever furnishes Indians the Best & Most Satisfactory Trade can always Control their Politicks."[29]

Of course, profit, more than statecraft, motivated American horse traders, and that required no official sanction. In addition to Nolan, Glass had been preceded in the West by several other American horse-trading parties. Little is known about them now, but in 1794–95, for instance, a twenty-seven-year-old Philadelphia gunsmith named John Calvert spent fourteen months pursuing horses with the Wichitas and Comanches before a Spanish patrol snagged him. Calvert was followed in 1804–1805 by a very active plains trader named John Davis and a Corsican carpenter, Alexandro Dauni. They were followed in turn by John House, one of Philip Nolan's mustangers, who successfully drove a herd back from the plains in 1805. Then there were trading parties led by Francisco Roquier in 1805 and John Cashily in 1806, who ingeniously planned to tell Spanish officials that the horses they were driving eastward were intended to help them bring their families west as new Spanish immigrants.[30]

Almost in the middle of the uproar over Jefferson's attempts to explore the Red River, Dr. Sibley licensed yet another horse-trading party, this one led by John Lewis and William Alexander and guided by Nolan's sign language expert, Joseph Talapoon. Lewis and Alexander seem to have been the Jefferson adminis-

tration's first experiment with traders as official government em-
issaries: they also took U.S. flags to the western Indians, and in
Sibley's name they invited the tribes of the southern plains to a
grand council in Natchitoches in 1807. In June 1807, three of this
party (the rest were still on the plains, running horses) arrived in
Louisiana driving a herd of mustangs. Did they pay the Spanish
tax on their horses? Of course not. As Sibley noted, a few years
earlier Spanish records had shown 1,187 horses officially *leaving*
for Louisiana, but somehow more than 7,300 horses had managed to *arrive* there. Helpless to stem the tide, one Spanish official estimated the number of the king's horses herded into the
United States during the early nineteenth century at a thousand
a month, which gives some idea of the volume of the economy.[31]

The paucity of surviving information on most of the horse
traders both before and after Anthony Glass permits some focus
on him. In apparent contrast to many of his contemporaries in
the economy, Glass was literate. Remarkably, Sibley had persuaded him to keep a journal, which he did—sporadically—during his ten months in the West. This document not only gives us
a sense of the early horse trade but also leaves an impression of
Glass as a sort of John Colter of the southern plains.

Glass was more solidly middle class than most American
horse traders. He and a brother were merchants in the river
town of Natchez, the terminus of the famous wilderness trail
of the same name that funneled western horses into Kentucky
and Tennessee. In 1808, he was about thirty-five and a recent
widower. Either legitimately, or perhaps as an explanatory ruse
in case Spanish officials captured him, the year before he had
inquired about emigrating to New Spain. How much experience
he had with horses, Indians, or the West is difficult to determine,
but there is little doubt that he viewed his 1808–1809 trading
expedition as high adventure.

If Glass's experiences were typical, the horse trade of the

early West was at least as much adventure as entrepreneurial enterprise. Judging from the speech he made before the assembled peoples of the Wichita villages in August 1808, the United States was convinced that these western tribes were already economic allies of the Americans, despite the conflicting territorial claims with Spain over the southern boundary of the Louisiana Purchase. Jefferson was their "Great Father," Glass told them, and as for him: "I have come a long Journey to see you & have brought with me some goods to exchange with you and your brothers—the Hietans [Comanches], for Horses if you will trade with us on fair and Equal terms."[32]

Establishing those terms took some effort and caused some arguments, but within a few days Glass was assembling his herd—twenty horses one day, thirteen the next, eleven a few days later, and apparently at that rate for week after week. There were also losses. Osage raiders, whom the Wichitas reported had driven off five hundred of their horses shortly before Glass arrived, took twenty-nine of his best horses late that August. A month later, during a second Osage raid on the Wichita horse herds, Glass was chagrined to find that "one of them was riding a remarkable Paint Horse that used to be [his] own riding Horse, which was stolen with those on the 22d of August."[33]

After two months of daily trade negotiations with the Wichitas, Glass's party—accompanied by a large Indian contingent—headed deeper into the plains in search of Comanche bands with whom to trade. While trade was his main goal, Glass clearly had yet another objective. The Wichitas had told him about a remarkable object far out on the plains, a large metallic mass that they and the Comanches regarded as a powerful mystery. Glass cajoled the Indians into taking him to the site, and after "observing considerable ceremony," they finally led the Americans to the place where the metal was. Glass was as mystified as anyone else, but what he was seeing, in fact, was a sixteen-hundred-pound iron-nickel meteorite, a major healing shrine for Indians of the southern plains. Fancying it a giant nugget of platinum, some of the members of Glass's party would return two years later and contrive to haul and float it back to civilization.[34]

Discontented with their inability to trade for horses from the Comanche bands they found, in mid-October Glass's party divided their goods. Several of the experienced horse traders among them headed off in search of particular Comanche trading partners from previous trips, but Glass continued southward, camping with increasingly larger numbers of Comanche bands from the north and west. He reported his disappointment: "trade dull[;] the Indians are unwilling to part with their best Horses." They were, however, willing to part him from his, stealing twenty-three one night in late December and smaller numbers later on.[35]

During the dead of winter 1809, with snow six inches deep on the plains, Glass finally attempted the mustanger's ultimate art—catching wild horses himself. Wild ones by this point "were seen by the thousands," and Glass, two remaining companions, and the Indians traveling with them built a strong pen and spent many days attempting to corral the wild herds around them. But "the Buffalo were so plenty and so in the way we succeeded badly in several attempts."[36]

Unfortunately—one suspects quite by design—Glass remained vague on the number of horses he ultimately drove back from the plains in May 1809, but the sense is of a herd of many hundreds of animals, including many of those that would fetch as much as $100 to $150. It is difficult to say just how typical his experience was. But in an economy for which few other day-by-day accounts exist, Anthony Glass's journal provides quite a remarkable look at an early-nineteenth-century western experience. He allows us to imagine a history where one had barely been imaginable before.

It would be a full decade later, when Spain and the United States finally agreed on the Red and Arkansas rivers as the official boundary between them (in the Adams-Onís Treaty of 1819), before another American horse trader would leave us an account rivaling Glass's. In the interim, scores—very likely hundreds—of unknown and undocumented American mustangers traversed the plains, running wild horses, trading for horses from the Indians, and encouraging such a general theft of horses across the West that one source estimates ten thousand were stolen from Spanish ranches in a single year.[37]

References exist for a few of these traders. Ezra McCall and George Schamp (who had been with Glass) were back on the plains in 1810. The Osages plundered Alexander MacFarland and John Lemons's mustanging party in 1812. Auguste Pierre Chouteau, Jules DeMun, and Joseph Filibert opened up a significant horse trade with the Comanches and Arapahos between 1815 and 1817. Caiaphas Ham and David Burnet became modestly famous horse traders in the same years, and so did Jacob Fowler (who left us a journal written in phonics) and Hugh Glenn. When Mexico finally achieved its independence from Spain and moved to open up its markets to the United States, the man who opened the Santa Fe Trail—William Becknell—could do so because he, too, was an old plains horse trader.[38]

What made these southern plains horse trade expeditions shadowy and northern plains fur trade activities well known was actually a simple difference. Because the horse trade featured live, not dead, animals, horses became their own transportation to markets. There was no need, as in the fur trade, for corporate investment in freight wagons, steamboats, or shipping. That difference not only created a documentary disparity for later historical writers but also affected the comparative fiduciary risk involved at the time.

Consider, for instance, one more example from the early

western horse trade, that of Thomas James of St. Louis, who gives us a final, fine-grained look at the mustanger's West before Mexico's revolution changed the ground. James, intriguingly, was both a mountain man *and* a mustanger. He had first gone west by ascending the Missouri to the Three Forks in 1809–10, but he did not make his first trip onto the southern plains until 1821. It was then that he rode from Fort Smith to the salt plains of present-day Oklahoma before he was confronted by Comanches under Spanish orders not to allow Americans to approach Santa Fe. Eyeing those splendid Comanche horse herds appreciatively, Thomas James got a sense of the possibilities.[39]

Invited to return the next summer to trade for horses, James did, and the result was a three-year expedition (1822–24) financed with $5,500 in goods. Ascending the various forks of the Canadian River, James's party of twenty-three finally met the Wichitas under their headman, Alsarea, and the trading commenced. Four yards of British wool blankets and two yards of calico, along with a knife, a mirror, flint, and tobacco, were the going rate for a well-broken horse, and James quickly bought seventeen that he knew would fetch one hundred dollars apiece back in the settlements. Eventually, the Wichitas introduced James to the Comanches, a Yamparika band under Big Star, and James got his first taste of horse trading Comanche style: they were perfectly willing to trade their best horses since they had every intention of stealing them back. According to James, despite the frustrations, the life of a nineteenth-century horse trader on the southern plains held a real allure. He was smitten: "I began to be reconciled to a savage life and enamored with the simplicity of nature. Here were no debts, no Sheriffs, no Marshals; no hypocrisy or false friendships."[40]

Once he had assembled a drove of 323 high-quality animals, James departed for the settlements, but not before Alsarea made a present of his own fine warhorse, Checoba, and urged James to return the next year to the headwaters of the Red, where the Wichitas grazed 16,000 ponies. That would have been the horse trader's promise of the Golden Fleece, but James never returned. Pushing his herd eastward, he lost all but 71 to stampedes and what must have been a biblical attack of horseflies. More attrition followed as he penetrated the woodlands. It is difficult to know how typical James's tribulations were, but when he finally reached St. Louis, he had just 5 horses left. That happened to be precisely the number he had started with.[41]

James's account, published under the title *Three Years among the Indians and Mexicans,* may not be entirely reliable. But if it is, his and Glass's accounts may help explain the lack of corporate interest in the horse trade. At least up until 1821, the trapping and trading of wild horses in volume on the Spanish border was a very risky business. Although Philip Nolan and his backers possibly made as much as forty thousand to sixty thousand dollars from an investment of seven thousand dollars in trade goods in 1797–98, the figures for other early traders look a lot less impressive. And Nolan's speculative profits do not take into account the work, fatigue, and risk factors in a dangerous wildlands vocation.[42]

The wild horse trade in the West did not evaporate after Mexico's revolution in 1821. If anything, as horses spread farther north and west, trading expanded geographically and perhaps even in volume. In the 1830s, Bent's Fort in Colorado based at least some of its economy on the horse trade of the Southern Plains tribes. And adventuresome Americans' interest in California in the 1830s had much to do with stories of the horse herds ranging across those golden, rolling hills. But whenever they rode, these later and more widespread mustangers would have based their artfulness on the West's horse economy of the period from 1775 to 1825.

The reason literary men such as Catlin and Audubon missed the full dimensions of the early western horse trade is that it was an example of what we might call a "concealed economy," which emerged where different empires—in this case a fading Spanish one and a vibrant, emergent American one—touched at their edges. In it, shadowy freelancers, Comanche and Wichita traders, Hispanic entrepreneurs, and Thomas Jefferson all ended up dealing with one another, at least indirectly, during the fluid time of our emerging national empire in the West.

Notes

1. Quotations in this paragraph and the following from George Catlin, *Letters and Notes on the Manners, Customs, and Conditions of the North American Indians,* 2 vols. (1841; repr., New York: Dover, 1973), 2:57–59. Catlin adds that wild horses were even then stocking "the plains from this to Lake Winnepeg, two or three thousand miles to the North."

2. John James Audubon, *Ornithological Biography, or An Account of the Habits of the Birds of the United States of America,* 3 vols. (Edinburgh: Black, 1835), 3:270–74. A few weeks later, Audubon sold Barro, "not without regret," for $120.

3. Nolan was a figure of considerable interest for twentieth-century historians of the Southwest. Secondary works addressing his life include Maurine Wilson and Jack Jackson's *Philip Nolan and Texas: Expeditions to the Unknown Land, 1791–1801* (Waco, Texas: Texian Press, 1987); Noel Loomis and Abraham Nasatir, *Pedro Vial and the Roads to Santa Fe* (Norman: University of Oklahoma Press, 1967); and Noel Loomis, "Philip Nolan's Entry in Texas in 1800," in *The Spanish in the Mississippi Valley, 1762–1804,* ed. John McDermott (Urbana: University of Illinois Press, 1974), 120–320.

4. William Dunbar to Thomas Jefferson, Natchez, August 22, 1801, and Daniel Clark to Thomas Jefferson, New Orleans, February 12, 1799, both in "[Documents] Concerning Philip Nolan," *Quarterly of the Texas State Historical Association* (April 1904): 315, 310.

5. This argument for the extent of Nolan's early journeys is based on the description of the southern plains that General Wilkinson would later provide to the Jefferson administration, almost certainly (although not definitively) from Nolan's own accounts. The description conveyed with striking accuracy the courses of both major headwater forks of the Red River, the existence of the Wichita Mountains, and the plateau of the Llano Estacado, along with the Pecos River and the Rocky Mountain Front in New Mexico. It appears in James Wilkinson to Henry Dearborn, Natchez, July 13, 1804, War Department, Letters Received, Main Series, Record Group M222, National Archives, Fort Worth, Texas.

6. Philip Nolan to James Wilkinson, Frankfort, Kentucky, June 10, 1796, and Philip Nolan to James Wilkinson, New Orleans, April 24, 1797, both in James Wilkinson, *Memoirs of My Own Times,* 3 vols. (1816; repr., New York: AMS Press, 1973), vol. 2, appendix 2. The primary sources do not provide an estimate of the size of the horse herd Nolan drove back from the West on this expedition, but his biographers believe that it was the biggest wilderness haul of his career as a mustanger. Wilson and Jackson (*Philip Nolan,* 34) set the figure for this Nolan trip at 1,296 horses.

7. Thomas Jefferson to Philip Nolan, Philadelphia, June 24, 1798, and Thomas Jefferson to William Dunbar, Philadelphia, January 16, 1800, both in the Thomas Jefferson Papers, Manuscripts Division, Library of Congress, Washington, D.C.

8. Various historians, including Noel Loomis, believed that Jefferson did get an interview with Nolan. But although Wilkinson's letter of introduction for Nolan arrived at Monticello in November 1800 (duly dated on receipt, as was Jefferson's habit), Nolan was once again running horses in the West by then. Using the letters between the various principals in the Thomas Jefferson Papers, I have been able to show that no meeting ever took place. The circumstantial evidence is that someone in Kentucky offered Nolan more money for the paint stallion than he could refuse. See Dan Flores, ed., *Jefferson and Southwestern Exploration: The Freeman and Custis Accounts of the Red River*

Expedition of 1806 (Norman: University of Oklahoma Press, 1984). The second edition of this book appeared under the title *Southern Counterpart to Lewis and Clark: The Freeman and Custis Expedition of 1806* (Norman: University of Oklahoma Press, 2002).

9. Philip Nolan to Jesse Cook, Natchez, October 21, 1800, quoted in full in Loomis and Nasatir, *Pedro Vial,* 217–18.

10. Wilson and Jackson, *Philip Nolan,* 65–76.

11. For the story of this expedition, see Dan Flores, "A Very Different Story: Exploring the Southwest from Monticello with the Freeman and Custis Expedition of 1806," *Montana The Magazine of Western History* 50 (Spring 2000): 2–17.

12. Bruce MacFadden, *Fossil Horses: Systematics, Paleobiology, and Evolution of the Family Equidae* (New York: Cambridge University Press, 1992); Richard Hulbert, Jr., "The Ancestry of the Horse," in *Horses through Time,* ed. Sandra Olsen (Boulder, Colo.: Roberts Rinehart Publishers, 1997), 13–34; Gaylord Simpson, *Horses: The Story of the Horse Family in the Modern World and through Sixty Million Years of History* (New York: Oxford University Press, 1951).

13. Francis Haines, "Where Did the Plains Indians Get Their Horses?" and "The Northward Spread of Horses among the Plains Indians," *American Anthropologist* 40 (January–March and July–September 1938): 112–17, 429–37; Gilbert Wilson, "The Horse and Dog in Hidatsa Culture," *Anthropological Papers of the American Museum of Natural History* 15 (1924): 125–311; Frank Roe, *The Indian and the Horse* (Norman: University of Oklahoma Press, 1955).

14. On the spread of horses in Texas, see Nettie Benson, "Bishop Marin de Porras and Texas," *Southwestern Historical Quarterly* 51 (July 1947): 16–40; and José Antonio Pichardo, *Pichardo's Treatise on the Limits of Louisiana and Texas,* 4 vols., ed. and trans. Charles Wilson Hackett (Austin: University of Texas Press, 1931–46). For the spread of horses in California, I relied on the California Manuscripts, Provisional Records, Letters Registers, 1794–1823, and the Herbert Eugene Bolton Papers (hereafter cited as Bolton Papers), part 1, both collections in the Bancroft Library, University of California–Berkeley (hereafter cited as UC-Berkeley).

15. Quotations from John Bartlett of the Mexican boundary survey and Texas Ranger John Duval, items 16771 and 16773 in the J. Frank Dobie

Papers, Ransom Humanities Research Center, University of Texas, Austin (hereafter cited as UT, Austin), and from Fray Juan Agustin de Morfi, "Journey among the Indians and New Mexican Diary," typescript in Bolton Papers, part 1, p. 449, UC-Berkeley.

16. Because of the quality of his work on the wild horses of the nineteenth-century West, I follow J. Frank Dobie, although he admits that his estimate is not scientific or even systematic and that "all guessed numbers are mournful to history." See Dobie, *The Mustangs* (Boston: Little, 1934), 108–109. On bison calculations, see Dan Flores, "Bison Ecology and Bison Diplomacy: The Southern Plains from 1800 to 1850," *Journal of American History* 78 (September 1991): 465–85.

17. See Richard White, "Animals and Enterprise," in *The Oxford History of the American West,* ed. Clyde Milner et al. (New York: Oxford University Press, 1994), 247–84.

18. The literature here is vast, but see, for example, William Swagerty, *Indian Trade in the Trans-Mississippi West to 1870,* vol. 4 of *The Handbook of North American Indians: Indian-White Relations,* ed. William Sturtevant, 20 vols. (Washington, D.C.: Smithsonian Institution, 1978–89), 351–74; Arthur Ray, *Indians in the Fur Trade* (Toronto: University of Toronto Press, 1974); and David J. Wishart, *The Fur Trade of the American West, 1807–1840* (Lincoln: University of Nebraska Press, 1979).

19. Joseph Jablow, *The Cheyennes in Plains Indian Trade Relations, 1795–1840* (New York: J. J. Augustin, 1950); Elliott West, "Called Out People: The Cheyennes and the Southern Plains," *Montana The Magazine of Western History* 48 (Summer 1998): 2–15; H. Clyde Wilson, "An Inquiry into the Nature of Plains Indian Cultural Development," *American Anthropologist* 65 (April 1963): 355–70.

20. The best discussion of horse-propelled ethnogenesis, or cultural re-creation, among the Comanches is Gary Anderson, *The Indian Southwest, 1580–1830: Ethnogenesis and Reinvention* (Norman: University of Oklahoma press, 1999). See also Thomas Kavanagh, *Comanche Political History: An Ethnohistorical Perspective, 1706–1785* (Lincoln: University of Nebraska Press, 1996); and Pekka Hamalainen, "The Western Comanche Trade Center: Rethinking the Plains Indian Trade System," *Western Historical Quarterly* 29 (Winter 1998): 485–513.

21. The best account (for the early nineteenth century) of Indian raids southward into Mexico for horses is by trader David G. Burnet, who

estimated that in 1818–19, the Comanches were stealing ten thousand horses a year there. See Ernest Wallace, ed., "Burnet's Letters," *West Texas Historical Association Yearbook* 30 (1954): 115–40. In "Ecological Aspects of Equestrian Adaptations in Aboriginal North America," *American Anthropologist* 85 (September 1983): 563–91, Alan Osborn explains the science of winter horse mortality on the northern plains as compared with the mortality farther south. For the raiding patterns that resulted, see Theodore Binnema, *Common and Contested Ground: A Human and Environmental History of the Northwestern Plains* (Norman: University of Oklahoma Press, 2001).

22. Both Wilson and Jackson, in *Philip Nolan* (9–10), and Terry G. Jordan, in *North American Cattle-Ranching Frontiers* (Albuquerque: University of New Mexico Press, 1993), argue that Americans learned the nuances of catching wild horses from residents of Louisiana Creole outposts such as Bayou Pierre, near present-day Shreveport.

23. See especially letter 15, Commandant General Teodoro de Croix's communication of the new regulation, in the collection of translated manuscript letters in the Bexar Archives (the Spanish Archives of Texas), Barker Texas History Center, UT, Austin. According to the commandant, "Another contributing factor in these [evils] has been the liberty with which everyone, up until now, has considered himself authorized to go out and build corrals or stockades, then round up, enclose and take possession of wild and unbranded cattle and horses." The best secondary account is found in Jack Jackson's *Los Mesteños: Spanish Ranching in Texas, 1721–1821* (College Station: Texas A&M University Press, 1986).

24. For examples of monthly figures on horses caught and taxed, see letter 45 (1784) and letter 51 (1785) in the translated series at the Bexar Archives, UT, Austin. Mustang total figures to January 1, 1787 (17,000 animals and 8,805 pesos), are from Pichardo, *Pichardo's Treatise,* 2:31–32. The quote is from Texas governor Domingo Cabello to José Antonio Rengel, San Antonio (Bexar), October 3, 1785, letter 50 in the translated series, Bexar Archives, UT, Austin.

25. Except where noted, this account and the quotations are from Jean Louis Berlandier, *Journey to Mexico during the Years 1826 to 1834,* trans. Sheila Ohlendorf, Josette Bigelow, and Mary Standifer, 2 vols. (Austin: Texas State Historical Association; Center for Studies in Texas History, University of Texas, 1980), 2:545–46. Zebulon Pike

offered an earlier, briefer description of this technique, to which he appended the salute, "For this business I presume there is no nation in the world superior to the Spaniards of Texas." Donald Jackson, ed., *The Journals of Zebulon Montgomery Pike,* 2 vols. (Norman: University of Oklahoma Press, 1966), 2:77–78.

26. The "squealing" quotation is from Father Bernabe Cobo, in a typescript translation of his *History of the New World,* Lawrence Kinnaird Papers, Bancroft Library, UC-Berkeley. Spanish horse-catching terminology is from Jackson, *Los Mesteños,* 465. Pike does not offer Spanish terms but refers to the effect associated with *hediondo.*

27. Pike rounds out these details by noting that the Spanish mustangers kept their captured animals without food and in constant motion until they submitted.

28. The account here is from Dan Flores, ed., *Journal of an Indian Trader: Anthony Glass and the Texas Trading Frontier, 1790–1810* (College Station: Texas A&M University Press, 1985). See also Elizabeth Ann Harper, "The Taovayas Indians in Frontier Trade and Diplomacy, 1779–1835," *Panhandle-Plains Historical Review* 26 (1953): 41–72. As prairie Caddoans, these people were related to the Pawnees farther north. Half a century before Glass came upon them, they had been persuaded by French traders to move from the Arkansas River to this location on the Red. By relocating, they were more accessible to Euro-Americans embarking westward from Natchez and Natchitoches.

29. See the epilogue in Flores, *Southern Counterpart,* for the story of the confrontation between the United States and Spain in 1806. The new policy toward American interlopers in Spanish lands seems to have been suggested by Texas governor Antonio Cordero. It was then approved by the commandant general of the northern provinces, Nemecio Salcedo. See Cordero to Salcedo, San Antonio, February 4, 1807, and Salcedo to Cordero, Chihuahua, July 12, 1807, both in the Bexar Archives, UT, Austin. Sibley's remark is taken from John Sibley to William Eustis, Natchitoches, November 28, 1812, in Julia Kathryn Garrett, ed., "Doctor John Sibley and the Louisiana Texas Frontier, 1803–1814," *Southwestern Historical Quarterly* 49 (January 1946): 415.

30. See Flores, *Journal of an Indian Trader,* 15–24; and Dan Flores, *Horizontal Yellow: Nature and History in the Near Southwest* (Albuquerque: University of New Mexico Press, 1999), 116–18.

31. John Sibley to W. C. C. Claiborne, Natchitoches, October 10, 1803, in *The Territory of Orleans, 1803–1812,* comp. and ed. Clarence Carter and John Bloom, vol. 9 of *The Territorial Papers of the United States* (Washington, D.C.: Government Printing Office, 1933), 75. The estimate of one thousand horses a month was made by Texas governor Juan Bautista de Elguezabal. Loomis and Nasatir, *Pedro Vial,* 66–67. Historian Jack Jackson (*Los Mesteños,* 470) also thinks that the extralegal horse trade from Spanish domains was often ten times the legal number during these years.

32. Anthony Glass, August 12, 1808, journal entry, in Flores, *Journal of an Indian Trader,* 47–48.

33. Glass, September 28, 1808, journal entry, ibid., 65.

34. Glass, October 9–14, 1808, journal entry, ibid., 68–69. The meteorite, known as "Red River," attracted the traders Schamp and McCall in 1810. The men laboriously hauled and floated it back from the plains. It ended up in the Peabody Museum of Natural History at Yale, where for much of the nineteenth century it was the largest iron-nickel meteorite in the world and the subject of many scientific papers. Meteorites such as these were understood by the prairie Caddoans to have come from the sky. People had long sought them out as healing shrines and fashioned them into arrow points and fetishes. Such meteorites are very likely the source of precious metals stories on the southern plains that go back all the way to Coronado's quest to reach Quivira. For the retrieval, science, and anthropology surrounding this particular meteorite, see the epilogue in Flores, *Journal of an Indian Trader.*

35. Glass, December 7 and 30, 1808, and February 6, 1809, journal entries, ibid., 73–80. The Comanche chiefs later managed to return some of Glass's stolen horses to him.

36. Glass, December 30, 1808, journal entries, ibid., 79.

37. Wallace, "Burnet's Letters," 115–40.

38. For more on other American horse traders, who often were not only illiterate but disinclined to call attention to themselves, see Flores, *Journal of an Indian Trader,* 85–91; and Flores, *Horizontal Yellow,* 116–18. Loomis and Nasatir also investigate many of the horse traders of the era, especially those who came to the notice of Santa Fe officials, in *Pedro Vial,* 248–64. William Becknell, who opened up the Santa Fe Trail in 1821, initially advertised for "a company of men

destined westward for the purpose of trading for horses and mules." The trip turned into one to open Santa Fe to American trade. John Aston, *History of Jack Stock and Mules in Missouri* (Jefferson City, Mo.: State Board of Agriculture, 1924), 10; and [William Becknell], "Journal of Two Expeditions from Boon's Lick to Santa Fe," *Missouri Historical Society Collections* 2 (July 1906): 56–67.

39. This account is from Thomas James, *Three Years among the Indians and Mexicans*, ed. Walter Douglas (St. Louis: Missouri Historical Society, 1916), 110–27.

40. Ibid., 119–234. The quotation appears on 223.

41. For comparison, Nolan reported that of the 250 horses he herded to Frankfort in 1796, he lost all but 42 to an affliction called "yellow water," a distemper that had even killed a horse he had brought for his patron, General Wilkinson. Nolan to Wilkinson, Frankfort, June 10, 1796, in Wilkinson, *Memoirs,* vol. 2, appendix 2.

42. The estimate of forty thousand to sixty thousand dollars for Nolan's herd in 1797–98 assumes a minimum of forty to fifty dollars each for twelve hundred horses.

6

Tales of the Texas Rangers

ROBERT M. UTLEY

The Texas Rangers vie with the Royal Canadian Mounted Police as a constabulary known and admired throughout the world. Both played a notable role in the past and continue to enjoy high reputation and a good press. Both attained legendary stature at least a century ago and still bask in its glow today.

In the popular conception, the Texas Rangers form an organized body of lawmen extending uninterruptedly back to the colonizing years of Stephen F. Austin in Mexican Texas. In truth, for at least four decades they were neither organized nor lawmen. Whether dating from 1823 (as modern Rangers like to think) or 1835 (as the contemporary record suggests), they began as citizen soldiers.

For nearly half a century, the citizen soldier contended with Indians who raided the settlements of the Texas frontier— mostly Comanches and Kiowas from north of the Red River— and this was the central and lasting purpose of their "ranging" units. During the years of the Republic of Texas, 1836 to 1845, citizen soldiers also gathered to fend off military incursions from Mexico, which had not conceded Texas independence, and after statehood they volunteered to fight as U.S. troops in the Mexican

Originally published in *American Heritage* 53, no. 3 (June–July 2002): 40–48. Reprinted by permission of Oxford University Press, Inc.

War. Finally, for both republic and state, the international border traced by the Rio Grande periodically drew companies of citizen soldiers to confront both Mexican bandits and raiding Indians.

Whatever the official designation, Ranger companies displayed certain common characteristics. The men volunteered to serve for a specified time, usually three or six months. They furnished their own mounts and arms. They wore no uniform. They bore no flag. They elected their officers. They enjoyed an easy camaraderie with one another and with their leaders. And they held military regulation and discipline in contempt. Only a gifted captain could form these mulish freemen into a fighting team.

Such a man was John Coffee Hays. In 1844, under his leadership, three ingredients came together to crystallize the evolving Ranger tradition. This mix occurred at the battle of Walker Creek, a ferocious fight with Comanche raiders in the hills north of San Antonio. The first ingredient was experienced fighting men, expert horsemen, and marksmen seasoned by the dangerous life on the edges of settlement. The second was Hays, who knew that men prickly about their individualism had to be led by example, not command. The third ingredient was a revolutionary weapon. At close range, the Comanche warrior employed his bow and arrow as a highly effective repeating weapon. What the Ranger needed was his own repeater. He got it in 1844. In 1839 the Texas navy had purchased 130 of Samuel Colt's revolving pistols. When President Sam Houston disbanded the navy in 1843, Hays equipped his men from the surplus stock. These "Paterson Colts" (they were manufactured in Paterson, New Jersey) held five .36-caliber paper charges containing powder and a ball in a revolving cylinder. Cocking the weapon turned the cylinder to line up a new chamber with the barrel and a hammer-activated percussion cap and also exposed a recessed trigger.

The Paterson Colts were fragile and delicate, but a Ranger armed with a Paterson and an extra cylinder could fire ten rounds in forty seconds, and Hays's men often carried two pistols and spare cylinders. At last they had the firepower to stand up to Comanches in mounted combat.

At Walker Creek, on June 8, 1844, Hays and fourteen men clashed with a Comanche force of seventy warriors. In a vicious close-range battle, with their five-shooters wreaking a deadly execution, the Rangers routed the enemy—the West's finest horsemen and among its finest fighters. The Comanches left behind twenty-three of their number dead on the field, and carried off, in Hays's estimate, thirty more wounded. Fewer than twenty escaped the battleground unhurt. Of Hays's men, one was killed and four wounded.

Jack Hays hardly looked the part of a frontier fighter or even an outdoorsman. Smooth-shaven, slim, and only five foot, eight, he impressed one observer as a "delicate looking young man." Moreover, he was modest, quiet, soft-spoken, and thoughtful, a man of few words either spoken or written. But he had no need to boast. His actions told all.

By 1845, when Texas joined the Union, Jack Hays had emerged as the preeminent Ranger captain. Others had gained distinction—Ben and Henry McCulloch, Richard Gillespie, and Samuel Walker—but Hays had become the ideal by which all subsequent generations judged a Ranger captain.

Still short-term volunteers, the Rangers had earned the admiration and respect of Anglo Texans. The Mexican War gave Hays and his comrades the opportunity to nationalize their tradition, to make the Texas Ranger known to all the nation. As federalized volunteers, they made hardly any concession to the regulations that bound other regiments. They clung to their traditional habits: short terms of service, no uniforms or flags, and scorn for the chain of command and military proprieties. They also inflicted atrocities on Mexican civilians as revenge for Mexican atrocities at the Alamo and elsewhere during the Texas

Revolution and the decade of the Republic. Generals Zachary
Taylor and Winfield Scott welcomed the Rangers' steadiness
in combat and their value as scouts; but both generals also be-
moaned the Rangers' consistent troublemaking. Taylor asked
"that no more troops . . . be sent to this column from the State
of Texas."

The rangers produced the first hero of the war. In April 1846,
even before Taylor won his victories at Palo Alto and Resaca de
la Palma, near the mouth of the Rio Grande, Sam Walker made
a name for himself by bearing dispatches across chaparral flats
infested by Mexican irregulars. His exploits earned the army's applause and quickly found their way into newsprint in the East.
President James K. Polk commissioned Walker a captain in the
Regular Army, and New Orleans admirers presented him "a fine-
blooded war steed" and "a very elegant and serviceable sword."

Walker's singular contribution to the war, however, lay in
the East. Samuel Colt, in Connecticut, seeking to interest a
hidebound Ordnance Department in his revolving pistol, approached Walker for an endorsement. Responding enthusiastically, the captain described how a handful of Rangers armed
with the Paterson Colt had bested five times their number of
Comanches at Walker Creek a couple of years earlier. "With
improvements," he asserted, "I think they can be rendered the
most perfect weapon in the World for light mounted troops."

Appealing directly to President Polk and the secretary of war,
Walker helped Colt circumvent the Ordnance Department's opposition to repeating arms and gain a contract. He also worked
with the gun maker on the improvements. The result was the
first six-shooter, which the inventor named the Walker Colt. It
was a heavy, powerful handgun, weighing four and a half pounds,
in .44 caliber, with a nine-inch barrel and a large cylinder to
accommodate six rounds backed by hefty powder charges. It

was sturdier than the old Paterson and easier to load. In striking power, it rivaled the regulation army musket and, at one hundred yards, even the rifle. In the hands of Texas Rangers, the Walker Colt fully met expectations. Colts blazing at Mexican lancers, Walker took a mortal wound at the battle of Huamantla.

After the war, Jack Hays emigrated to California, where he played an influential role in building the new state. His mantle fell on his wartime adjutant, John Salmon ("Rip") Ford. More than six feet tall, lean and blue eyed, voluble, and fun loving, Rip Ford had led a varied life: practicing medicine, studying law, dabbling in surveying and politics, editing an Austin newspaper, and serving Hays effectively in the Mexican War.

Rip Ford began his career as a Ranger captain in 1849, when he was thirty-four. Throughout the 1850s, he proved a successful and respected leader, a terror to Comanche raiders, and a worthy successor to Hays. His most significant feat occurred in 1858, when he surprised and routed the Comanche band of Iron Jacket at the battle of Antelope Hills, on the Canadian River in the Indian Territory north of Texas.

The U.S. Army had built forts and garrisoned Texas, but neither federal troops nor the Rangers could slow the pace of Comanche raiding. They scored occasional successes, but the Texas frontier endured the ravages of Indian raids for nearly half a century. Not until the army's Red River War of 1874–75 did the northern raiders settle on a reservation and leave Texas alone.

The Red River War coincided with the beginnings of the second phase of Ranger history—law enforcement. In 1874 the Texas legislature authorized what administratively came to be known as the Frontier Battalion. The authors of the law meant to create a permanent military force to do what the citizen soldier had done, only better. The Rangers of this outfit displayed many of the defining features of their predecessors, but they were no longer citizen soldiers. Although the Frontier Battalion was designed to fight Indians, when the Indian menace subsided it recast itself as a corps of lawmen. Thereafter, Texas Ranger meant "state lawman" rather than "Indian fighter." Unlike the citizen soldier, he contended with offenders against the laws of Texas.

Major John B. Jones, the architect of the Frontier Battalion, presided over its transformation into a state law-enforcement agency. The rangers owed their march toward institutional continuity to him more than any other man. Like Hays, Jones didn't look like a Ranger. Spare, with a high forehead, penetrating eyes, and a drooping mustache, he dressed impeccably and sat his horse erectly. He was forty in 1847, a bachelor, dignified and humorless, religious, a user of neither tobacco nor alcohol, soft-spoken, courteous, kind, and indefatigably determined to a fashion an organization capable of carrying out its assigned mission.

Jones succeeded in asserting mastery over administrative, logistical, financial, and political concerns in Austin while exercising operational control of his companies and riding the frontier several times a year. At the same time, he reshaped the Texas Ranger tradition without destroying it. Rangers still provided their own horses and arms. They still wore no uniforms. They still enjoyed an easy camaraderie with one another and with their officers. Yet they were no longer citizen soldiers springing to arms to meet a threat and then returning to their homes; they were men recruited to serve for as long as the money held out. They were, in short, a special breed of soldier, drawn not just from the frontier but from anywhere in the state and trained in the hard school of experience. Despite informal relationships within a company, moreover, they served in a plainly military organization, one in which Jones insisted on system, order, discipline, subordination, accountability, and diligent performance of the mission.

Although the law authorized a battalion of 450 men—six

companies of 75 men each—the legislature never appropriated enough money to sustain such a force. By the close of 1875, it had peaked at five companies, each consisting of a captain and 21 Rangers.

John B. Jones shared the beginning of a new Ranger era with an even more improbable figure than he, Leander H. McNelly. McNelly headed a militia company called out by the governor to suppress the violent Sutton-Taylor feud. In most essentials, the company resembled those of the Frontier Battalion. The men regarded themselves as Rangers, and so did the public—calling them "McNelly's Rangers." In one respect, however, the captain himself, no other company resembled McNelly's Rangers. McNelly's full brown beard and bushy mustache failed to offset his gaunt face and frail body. Although wracked by tuberculosis, Leander McNelly possessed in full measure the ingredients of leadership that had endowed previous great captains. One of his recruits recalled, "The way Captain fixed control over this bunch can't be told. I still don't know how he did it, but he did. One thing, he didn't waste a word or a move. He appeared to know exactly what he wanted to do and how to go about doing it. I got the feeling that here was a man who could tell you what to do and you'd do it and never have any suspicion that he might be wrong."

McNelly failed to suppress the Sutton-Taylor feud but soon found himself combating Mexican cattle thieves on the Rio Grande. Like most Anglo Texans, he looked on Mexicans as inferior and all their able-bodied men as bandits. He maintained his own secret spy service south of the border, and he resorted to unconventional methods to extract information from captives. As the federal commander in Texas observed of a McNelly success, "The officer of the State troops in command had learned the whereabouts of this raiding party by means which I could not legally resort to, but which were the only means of getting at the actual facts. He caught one of the number and had him hung up until he was made to confess where the rest of the raiders were." McNelly's interrogator and sometime executioner was Jesús Sandoval, who regularly served his captain with methods the army could not legally resort to.

McNelly's most spectacular feat was an inglorious exploit that earned him glory. On November 18, 1875, going after stolen cattle, he led his thirty Rangers across the Rio Grande near Las Cuevas. They charged into a village mistakenly thought to be the refuge of the thieves and shot down a dozen or more men unfortunate enough to be caught in the streets. A large Mexican force drove the invaders back to the river, and the two sides exchanged fire all day. McNelly refused the "advice" of U.S. Army officers on the Texas side to withdraw, even when confronted with four hundred troops gathering to defend Mexican sovereignty. For two days he held his position. Only when the Mexican leader promised to turn over the stolen herd and the thieves the next day did McNelly boat his little company back to Texas.

As it turned out, the Mexican officials delivered only a third of the cattle and none of the bandits. Even so, McNelly's reputation soared. Texans admired brave men who threw aside legalities to right wrongs by direct action. The unpleasant realities—that the Rangers had killed a dozen or so Mexicans of uncertain guilt, that McNelly's stubborn refusal to withdraw from Mexican soil had almost gotten his command obliterated, and that the return of a few score stolen cows was less a victory than a formula for backing down without losing face—were drowned in public applause for a handful of bold Rangers who had outfought and outfoxed overwhelming numbers.

Tuberculosis killed Leander McNelly in September 1877, and his company was later incorporated into Major Jones's Frontier Battalion, but McNelly's exploits had pumped new life into a legend subsiding since the glory days of Hays and Ford. The colorless Jones, destined for legendary status in a later generation, laid the groundwork for the rise of Texas Rangers in popular esteem. Elevated to adjutant general of Texas (to whom the Rangers reported), he died in 1881. His two successors, however, kept inflating the legend even as the state legislature cut appropriations and reduced the number of Rangers.

Adjutant Generals Wilburn H. King (1881–91) and Woodford H. Mabry (1891–99) tried to cover the state with fewer than fifty men but extolled their virtues and successes in ringing rhetoric that was short on specifics. These were the years of stars such as Lam Sieker, Sam McMurry, Frank Jones, Ira Aten, John A. Brooks, John R. Hughes, and John H. Rogers. The handful of Rangers contended with cow thieves, fence cutters, train and bank robbers, railway and mine strikers, family and political feudists, vigilante mobs gone bad, and Mexican bandits.

Border Mexicans, reared on stories of McNelly and the excesses of Rangers during the Mexican War, loathed *los rinches,* who were believed to treat every Mexican male as a bandit. It was a loathing justified only by a few well-publicized incidents. Moreover, to Mexicans, *rinches* meant all Anglo lawmen, not just Rangers, who were so few that not many operated on the border.

One who helped keep the torch blazing was William J. McDonald, who captained a company from 1891 to 1907. "Captain Bill" possessed courage, bravery, dedication, persistence, mastery of horse and gun, and criminal investigative skill. Six feet tall, lithe, and wiry, he projected authority with riveting blue eyes deeply set in a face framed by big ears and adorned with a mustache merging into muttonchop whiskers. More than any other Ranger captain, he was a showman, a self-promoter who reveled in notoriety. He cultivated politicians and newsmen and made certain that his exploits received public acclaim, often at the expense of his men.

McDonald gained a merited reputation for talking down mobs. "I used to tell him," recalled one of his men, "'Cap, you're going to get all of us killed, the way you cuss out strikers and mobs.'" "Don't worry, Ryan," was the response. "Just remember my motto." He repeated his motto often enough to bequeath it to all successive generations of Rangers: "No man in the wrong can stand up against a fellow that's in the right and keeps on acomin'."

Bill McDonald also was the inspiration for an enduring Ranger myth. The tale survives in many versions, but in all of them an impending riot leads to a call for Rangers. One arrives, and when asked where the others are, he answers that there's only one riot. Since 1961, an imposing eight-foot statue of a steely-eyed Ranger has dominated the terminal of Dallas's Love Field airport. The pedestal bears the inscription "One Riot, One Ranger." Pneumonia killed Captain Bill in 1918, but even in death he continued to proclaim his motto. His tombstone in a Quanah cemetery bears the inscription "No man in the wrong can stand up against a fellow that's in the right and keeps on acomin'."

Throughout the twentieth century, the Texas Rangers reveled in McDonald's righteous motto. At the same time, they committed atrocities against Mexicans that brought the force to the edge of extinction, suffered ruinous politicization at the hands of the notorious governors James E. and Miriam A. ("Pa" and "Ma") Ferguson, and as late as the 1960s deployed under orders of Governor John B. Connally as strikebreakers against unionized Mexican agricultural laborers in South Texas.

On the positive side, the Rangers tamed oil boomtowns, aggressively carried out Prohibition laws, and warred on gangsters. One of their number, although flushed out of the force not long before by politics, set up the ambush that killed Bonnie and Clyde.

The move toward a truly professional law-enforcement agency began in 1935, with the creation of the Department of

Public Safety. This reform removed the Rangers from the adjutant general's command and combined them with the highway patrol. Since then, they have served as the state's criminal investigation arm, often with dramatic success. At the same time, they only grudgingly admitted minorities to their ranks and resisted women until forced into a feeble tokenism.

Over the past century, two competing images of the Texas Rangers emerged, both in scholarly studies and in popular thought. At the beginning of the twenty-first century, they still war with each other, one sustaining the bright legend, the other inspiring periodic attempts to abolish the Rangers altogether.

In 1935, Professor Walter Prescott Webb of the University of Texas gave scholarly respectability to the first image. In his conception, "[t]he real Ranger has been a very quiet, deliberate, gentle person who could gaze calmly into the eye of a murderer, divine his thoughts, and anticipate his action, a man who could ride straight up to death." Webb's Ranger knew no fear and called on unlimited reserves of courage.

Beginning in the 1960s, revisionist scholars drew a darkly contrasting portrait. It features a brutal, lawless Ranger, one who as a soldier indiscriminately slaughtered Indians and Mexicans and as a lawman systematically practiced *ley de fuga* ("law of the fugitive"), in which prisoners were routinely shot while supposedly trying to escape. This Ranger shot first and asked questions later. Today he would be called a rogue cop.

Not surprisingly, Ranger history yields a few dauntless men who fit Webb's definition as well as a few of the rogue cops of his challengers. But the vast majority of Rangers of then and now come across as real people with their share of talents and shortcomings, individuals who have sometimes lived up to the legend.

The legend has burned brightly for more than a century. The effusions of Adjutant Generals King and Mabry helped inspire popular fiction, verse, and balladry celebrating the strong, silent,

fast-shooting lawmen of legend. In 1892, a frontier housewife
composed her own six-stanza homage, which concludes with the
following lines:

> He may not win the laurels,
>   Nor trumpet tongue of fame,
> But beauty smiles upon him,
>   And ranchmen bless his name.
> Then here's to the Texas Ranger,
>   Past, present, and to come,
> Our safety from the savage,
>   The guardian of our home.

Even as the twentieth-century Ranger came under severe
criticism and verged on extinction, the Old West lawmen
flourished in print and film. Comic books and pulp westerns
continued to star the Rangers. Zane Grey's *Lone Star Ranger*
(1915), dedicated to the Rangers, reached the theaters twice as
a silent and once, in 1930, as a talkie. Films featuring the Texas
Rangers appeared as early as 1910 and have never stopped. Mike
Cox's "Texas Ranger Filmology" lists 118 Ranger movies as having been released between 1910 and 1995.

The Lone Ranger galloped into radio in 1933. With *William
Tell* as the overture, the masked rider of the plains and his faithful
Indian companion, Tonto, warred against frontier evil and with
a silver bullet disarmed bad men without ever drawing blood.
With radio giving way to television after World War II, Clayton
Moore and Jay Silverheels appeared in 1949 in a long-running
series that gave visual form to the heroes of the radio generation. The Lone Ranger still lives. Internet Web sites provide the
most arcane detail any aficionado could want about this giant of
popular culture.

The Lone Ranger did not dominate television portrayals of
the Rangers. Series came and went, and feature-length films ex-

ploited and fueled the legend. In 1989, the television miniseries drawn from Larry McMurtry's *Lonesome Dove* gained a huge audience, giving graphic expression to the first of four books about the Rangers that enjoyed triumphant sales. Chuck Norris starred in the top-rated series *Walker, Texas Ranger,* a foolish epic so implausible that it probably embarrassed every modern Ranger but which ran for eight years.

Late last year Hollywood brought out the saga of Leander McNelly. "An epic adventure of love and courage in a rugged land," ran one publicity statement, "Texas Rangers revives the great tradition of the pure American Western." (This may be so, but the producers upended the script and made McNelly the unlikely foil for a nasty squad of punks in the *Young Guns* tradition.)

The legend offends some Texans, who regard the Rangers as an anachronism, a survival from frontier times that should have been abolished long ago. But to many more Texans they are still the embodiment of men in the right who just keep acomin'. This appealing vision fortifies public opinion and promises the abiding affection and political support of the majority of Anglo Texans. (A burgeoning Hispanic population, verging on the state's majority, may one day change this dynamic.) Despite the continuing efforts of scholars to recast the image of the Texas Ranger, in the legendary ideal inspired by Jack Hays and fleshed out by the Old West lawmen, he still rides in the popular imagination—in Texas, in the nation, and around the world.

7

The Last Empire

WILLIAM BROYLES, JR.

The two men seem to be floating quietly on a sea of cattle. They ride through the herd slowly, without rippling its surface. The rust-colored Santa Gertrudis cattle make room for them, then close back in from every side, jamming the riders' legs against the flanks of their horses. Their hands are folded across their saddle horns; only their cowboy hats move, almost imperceptibly, as they study the cattle. The vaqueros surrounding the herd sit motionless, slumped into their saddles, silhouetted against the early morning sun. As the herd mills about, a cow or calf occasionally escapes, but the vaqueros chase it back, then resume their posts. When the two men in the middle of the herd decide which cows they will cut out of it, this pastoral scene will explode.

It is late July, roundup time on the King Ranch in South Texas. By nine in the morning, the temperature is approaching one hundred degrees. The deep azure sky is unmarked by clouds. The herd sends up a cloud of dust that mutes the harsh sunlight so that the cattle and the vaqueros are bathed in a subtle haze. The sound is deafening. Horses neigh and sputter. The cattle are in full voice, up and down the register from high tenor to deep bass. Upwind, where a few Longhorns form the nucleus of a second

---

Originally published in *Texas Monthly* (October 1980): 150–73, 234–78. Reprinted by permission of *Texas Monthly* Magazine.

herd, other cattle add their voices with the antiphony of a fugue.

Only the men are quiet. If a calf escapes, they may wave their cowboy hats and whoop at it as they gallop in pursuit. But to communicate with each other is considered unnecessary and in bad form. Every now and then one of them will point out a cow to be cut, briefly lifting one knobby finger over the saddle horn. But mostly they move with the precision of a silent drill team. They have all done this work many times before. Both men and horses know their roles. Almost all the vaqueros were born on the ranch. Some are fourth- and fifth-generation Kineños, or King's men, as they have been known ever since a steamboat captain named Richard King persuaded an entire Mexican village to cross the Rio Grande and work at his cow camp on the prairie almost 130 years ago.

The roundup is the last remaining tradition of the open range. At the King Ranch's Norias Division—238,000 acres that stretch westward from the Gulf of Mexico—the ritual hasn't changed in more than a century. The technology is ancient but effective: spurs, chaps, ropes, brands, horses. The cattle trucks are discreetly hidden behind a mesquite thicket as if in apology for their intrusion on this frontier tableau. At the ranch's other nearby divisions, as in most of the American West, cattle are worked in pens and sometimes even gathered by helicopter. But at Norias, where the sandy pastures are choked by mesquite, huisache, ebony, shin oak, and granjeno, cattle are still worked on horseback, in the open. To gather this herd took the Kineños a week of hot and dusty labor in thickets so deep and thorny that another vaquero fifteen feet away was invisible.

One of the two men bobbing in the middle of the herd of a thousand or so cattle is Stephen Kleberg, known to everyone as Tio, which is Spanish for "uncle." His great-grandfather married the youngest daughter of Richard King, the founder of the King Ranch. Since 1886, the year after King died, a Kleberg has run the ranch. In 1974, there were four male Klebergs who outranked Tio on the ranch, but so many changes have come to the ranch since then that for the past year Tio has been the senior Kleberg. He is thirty-four years old, with bright blue eyes, fair skin, and a blond handlebar moustache that spills down the lower half of his face. He is not tall—about five foot, seven or so—but wiry and erect, like a boxer. On horseback he is a study in shades of russet and tan. His narrow shotgun chaps are a weathered rawhide, his hat is beige, and around his neck is a red bandanna. His horse is the same deep red as the cattle.

The man with him is Lavoyger Durham, the boss of the Norias Division. Two years older than Tio and his opposite in looks, Lavoyger is tall, with dark skin and hair and a strong, jutting jaw. Like Peter McBride of the Encino Division next door, Lavoyger is a third-generation foreman. He is related to Tio and to the vaqueros, a man from both of the great family traditions of the ranch. His grandfather was a Texas Ranger who married Richard King's niece and went to work on the ranch in 1878; his father, Ed Durham, ran Norias before him and married the daughter of one of the head Kineños.

Watching them closely is Joe Stiles. Joe is thirty-three, tall, bowlegged, and squinty-eyed. His father is the foreman of the Santa Gertrudis Division outside Kingsville, sixty miles north of Norias. Joe manages the ranch's Quarter Horse program, which accounts for his close attention to Tio's riding. The horse Tio is using to cut cattle on this rough pasture is Mr. San Peppy, the ranch's prize stallion and a $4 million Quarter Horse. But like everything on the ranch, Peppy has no value unless he can work. "I'd rather he died cutting cattle," Joe says, "than in a show barn."

Three experienced in-laws in their sixties direct the ranch's larger corporate fortunes, but the ranch itself and its 130 years of tradition are in the hands of these young men and others like them, a new generation in its twenties and thirties with its own ideas about how to do things. The ranch, for example, now contains one of the largest *farms* in South Texas; it has its own feed mill and feedlot and a completely reorganized Quarter Horse program. It has cut back its huge Australian operations, disbursed most of its oil royalties to the family, and bought out its two major stockholders. It is a very different place than it was just six years ago.

The Most Famous Ranch in America

The four divisions of the King Ranch cover 825,000 acres, an area considerably larger than Rhode Island. Its 60,000 head of cattle could provide every male American with a quarter-pound hamburger. Keeping those cattle in their pastures is 2,000 miles of fence, enough to stretch from the ranch's headquarters in Kingsville to Boston. There are 2,730 oil and gas wells on the ranch, more than have been drilled in Saudi Arabia. Its 350 windmills keep twenty men busy full time. The ranch originated cattle prods, dipping vats, elaborate pens for working cattle, hunting cars, wire-mesh fences instead of barbed wire, and, most dramatic, the first American breed of cattle and virtually a new breed of horses. As if that weren't enough, in the 1950s the ranch leaped over oceans to establish itself on 8,000,000 acres around the world, a ranching empire the size of Massachusetts and Connecticut combined.

Richard King bought his ranch with money he had earned piloting steamboats on the Rio Grande, and to this day the ranch draws on some of the best qualities of the two cultures on either side of that river. The business standards—the computers, the sophisticated management, and the insistence on state-of-the-art technology—are resolutely American. The sense of family, the deference and loyalty, the dedication to the land, and the methods of working cattle are distinctly Mexican. English is the language of the office, Spanish that of the range.

The ranch is in many ways an anachronism, an aristocracy in an age when tradition and authority and class systems seem irrelevant. In quiet defiance of that age, the ranch continues to function on the basis of inheritance, of both property and position. One generation succeeds the next in every job, from cowboy to foreman to owner. This continuity is by no means assured. The ranch's paternalistic traditions tend to excite the attention and outrage of government agencies. And estate and inheritance taxes work inexorably against the preservation of such an extensive family enterprise. The family itself, grown large and diverse, no longer finds its complete fulfillment in a more or less unremarkable piece of prairie, no matter how vast or historic.

But some things remain constant, no matter how much the world changes. Far from his desk and all its complexities, Tio Kleberg has such immutable matters on his mind as he rides into the herd. His immediate task is to separate the cows without calves from the tight, moving mass of the herd. Picking them out is a decision based on subjective observation ("They just look different," Tio says), and only Tio and Lavoyger do it. A mistake could mean losing future calves or allowing a nonproductive cow to continue to consume the ranch's grass.

The economics of the cattle business are deceptively simple. Grass is the feedstock, cows and bulls the capital, meat and hides the product. In a drouth or a hard winter, for example, the rancher soon runs short of grass. He can supplement it with feed, but if feed is too expensive and beef too cheap, buying feed won't pay. In that case, he may sell off not only his yearling crop but a good many mother cows and young calves as well. As a result, the market will be flooded with beef, and the price will drop still further until the shortage of mother cows produces a smaller calf crop and drives prices back up. As big as the King Ranch is, it can't influence this cycle any more than the smallest rancher can. Cattlemen accept it as simply another affliction of their business, like drouth and disease, range fires and brush.

Tio and Lavoyger are in no hurry. They move slowly with the

flow of the cattle. Then one points briefly to a cow, the other nods, and they begin threading that cow through the hundreds around it to the edge of the herd. Once the cow is out where the herd is not so tightly packed, Tio begins to transfer authority to the horse. Mr. San Peppy positions himself sideways to the cow, fixing it out of the corner of his eye. When the cow's ears stand up, the horse knows he has its attention. Tio loosens the reins and grasps the saddle horn, letting Peppy take over. The next few seconds are like a dance before a mirror. If the cow heads left, Peppy is there. If it swerves to the right, Peppy pivots off his hind legs to meet it.

Crouched so low that his belly seems to be touching the ground, his mane swirling, the horse drives the cow backward, away from the security of the herd, out into the territory controlled by the vaqueros. The instant the cow is turned away from the herd, one of the vaqueros runs it across the pasture to the new herd. Santa Gertrudis cattle are surprisingly agile and fast, so this process often demands wild rides at full gallop across rugged ground and through mesquite thickets.

After the barren cows are cut, Tio and Lavoyger take a break to talk briefly to their children while Joe Stiles and Tio's cousin Martín Clement begin cutting out the yearling calves for sale. Because it is summer, children—the Klebergs', the foremen's, and vaqueros'—are everywhere. The roundup is an important part of their education. The teenage sons of the vaqueros are helping with the roundup, and the cow boss, known as the *caporal*, watches them closely. The roundup is like a tryout for future jobs as vaqueros, and the young Kineños are eager to show off their skills. The older vaqueros feel responsible for how well the younger ones work. They do not hesitate to take a father aside and speak to him about his son's mistakes, offering him criticism and encouragement. They fully expect that the father will do his duty and that the son will listen and obey his father. That is how it was done for them and for their fathers before them. It is the King Ranch way.

The Family

The Klebergs live by the same ethic. They give each other gentle and not-so-gentle suggestions on child rearing, they criticize errant behavior, and they teach vital skills and underscore moral points. The stability of the ranch has allowed the development of the sort of extended family that is rare in America. It is a family that through five generations has had the same purpose—to sustain its ownership of this great tract of earth. On one level, the task at hand in this Norias pasture has to do with cattle. On quite another level, it has to do with the future of the ranch.

Tio finishes a brief talk with his older son about the way he was handling his horse and then rides back to the herd to watch his wife, Janell, and his younger brother, Scott, cut out the yearling calves. Scott is twenty-two and is studying range management at Texas A&M; everyone in the family expects great things of him when he comes home to work at the ranch. Precisely because of that, Tio watches him closely. To Tio's mind, Scott is following the yearlings he is cutting about two or three feet farther out of the herd than necessary. "Park him! Park him!" Tio yells. Scott concentrates and on the next calf has already turned back into the herd when the vaquero picks the calf up. Tio smiles, satisfied.

Janell and Martín take a turn next. When they finish, they ride over to the horse trailer. Martín complains about how hard it is to buy cowboy hats for the ranch's commissaries. "The folk in discos just keep cornering the market," he says. Janell's face is streaked with sweat and dust. Beneath her cowboy hat, her blond hair is a dirty gray.

Janell met Tio at Texas Tech. When she came back to Kingsville with him nine years ago, she felt she was entering a completely different world. No one told her to learn to cut cattle. She did it on her own, to be part of the work of the ranch. She pats her horse and looks out at her children bouncing around on their horses. "What you have to understand if you work for this family," she says, "is that none of this is yours—not the land, not the houses, not the horses that you grow to love. That's hard to remember. And it's hard to teach your children. Like us, they tend to think it's theirs. It's not. Everything belongs to the ranch, and the ranch belongs to the family. Keeping the family and the ranch together is more important than any of us."

The ranch and the family, however, are not always one and the same. The ranch's story is straightforward enough; it is the progress of a piece of earth from primitive wilderness to productive pastures, an account of will and technology pitted against nature. The family, however, has not enjoyed an easy journey to its current preeminence. To sustain anything through five generations, much less a ranch in a harsh, unyielding country, is to overcome suffering, hardship, and conflicting ambitions—and it is, at times, to overcome success.

There is blood and power in the King Ranch's history, but there is surprisingly little duplicity, rapaciousness, or greed. The land itself was acquired legally, purchased from presumably willing sellers. Compared to the great fortunes built by devious and ruthless robber barons like the Rockefellers, the Morgans, and the Mellons, the King Ranch is a monument to probity, neighborliness, and hard work.

Part of the story of the King Ranch is how one family conquered and sustained a great ranch, and part is how that family conquered and sustained itself. The past six years of the ranch's history have been tumultuous, even by its own standards. Both of the men who had run the ranch since 1918 died. And the two most obvious successors left the ranch and filed suit against it. To carry on, the family has had to rejuvenate itself once again. A frontier character named Richard King overcame great challenges to found this empire. The men and women who run it today have perhaps an even harder task. They must hold it together—against all the pressures, from inside and outside the family, that would tear it apart.

The Call West

The man who began the King Ranch and one of America's most durable families had no family ties himself. In 1833, at the age of nine, he was apprenticed to a jeweler in New York City. He never saw his family again and never divulged anything about them, except that they were Irish. The young boy could not abide the close, tedious work of the jeweler's shop or the rigid medieval bonds of apprenticeship. Even at that age, he was drawn toward open spaces. At eleven, he stowed away on a sailing ship bound for Mobile, and for the next ten years he worked on steamboats in the rivers and coastal waters of the eastern Gulf of Mexico. The steamboaters were his parents and the frontier was his school-room. The boy learned its tough and demanding lessons well, and he grew into a young man with a quick mind and quicker fists.

During the Seminole wars of 1841, he served on an army steamboat and in Florida met a man who would be his friend and partner for the rest of his life. Mifflin Kenedy was seven years older than King and seemed to have little in common with him. Kenedy was a devout Quaker and a studious, reflective man. His great strength—he could throw a massive anchor overboard by himself, a task that normally required three men—allowed him to remain aloof from the brutish steamboating world, where a man could get his eyes gouged out if he forgot to offer his neighbor a drink. Kenedy saw something special in King and took him under his wing.

After Kenedy went to Texas in 1846, he wrote King that the Mexican War had created a boom for steamboaters on the Rio Grande. For Richard King, who had no family, no money, and no roots, that news was enough. He went to Texas. The Rio Grande was in rugged, uncharted country torn by war. Opportunity was there for the taking. The extent of that opportunity, however, could hardly have been apparent to the twenty-two-year-old steam-boater as he trudged across the sand at the mouth of the Rio

Grande toward the few shanties and hovels—made of sticks and covered with mud and seashells—that had sprung up around the stacks of cargo waiting to be moved inland.

King spent the rest of the war piloting steamboats up an down the Rio Grande for the U.S. Army. When the Mexican War ended in 1848, King bought a surplus steamboat and went into business hauling freight and passengers. A year later, he and Kenedy joined a border entrepreneur named Charles Stillman in a shipping company they called M. Kenedy & Company. King provided the muscle and designed new boats for the twisting, shallow, windswept river; Stillman put up the capital; Kenedy contributed the diplomacy and the management. By 1852, they had run their competitors off the Rio Grande. There was a good deal of legitimate freight in their business, but their primary trade was smuggling. A burdensome tariff system imposed by Mexico made smuggling the accepted way of doing things, as it had been in the American colonies before the Revolution.

The conflict between Americans and Mexicans on the border had culminated in more than a decade of war, from massacres at the Alamo and Goliad in 1836 to the American atrocities during the invasion of Mexico in 1848. A great deal of blood had been shed on both sides. For thirty years after the Mexican War, the border seethed with armed bandits, Mexican guerrillas, and raiders. One man's hero was another man's villain; the most vicious bandits were honored in Mexico, the most brutal Texas Rangers elevated to sainthood in Texas.

Politics along the Rio Grande were Byzantine—intrigue, revolution, and counterrevolution hung as heavy in the air as the heat. Betrayal was expected, allies were untrustworthy, a loyal friend and partner was extremely rare. Every decade brought new schemes to make part or all of Mexico a new republic, a protectorate, or even a state in the United States. King and Kenedy were deeply involved in border intrigues, but it was not until they supported Porfirio Díaz, who would be dictator of Mexico for more than thirty years, that they ever backed a winner. The border was a difficult, complex place. Poised between two cultures, beyond the domination of either, Richard King was right at home.

A Rose amid Thorns

Life on the border was primitive. Men and animals shared the same drinking water. Outbreaks of cholera and typhoid periodically swept through the river towns, turning them into charnel houses. Dysentery and other debilitating diseases were endemic. Treatment was primitive, anesthesia unknown, and opium the most common medicine. When it rained, the streets became quagmires. When the wind blew, the sand covered food and furniture, coated sweaty bodies in grime, and filled bedclothes with grit. The heat was everywhere, humid and inescapable. Richard King must have lain awake many nights, simmering in his own sweat, tormented by flies and mosquitoes, wondering why he hadn't followed the forty-niners out to the easy pickings of the California goldfields.

But he stayed, laboring through the hottest part of the day, commanding the world from the wheel of his steamboat, ignoring the custom of taking a siesta, dripping sweat into his ledgers, and drinking the Rio Grande water that killed many of his contemporaries. Water wasn't all he drank, of course. The most prevalent and important frontier institution was not the church or the school but the bar. Bars were the setting for business deals, social meetings, and the political schemings that permeated border life. In such a bar, Richard King celebrated his twenty-sixth birthday. Spying a stranger, King walked over to offer him a drink. King's greeting—first recorded in Tom Lea's two-volume history of the King Ranch's first century[1]—summed up his world: "People who come to Texas these days," King said, presumably with a smile, "are preachers or fugitives from justice or sons of bitches. Which one of those fits you?"

One sweltering day in 1850, Captain King had wrestled his war surplus steamboat up the river, past snags and mud bars, fighting the wind, and he was ready for a few drinks. But an old steamboat was docked in his customary berth. Fuming, King brought his boat in and began stamping and cussing around the waterfront. As he ranted about the effrontery of putting a rat-infested scow in *his* berth, a young lady of seventeen emerged from the boat and, with some indignation, put King in his place.

Her name was Henrietta Chamberlain, and her father was a widower, a Presbyterian missionary from New England who had answered the call to become the first Protestant minister on the Rio Grande, rich waters for the fishing of lost souls. Richard King, who had seldom seen the inside of a church, became an eager, if not wholly sincere, participant in the Reverend Mr. Chamberlain's pioneer Presbyterian church. And if his attention strayed from the preacher's Calvinist pronouncements to the preacher's comely daughter in the choir, who could blame him? Anglo women were scarce on the border. They were therefore highly prized, fought over, cherished, and treated with a formal gentility that was as much a part of the frontier as its spontaneous violence. For Captain King, the preacher's sweet daughter was everything he himself was not. Against competition from every unmarried man on the border, he set out to win her. As the courtship progressed, he also began exploring the land beyond the muddy river that was his home.

The Rancho

In the spring of 1852, Richard King took a trip. Henry Lawrence Kinney, the imaginative frontier smuggler and rogue who had founded Corpus Christi, had decided to boost the town's fortunes with a world's fair. King had been running his steamboats up and down the Rio Grande for five years and was eager to see Corpus Christi and the country on the way. What he saw were miles of sand flats and then, north of what is now Raymondville, a vast and trackless sea of grass sprinkled with little copses of hackberry, oak, and, occasionally, mesquite. This was the southern tip of the Great Plains in its virgin state, before it had been despoiled by fences, by towns and railroads, by the invasion of mesquite and huisache brush.

The plains were the natural habitat of wandering animals that fed upon its grasses. To the Indians, that meant buffalo. To the Mexicans and then the Americans, that meant cattle—tough, rawboned Spanish cattle called Longhorns that need almost no care. Because there was so little water, the cattle roamed over great spaces. The men who tended them were therefore spread thin and, like the cattle, had to fend for themselves. They had to be mobile, tough, and willing to live out on the plains alone.

When King got to Corpus Christi, a friend of his, a Texas Ranger named Legs Lewis, proposed that they establish a partnership to operate a cow camp on the plains. King would supply the capital; Lewis would work the place and, above all, guard it. That was the theory, but King would quickly become more involved than would an absentee investor. They chose as their headquarters a little rise on the banks of Santa Gertrudis Creek, the site of an old Mexican rancho about forty-five miles west of Corpus Christi. King had camped there on his journey north.

While Lewis tended to the building of some jacales (rough huts made of sticks and adobe), King set out to buy the land from its Mexican owners, who after the Mexican War had found themselves in possession of a worthless desert in another country. His first purchase was a Spanish land grant called the Rincón de Santa Gertrudis, 15,500 acres where Santa Gertrudis Creek empties into Baffin Bay, where the town of Kingsville now stands. King purchased the land in 1853 for $300, or a little less than 2 cents an acre. The next year he bought a larger Spanish grant, 53,000 acres due west of his first one, running ten miles along Santa Gertrudis

Creek. He paid $1,800 for it, or a little over 3 cents an acre. At that time, the Great Plains were still known as the Great American Desert. Many of King's business associates told him that even at those prices he had been taken, that the land he had bought would never be worth anything. But King had other ideas.

Buying the land was one thing, holding it another. Their cow camp was in the strip of land between the Nueces and the Rio Grande, the most dangerous part of the frontier. Scarcely a dozen years before, the Texas General Land Office map had borne the notation "of this area, nothing is known." A Texas Ranger who fought in the Nueces Strip described King's first ranch: "The men who held the cow camp on the Santa Gertrudis were of no ordinary mold. They had come to stay. It was no easy matter to scare them. The Indians still made descents on the country . . . and they had the advantages of numbers and movement. But the brave men who held the ranch had determined to make a ranch on the Santa Gertrudis or leave their bones to tell of their failure."

Winning the land, first from the Indians, then from the raiding armies of Mexican cattle bandits, would take Captain King more than two decades. The struggle to establish his ranch engaged not only his will and courage but also his greatest quality, a clear-eyed practicality that combined observations from different realms of his experience into something useful. King knew nothing about cattle. That was one of his greatest assets. He didn't know the accepted way of raising livestock, so he invented his own.

Richard King was the first to grasp the distinctions—in scale, in spirit, and in setting—between ranching cattle and raising cattle as a sideline to farming. The Anglo settlers making their way west through the Southern forests often brought cattle, sometimes in large numbers. They rode horseback, after a fashion; they had roundups; they even drove their cattle to market as far away as New Orleans. They had, in short, all the elements of a ranch, but they didn't have *ranches*. And most of them saw the Mexicans and their culture as a barrier to be pushed aside, nothing more. They learned no more from them than they did from the Indians.

King was different. He did not establish a Southern cattle farm, worked by slaves. His manner was American, but his model was Mexican. He did not look back east for his inspiration; he looked across the Rio Grande. His first cattle came from border ranches, and so did his first hands, Mexican vaqueros from a long tradition of Spanish cattle ranching that had little in common with Anglo-Saxon farming.

The Spanish relied on three institutions to shape their conquest in the New World: the presidio, or fort; the mission; and the hacienda. The Mexican hacienda and its smaller cousin, the rancho, were self-contained, subsistence operations, inextricably tied up in the system of servitude and patronage that underlay the stability of village life. Richard King saw the merit of the ranching equipment and techniques his vaqueros brought with them—their lassos, their saddles and chaps, their way with cattle—but subsistence was not what he had in mind.

In 1854, King took a momentous step: he journeyed into Mexico and, in a scene out of Kipling's *Man Who Would Be King*, persuaded the elders of a dusty village to come back to Texas with him, where he would be their *patrón*. With the elders came the whole village in an *entrada*—men, women, and children, donkeys, chickens, and carts loaded with possessions. That entrada was the beginning of a complex, almost feudal network of relationships that exists on the ranch to this day and that sets it apart from the other great ranches in America. Its roots go not only to Plymouth Rock and the Pilgrims but also to Cortez and the conquistadores. On his struggling ranch on the edge of the frontier, King forged—by trial and error, courage, determination, and hardheadedness—a synthesis of aristocratic Mexican husbandry and democratic American marketing and business. He was not alone, of course; other men were ranching in Texas, but none with the scale and permanence he envisioned. More than anyone else, the steamboat captain who knew nothing about ranching created the cattle kingdom.

Buy Land and Never Sell

Drouth in the 1850s had dried up the Rio Grande, so business on the river was slow. King spent more and more time on his rancho, stocking it with cattle and horses and supervising the construction of a dam that was the first major capital improvement between Corpus Christi and Brownsville. King's carefully kept ledger books reveal that in 1854 he spent more than $12,000 on his ranch—forty times what he had paid for the first 15,500 acres.

He also found time to continue his courtship of Henrietta. Doubtless, this rough, unlettered riverboat captain was not the sort of man Preacher Chamberlain had had in mind for his daughter. Yet eventually King convinced both father and daughter that he possessed virtues not immediately obvious to civilized folk. In December 1854, King and Henrietta were married. For their honeymoon, Captain King took his bride to the Santa Gertrudis, the heart of the frontier, where few Anglo women had been before. They rode in a stagecoach flanked by armed vaqueros, camping out at night under the stars, cooking over open fires. After four days, they crossed the creek, and Henrietta King saw what her friends in Brownsville called King's Folly: a cluster of jacales, a stockade, a brass cannon, some mesquite corrals, and her new house—an adobe hut so tiny that she had to hang her pots and pans outside. She would make her home on the Santa Gertrudis for more than seventy years.

The frontier turned the men hard and brittle as caliche, but it had a different effect upon the women. As Walter Prescott Webb, the great historian of the West, wrote, "The Plains—mysterious, desolate, barren, grief-stricken—oppressed the women, drove them to the verge of insanity in many cases." Henrietta

Chamberlain, however, had been raised to overcome hardship with faith. If her husband's mission was to win the West, hers was to civilize it.

Even in a mud hut, Henrietta was a model of propriety, demanding at least the appearance of civilized behavior from the frontiersmen who crossed her threshold. She called her husband "Captain King" all their married life. The embodiment of the triumph of will over circumstance, she was stern and unforgiving of the weaknesses of the flesh. She wrapped herself in her sense of duty as tightly as in her corset, and her husband, whose flesh was so much weaker than hers, struggled mightily to live up to her standards. Even on the frontier, they were perfect Victorian types, he the adventurer and she the preacher's daughter, called on by fate to play their roles in a world whose every reality worked against the stable values she lived by. But if Henrietta King had not been so rigid, it is quite possible that Richard King, and certainly the generations that followed him, would never have won or held their great ranch.

In 1855, only a few months after King and Henrietta were married, Legs Lewis, King's partner, was killed by a jealous husband. Lewis's death meant that King had to work the ranch on his own or lose it. The capital kept coming from the river, but King saw the ranch as his future. "Land and livestock have a way of increasing in value," he told Mifflin Kenedy. "Cattle and horses, sheep and goats, will reproduce themselves into value. But boats—they have a way of wrecking, decaying, falling apart, decreasing in value and increasing in cost of operation." To that credo King added a piece of advice from his friend Robert E. Lee, who was stationed in Texas until the Civil War. "Buy land," Lee had told the young rancher, "and never sell."

King did just that. He was always enlarging his holdings, and he kept lawyers busy perfecting his titles, making sure his purchases were absolutely legal. He found the best lawyers he could and gave them succinct instructions. "Young man," he told one years later, "the only thing I want to hear from you is when I can move my fences." In 1860, after Mexican raiders destroyed Mifflin Kenedy's ranch near the Rio Grande, King and Kenedy became partners in the Santa Gertrudis. They continued M. Kenedy & Company as their steamboat operation, but their new ranching business bore the name R. King & Company.

King tried everything to make the land yield a profit. He dug dams and impounded water. He experimented with sheep. He raised horses and mules for the army and for distant cities. And he raised cattle—tough, hefty, bad-tempered Longhorns that were sold to other ranchers as breeding stock or were slaughtered for their hides and tallow. The carcasses were either used to feed his pigs or dumped on the prairie or in the bay. He tried injecting salt into the meat so he could ship it to market and avoid such waste, but it didn't work. For almost twenty years, King spent nothing on fences, feed, or veterinary services. Ranching in those days was simply harvesting the plains. And King was willing to forgo immediate profits in the deep conviction that land, the more the better, would one day pay.

Heroes and Villains

The Civil War did three things for Richard King: it gave him the opportunity to amass a fortune, it put the final touches on his formidable character, and it led to the opening of the great Northern markets for beef that confirmed his faith in ranching and made his name known throughout America. King and Kenedy were staunch Confederates, in sentiment if not in service. The Santa Gertrudis became a major depot for the Southern cotton sent to Europe through the Confederacy's back door at Matamoros. The two men also got rich selling supplies to the Confederacy, and they made sure they were paid in gold. For them the Civil War was as big a bonanza as the Mexican War.

Their fortunes were not made without risk. The Nueces Strip crawled with draft dodgers, bands of guerrillas, Mexican raiders, French agents from the emperor Maximilian in Mexico, and Comanches. The Union army raided the Santa Gertrudis in 1863, aiming to put the rebel cotton depot out of action. King slipped away, but his faithful Mexican retainer, Francisco Alvarado, was shot dead at the feet of the pregnant Mrs. King as he opened the door.

Tom Lea valiantly defends King's leaving his wife to the mercy of the Union raiders. Yet King's decision to make money from the war rather than fight in it makes his character suspect, and allowing his servant to be slain in his place does not bring glory to the King name either. But to see him simply as a war profiteer running out on his family to save his own skin would be too harsh. To have stayed and fought would have been suicidal, and to have fled with his wife into the prairie could have endangered both her and the baby. There was no easy decision.

After the raid, the Kings abandoned the ranch. Just two months later, Henrietta King gave birth to their second son, whom she named Robert Lee King. Her husband was not present for the birth. He had again gone underground, and he spent the rest of the war keeping Confederate supplies moving past the Union cavalry. Although he was scarcely forty, he became known as "the old captain," a remorseless, driven frontier figure. After Appomattox, King crossed the river into Mexico with his gold and prepared to move all his operations south of the border. But he was pardoned by the Union and went back to rebuild his ranch.

It was no easy task. The Reconstruction Administration disbanded the Texas Rangers and all but ceded the Nueces Strip to the Mexican bandits, who renewed their raids on the hated gringos with brutal intensity. The next ten years were filled with both opportunity and danger. One of the great booms of American history—the cattle drives—was just beginning. But the raids drove many of King's neighbors out of business, and his whole empire was threatened. He lost thousands of cattle during these cattle wars. It seemed, in fact, as if the Mexicans were about to win back the land south of the Nueces that they had lost in the Mexican War.

The leading raider was a rogue named Cheno Cortina, an upper-class border character who had fought the Americans in the Mexican War and then lost his family's land in and around Brownsville. Cortina—red haired, green eyed, charismatic, cruel, and thoroughly opportunistic—kept the border in upheaval for almost twenty years. He liked to say, "The sight of a gringo makes me think of eating little kids." Cortina became King's greatest nemesis. "The gringos are raising cattle for me," he would boast. The raids got so bad and King became such a prominent target that he was ambushed on his way to meet with the American commission investigating the raids, and a young German riding with him was killed. In desperation, King went so far as to join the Republican Party in the vain hope that he could get help from the Reconstruction Administration, which seemed quite happy to see the former Confederates suffer.

Finally, in 1877, at the end of Reconstruction, the Texas Rangers were reassembled. In one encounter, a group of Rangers fought a pitched battle with a dozen cattle raiders who were driving a large herd of King Ranch cattle. The Ranger killed every raider and dumped the bodies in the square at Brownsville as a sign that times had changed. It set the tone for the bitter role the Rangers played on the border, but it worked. The raids slacked off, and when Porfirio Díaz seized power in Mexico in 1876 (with King's help), he made sure that they ended. King's empire was saved.

The Cattle Kingdom

In 1870, after a few years of amicable negotiations, Richard King and Mifflin Kenedy dissolved their partnership in R. King & Company. Kenedy bought the neighboring Laureles Ranch from Charles Stillman, who had retired to New York (where he founded, among other institutions, the National City Bank). The steamship business was winding down as the river silted up and competitions from a border railroad started to eat away at profits. Both Kenedy and King began devoting most of their time to their own ranches.

Having assembled almost 200,000 acres in the area of the Santa Gertrudis, King turned his attention to buying up the huge San Juan de Carrecitos grant. The grant covered 350,000 acres sixty miles south of the Santa Gertrudis and contained an old water hole called El Sauz, where King had camped countless times on his journeys to and from Brownsville. This land was not as rich as the Santa Gertrudis, but its sandy soil still supported native grasses in addition to sacahuiste, which cattle could eat in a drouth. King gave his lawyers standing orders to buy up rights and titles to the San Juan de Carrecitos grant whenever they could.

After the Civil War, the United States embarked on a period of furious industrial expansion. Railroads pushed across the continent. Huge empires of steel and oil were built. And to the cities of North and East came millions of immigrants from Europe and rural America. These new city dwellers needed meat. That demand found its supply in the Nueces Strip, where hundreds of thousands of cattle, untended during the war, were available for as little as $5 a head. The trick was to get the $5 steer to the $40 market. For a few years, the men who could do that reaped enormous profits. King sent more than one hundred thousand cattle north on the cattle trails during the 1870s. By the most conservative estimate, his profit over the decade was well over $1,000,000. One year, when he sent thirty thousand head, he made close to $400,000.

So immense were these cattle drives that the spillover from them was enough to stock ranches from Oklahoma to Montana. Yet the very success of the cattle kingdom spelled its doom. More and more cattle were raised in the Midwest, making it less profitable to ship cattle there from South Texas. Hardiness on the trail became less important and demand for better cuts of meat grew; the Longhorn was on its way out.

To raise better cattle, the rancher needed fences so he could control his stock. King and Kenedy were among the first to fence their holdings, using cypress and pine from Louisiana. By the late 1860s, King had built a fence more than five hundred miles long completely around Santa Gertrudis. To ride round it on horseback took ten days. The end of the open range meant that the rancher had to become an agricultural businessman, concerned less with winning the wilderness than with repairing his fences and keeping track of the breeding progress of his stock. Captain King brought in fine English Durhams in the early 1870s, beginning a breeding program that has continued for a century. Looking for better means of transport, King and Kenedy helped found a railroad from Corpus Christi to Laredo that passed within twenty miles of the Santa Gertrudis headquarters. The railroad arrived in 1881. Four years later, the trail drives came to an end.

A Frontier Relic

Life on the ranch became steadily more civilized. There was a cook and a Virginia governess for the three girls. Mrs. King saw that the five children all went away to proper Presbyterian schools. King often visited them when he was in St. Louis disposing of his herds. He was a striking figure, with his limp from an old river injury, his beard stretching down to the second button on his shirt, his pants rumpled, his boots always scuffed. He chided his daughters for being ashamed of his rough appearance—and then gave them expensive gifts in the manner of a father who had spent more time on his empire than on his family. Once he even gave his wife a pair of diamond earrings, which she, totally in character, did not wear until a local jeweler had painted them with black enamel so they would not appear ostentatious. Of the two boys,

Robert Lee was far more interested in the ranch. In 1883, Richard, Jr., married a Missouri girl and transformed La Puerta de Agua Dulce Ranch, north of the Santa Gertrudis, into a farming and cattle operation along midwestern lines.

A few months before his brother's marriage, Robert Lee died of pneumonia at the age of nineteen. The death of the boy in whom Captain King had placed such hope destroyed his faith in the future. He looked around his great empire and could take no solace from it. He wrote his wife, "I am tired of this business, as I at all times have made a mess of everything I have undertaken . . . and now I want to quit the Rancho business and will do so." Over the years, his friend Kenedy had come to a similar point of despair and had already sold the Laureles to a group of Scotsmen. King went so far as to show the Santa Gertrudis to some European buyers, but the sale never went through.

King was the great cattle baron of Texas, the master of the plains, owner of six hundred thousand acres, forty thousand head of cattle, six thousand horses, and twice that many sheep and pigs. But his heir was dead, and his very successes were changing the frontier world he loved. King eventually had to hire an Irishman to have fistfights with when he was in the mood, so quiet had Texas become. His benders with Rose Bud Whiskey became more extreme, his trips to Brownsville and other places more frequent. To inaugurate the railroad from Corpus Christi to Laredo, for example, he traveled west in a private car filled with dignitaries. Along the way, he spiked the lemonade, and the whole party—the leading citizens of South Texas—ended up marching through Laredo behind a big bass drum, singing at the top of their lungs and challenging all comers to a fight.

King remained a rough frontiersman, a natural leader, violent, passionate, and unpredictable. A more sensitive, gentle man could not have driven out the Indians, dominated outlaws and bandits, inspired vaqueros and cowboys, and won the frontier without any of the supports of civilization. "I have to make 'em think I'm a man-eater," he used to say. "If I don't they'll kill me."

The Pioneer's Farewell

Even though he despaired over Robert Lee's death, King managed to find a worthy successor, a man much different from himself. His only surviving son, Richard, Jr., was not by temperament a rancher. Two of his daughters had moved away and were not always on the best of terms with their demanding mother. But the youngest daughter, Alice, had stayed home, helping her mother keep a God-fearing house. In Corpus Christi in 1881, King had met a young lawyer named Robert Justus Kleberg, who was on the opposite side in one of King's many lawsuits. Kleberg had carried the day, and on the night of his victory, he received a visit from the stern rancher, whose hard eyes had followed him throughout the trial. Captain King had a proposition for Kleberg: he wanted Kleberg to take on some of the ranch's voluminous legal business.

Kleberg accepted the offer and asked when he should start. "Right now," King said, and the two left for the ranch on a buckboard in the middle of the night. At the ranch, Alice served coffee and cakes and then went back to bed, after getting a quick look at the man who would become her husband, the father of her five children, and, with her, the next link in the lineage of the King Ranch.

It wasn't just Robert Lee's death and the end of the frontier that were destroying Richard King. Something else was, too—stomach cancer. Alice and her mother both tried to care for him, but by 1885 King's rugged body could battle the disease no longer. His hair and beard had turned gray; his complexion was ashen. When he left the Santa Gertrudis to see his doctor in San Antonio, everyone knew he would not be back. The man who had conquered the West had to be helped to his stagecoach. His last instructions to his manager were "Don't let a foot of the dear old

Santa Gertrudis get away from us." At the Menger Hotel in San Antonio, next door to the Alamo, he died at dusk on April 14. He was sixty years old.

Big Boots to Fill

Shortly after her husband's death, Henrietta King, to whom he left everything he owned, gave her daughter's fiancé a mission: to run the ranch. It was not the best of times for a young lawyer of thirty-one to become a rancher. Cattle prices had fallen disastrously, from $40 a head to $5. The trail drives and the profits they had brought were over. Drouth gripped the prairie and would not let loose for almost a decade. King's relentless land buying had put the ranch deeply in debt. One of Robert Kleberg's first tasks as manager of the Santa Gertrudis was to disobey Robert E. Lee's advice: he sold land, about twenty thousand acres of it. Those odd pieces here and there went to cancel several debts, one of which had even dragged the widow King into court with a collection suit.

Robert Kleberg was not of the pioneer stock that had moved into Texas from the South. His family had come directly from Germany in 1834 and had begun life in America as new to it as the first settlers in New England. His father was a lawyer, and his mother was from a family of educated and distinguished Prussian aristocrats. They brought to Texas its first piano, as well as fine paintings, engravings, books, and music. Robert Kleberg received his law degree from the University of Virginia, then returned to Texas to practice. Possessed of a Prussian rationality and a stolid determination, Kleberg also had a bit of gemütlichkeit; he drank his share of beer and would even sing popular songs in public if called upon at weddings and other occasions. But what he brought most to the ranch was a strong sense of family, an unshakable belief in education, and a determination to plan for future generations.

It took a while for Kleberg to adapt to the ranching end of his new life. He was, after all, a lawyer and something of a scholar, a far cry from the larger-than-life character whose boots he had to fill. He spoke no Spanish at first, a distinct handicap in a kingdom whose subjects conversed in that tongue. He was only a passable horseman. He preferred to travel in a buckboard, dressed in his woolen suit and tie like a proper city lawyer, ignoring by a supreme effort of will the stupefying South Texas heat. But if he felt doubts about his new role, his firm sense of duty kept him going. He threw himself into ranching as vigorously as he had into the study of law, and he soon put his own stamp on the greatest ranch in the West.

In the year after Richard King died, Robert Kleberg took another step that tied him to his new destiny forever. In a small and private wedding ceremony, he married Alice King. The only guests from outside the family were Mifflin Kenedy and another of Captain King's partners, Uriah Lott. One represented the young couple's past, the other its future. Kenedy had been Richard King's lifelong friend and partner. Lott, in contrast, was a man of the new West. He was a railroad builder, a speculator on a grand scale, a man who recognized the benefits—and profits—that would come from opening up South Texas. Mifflin Kenedy had brought Richard King to the frontier; Uriah Lott would help his descendents bring the frontier to an end.

The new master of the King Ranch was eager to see Uriah Lott put to use. Like Lott, Kleberg saw the vast expanse of South Texas not as the open range but as the site of towns, farms, schools, and cities. He saw it civilized. The key to connecting South Texas to the rest of the world was a railroad from Corpus Christi to Brownsville, and the key to getting that railroad was finding water. Kleberg tried everything from prayers to dynamite. Finally he found a company in the Midwest with new drilling equipment that could penetrate far deeper than he had ever been able to drill. He ordered it at once and in 1899 set to work.

One rainy morning a vaquero appeared at the ranch house, breathless with his news. The new drill had struck water! Kleberg leaped into his buckboard and, whipping his horse, charged across the prairie. He stood at the well—water streaming down his face, his clothes soaked and muddy—and he cried. "The men," he recalled, "wondered why I cried when we finally saw what we had all been praying for. But I knew at once a definite source of water was available I could induce railroad construction, which in turn could lead to the development of South Texas."

With those wells, Robert Kleberg got his railroad and his town. Uriah Lott lined up the investors and the real estate. The ranch donated land both to provide a right-of-way and to pay the railroad contractors. As the railroad was being laid out, Kleberg lost no time in developing his land. He and the widow King rode out from their ranch house, a lonely sentinel on the prairie twenty miles from the nearest railhead and forty-five from Corpus Christi. They stopped at a spot where Richard King had spread his blanket for Henrietta on roundup picnics years before, where Comanches and the wild Longhorn had once held sway. In the distance, some cattle grazed, and all around there was no sound except the wind rustling in the hackberry and huisache trees along the creek bottom. Kleberg dismounted first, then helped Mrs. King down. "Here," he said, according to family legends, "we will build our town."

His vision was the same vision that had been transforming the wilderness of America into civilization for almost three hundred years. Before long, there were streets, churches, and *people*. These were city people—blacksmiths, teachers, salesmen, carpenters, the same sort of people who could be found throughout turn-of-the-century small-town America. Bringing civilization to the banks of the Santa Gertrudis—even in the form of a fairly primitive ranching and railroad town—was among Robert Kleberg's greatest achievements. To Henrietta King, it was the fulfillment of a dream a half century old. She donated the land for churches and schools out of her own lots, since to have churches in what had once been the frontier was the reward for all her hardships and the confirmation of her faith. The town was named Kingsville, after the region's last real frontiersman, but with its founding the South Texas frontier was no more.

Kleberg didn't stop with the town. He set aside land for demonstration farming of cotton, vegetables, and citrus. He planted countless species of fruit, from grapefruit to olives and date palms, and found that oranges and grapefruit grew well and bore prolifically. Kleberg's early experiments created the South Texas citrus industry. He was, at heart, a businessman. He wanted to *use* the land more than a rancher did, and he couldn't abide just leaving it to be harvested by cattle and horses.

By the time of his death in 1932, the ranch had doubled in size, to more than one million acres. He bought big tracts and small, often during drouths and depressions when prices were low. He bought the Laureles Ranch from the Scots who had bought it from Mifflin Kenedy. He brought in South African grasses to improve his pastures. For years, horses had been a major source of income for the ranch; as many as twelve thousand a year were sold to the army and to cities, businesses, and individuals all over America. Kleberg bred Clydesdale and Percheron horses, and business remained brisk until the automobile made draft horses obsolete.

One of the difficulties facing ranchers at the turn of the century was mesquite, which as a result of large-scale horse operations had spread like a weed across valuable grassland. (Horses ate the mesquite beans, which were warmed to incubation in their digestive tracts and then nourished to rapid growth by their manure.) Kleberg worked out the first rudimentary way to plow up mesquite and clear choked pastures.

The two biggest problems with the ranch, however, were water and cattle. Kleberg alleviated the water problem with his artesian wells; windmills soon were constructed all around the ranch, each serving its own pasture and allowing even more selective breeding operations. Yet the English breeds that the ranch imported had an unfortunate habit of dying once they got to South Texas. They lost weight, gave birth to stillborn calves, and declined into stupor and death. Through perseverance and a lawyer's patient accumulation of evidence, Robert Kleberg discovered that the cattle were suffering from a disease spread by ticks that came to be called Texas fever. For almost two decades, he worked to develop techniques to eradicate it. He built the first cattle dipping vat and initiated other preventive programs, almost single-handedly bringing the disease under control.

The Price of Inheritance

The widow King, though frail, survived her husband by forty years. When Robert Kleberg and Alice King were married in 1886, Henrietta King accompanied them on their honeymoon. This sharing of their postnuptial rite established a pattern that continued until her death in 1925. Mrs. King's bedroom in the old frame ranch house was directly across the hall from theirs. When that house burned in 1912, the custom of close family living carried over to the grand hacienda, known as the Big House, that looms over the Santa Gertrudis to this day.

Mrs. King presided at the dinner table and was quite free with advice on how the young couple should raise their five children. They never had a life of their own until they were near death; that was the price they paid for their inheritance. For decades, the King Ranch was known as "the widow's ranch," and Mrs. King, dressed always in black, set the tone for it. Twice a year she toured the ranch in her heavy black Rockaway stagecoach, and she was, in fact if not always in practice, the boss of the place. She gave Robert Kleberg authority and respect, but she never stepped entirely aside. A woman of unflagging charity and Christian determination, she still expected to receive her due as pioneer, founder, and owner.

At times, she no doubt made the Klebergs' lives utterly miserable.

But Mrs. King's fussy presence was only a minor source of misery compared with the South Texas climate. It was no more fit for proper Victorians than the steamy plains of India were. The vaquero men and women wore light cottons. The Kleberg men suffered under wool trousers, high boots, stiff collars, suspenders, and wool coats. The women of the family were gussied up in layers of chemises, petticoats, whalebone corsets, and heavy cloth from head to foot. Dressed like that, simply to survive a South Texas August was a triumph. Mrs. King would not allow the men to dine at her table in shirtsleeves, no matter how hot the day. And so they would sit through dinner, sweating profusely. If the windows were opened, the wind would cover the plates with dust. If it was a bit cooler, the mosquitoes would descend in clouds. Even so, after dinner the family members would entertain each other, putting on skits, telling stories, reading aloud, and singing songs, always closing with Mrs. King's favorite, "Rock of Ages."

The new generation, the Klebergs' two boys and three girls, grew up on the ranch in spirit even though they spent the school year in Corpus Christi. Their father delighted in sending a stagecoach drawn by magnificent white horses to meet them at the train stop. The horses whisked them away on what must have been a heady ride across twenty miles of prairie to the threshold of the ranch house. When the railroad finally came to Kingsville, the railroad manager sent a special engine and caboose every Friday to take the children from Corpus Christi out to the ranch.

Alice King Kleberg, for her part, stayed in her mother's shadow and deferred to her husband, a model of self-denial. But she harbored in her heart a warm spot for her father's flamboyance. Her first son, Richard Mifflin Kleberg, was her favorite. He was dashing, talented, and athletic. He mastered languages, golf, the guitar, and the piano, all with ease. He was a natural diplomat with a flair for dramatic gestures and could deliver moving speeches in

Spanish, German, and English. He would sit with his mother for hours, playing his guitar and singing songs.

But Robert Kleberg, while he admired his elder son's talents, placed his faith in Robert Kleberg, Jr., his second son. Bob had to work harder for what he got. Shorter than Richard, he was also less athletic and graceful. He had a terrible ear for languages and music and a soft, squeaky voice unsuited to public speaking. He liked books but did not take to schools. He pulled his share of pranks, but in contrast to Richard, he was a serious and earnest young man, just the sort to inspire confidence in his father and the widow King.

Richard Kleberg, as befitted his talents, became the ranch's emissary to the world at large. He looked after its interests in Congress from 1932 to 1944 (and gave a young Texan named Lyndon Johnson his first job in Washington). Richard Kleberg was something of a legend there. He often drove up to the Capitol in a stripped-down King Ranch hunting car like the one Buick made for him, trimmed in sterling silver, with compartments for guns, ammunition, and liquor.

Bob, however, was given the responsibility of the ranch. Captain King himself had skipped over the most obvious heir in favor of a man better suited to the task. That tradition, more than anything else, enabled the family to sustain itself when an aristocracy that gave everything to the firstborn would have failed. And no one proved that tradition's worth more eloquently than Bob Kleberg.

In the Captain's Image

One hundred years, almost to the day, after Richard King established his first cow camp on the Santa Gertrudis, Bob Kleberg stood on a rise in Queensland and gazed out on the vast red-dirt sweep of the Australian outback. The country was raw desert, worked desultorily by a few settlers and Aborigines whose occasional travels sent whirlwinds of dust across the steppes. But Bob Kleberg saw in that Australian wilderness precisely what his grandfather had seen in the grassy, godforsaken Wild Horse Desert of South Texas; he saw the makings of an empire. By the time he finally satisfied that vision, he had added 8,000,000 acres of Australian land on long-term leases to the 825,000 or so his family owned in Texas.

He also left his mark on every aspect of the original ranch. He led it through the tumultuous decade following the death of Henrietta King in 1925. He survived bitter court battles with his cousins over the division of the ranch. He weathered the Depression and its catastrophic effect on ranch profits. He engineered a deal with Humble Oil for the ranch's oil and gas rights that put it permanently on a sound financial footing. And he developed an entirely new breed of cattle that was to the cattle business what the Model A Ford was to the car business. He was, by any definition, a genius.

Like his brother and sisters, Bob Kleberg grew up on the ranch. He learned to ride at four and to cut, rope, and shoot soon after. His mentors were his cousin Caesar Kleberg, ranch foreman Sam Ragland, and the Kineños. Caesar was the family eccentric. He ran the southern sector of the ranch from a weathered old ranch house at Norias that had neither electricity nor plumbing. The railroad tracks cut through the front yard. The bathtub was on the front porch, and cots did for beds. The place was so cluttered, rumor said that nothing that went in ever came out except, occasionally, Caesar himself.

As a boy, Bob lived with Sam Ragland in the foreman's cottage next to the Big House. Ragland and Caesar, as well as Kineños such as Augustín Quintanilla and Faustino Villa, who had been with Captain King on the river, made the younger Kleberg son their apprentice. He was a quick learner. With their help, he trained his eyes, his ears, and his nose to pick up the subtle variations that told him, as if by instinct, which calves would breed best, which clouds carried rain, which plant stung, and which one healed. Bob's early ambition was to be an inventor, and later the stirrings of youthful independence caused him to announce that he was going to be an engineer. But the onset of his father's palsy and World War I changed that. He came home to run the ranch in 1918 after only two years of college, and for all practical purposes he did not leave it for twenty years.

The Ranch Divided

In 1925, at the age of ninety-two, the widow of the King Ranch died. At Henrietta King's bier were bankers from the East, railroad executives, oilmen, and politicians. There were also hundreds of Kineños, some of whom had ridden for two days from the ranch's far divisions. Unbidden, they led the funeral procession into the town cemetery, a few miles from where her husband had first brought her to the uninhabited frontier more than seventy years before. Then they circled the open grave on horseback at a fast canter, their hats held at their sides.

Mrs. King's death threw the ranch into crisis. The estate taxes and the Depression that soon followed dragged the ranch more than $3 million into debt, to the edge of financial ruin. More ominously, the huge empire built by the riverboat captain had to be divided among his heirs for the first time. That complex and, in some cases, bitter process consumed an entire decade. It was Bob Kleberg's first great test.

Mrs. King's will called for her daughter Alice to receive the northern tier of the ranch, the Santa Gertrudis and Laureles divisions. The southern sector was divided among her other heirs, with the children of Richard King, Jr., receiving the Santa Fe Ranch to the west. The Atwoods, heirs of Mrs. King's eldest daughter, Nettie (from whom the widow had long been estranged, never having approved of her daughter's marriage to an army officer), received

El Sauz on the south. The Klebergs got the northeastern portion
known as the Norias Division, to which they added the shares of
two other heirs who sold out to them. In the early 1920s, knowing
that his family was going to lose most of the sandy pasture in
the southern sector, Bob Kleberg had bought a sandy ranch south
of Falfurrias to create another division, the Encino, just north of
the Santa Fe Ranch. Of the ranch's 1,200,000 acres, the Klebergs
ended up with more than 800,000.

Throughout the ten years between Mrs. King's death in 1925
and the final partition in 1935, Bob Kleberg, the youngest trustee,
ran the ranch for the heirs. He ran it without hesitation and with
a zeal that angered the Atwoods. They fought the will bitterly,
challenged his trusteeship, raged over his imperial manner, and
fumed that he charged his freewheeling escapades to the estate.
Led on by their Chicago lawyer, the Atwoods refused to take El
Sauz and sued the ranch for nearly twenty years, all the while
living in comparative poverty on a modest allowance Mrs. King
had given them in her will. Estranged, lonely, and resentful, one
of them bequeathed her estate to a Chicago policeman who had
treated her kindly. The lawyer ended up with well over half of El
Sauz in return for masterminding what was, by the time it was
finally settled in the 1950s, the longest suit in Texas history.

To manage their holdings, in 1934 the Klebergs incorporated
the King Ranch (which meant that the descendants of Richard
King, Jr., would no longer be a part of the ranch that bore their
name). Each of the five children of Alice King and Robert Kleberg,
Sr., got one-fifth of the stock, which they pooled in a trust set
up to last until 1954, when they or their heirs would control the
stock individually. The intent was clear: after suffering through the
tense decade following Mrs. King's death, Bob Kleberg, his older
brother, and their three sisters were pledging to keep the King
Ranch together.

The incorporation of the ranch was the beginning of its modern history. It was no longer one man's empire. Instead, it belonged to a growing family whose members would have to agree on its destiny. In 1934, there were only five stockholders; in two generations, there would be more than sixty. Corporate politics, meaning family politics, would decide the ranch's future, even if the will, the charisma, and, above all, the longevity of Bob Kleberg would obscure that fact for four decades. Back in the early 1930s, however, Bob worried less about how his heirs would run the ranch than about making sure they would have something to run. Neither the Atwoods, the land, nor the future was the biggest thorn in his side—money was.

Playing the Oil Card

Ranchers have traditionally been land-poor: long on acres, short on cash. Ever since the brief halcyon years of the cattle boom following the Civil War, the King Ranch had seldom earned more than $100,000 or $200,000 a year in profit from all its ranching operations. Some years it lost money. In the 1930s, however, drouths so parched the ranch's pastures that its cattle were starving. Yet there was no point in buying feed for them—fat steers were selling for a pitiful three and a half cents a pound. The King Ranch unloaded thousands of head of cattle and earned in return barely enough to pay for shipping them to market.

It was a grim period. Bob's cousin Richard King (who was still with the ranch then) spent all his time on trains, trying to stay ahead of the ranch's creditors by floating new loans to pay off the one ones coming due. Throughout the crisis, the elder Kleberg, the old German lawyer who had bested a riverboat captain in court, still got in his car every afternoon and had himself driven around the ranch, his blue eyes staring out at the barren plains, his once fertile mind having been made helpless by a stroke.

The pressure on Bob to sell off big chunks of the ranch, to throw into the fire the only asset it had left—its land—became

overwhelming. No one saw any other way out. But Bob, obsti-
nately and unreasonably, refused to sell land. "Selling is easy," he
would say. "Collecting is hard." He looked instead to something
else the ranch possessed—beneath its surface. He looked to oil.

In 1933, Bob Kleberg tried to persuade several oil companies
to take a lease on the ranch. Gulf, Shell, and Texaco turned him
down. Humble Oil did not: in return for a loan that would assume
all of the ranch's $3 million debt, then held by numerous inves-
tors in the form of King Ranch notes, and in return for a royalty
interest and enough bonus payments to meet the interest on the
loan, Bob granted Humble the right to search for oil and gas on
the more than one million acres the family controlled before the
partition. When the deal was closed, Humble had possession of
what was then the largest oil and gas lease in the world. And the
ranch—provided, as many oilmen doubted, that there was oil
under its pastures—was on a sound financial footing at last.

Using the primitive geological survey methods of the time,
Humble spent the next six years trying to discover just where to
drill its first well. "It was like firing a rocket into space not knowing where the planets were and expecting to hit something," a
veteran of the early exploration recalled. In 1939, Humble began
drilling in the sections adjacent to proven fields outside the ranch.
Not until 1945, twelve years after the lease was signed, did they go
after new fields with their first wildcat well. It hit. Two years later,
the ranch had raked in $3.25 million in royalties from fields that
the *Oil and Gas Journal* estimated would be second to East Texas
in oil and second to Amarillo in natural gas. By 1953, there were
650 producing wells on the ranch.

The relationship between the King Ranch and Humble was
based on a simple understanding: the King Ranch might be an
oil field to Humble, but it was still a ranch to Bob Kleberg. For
example, when the first oil well was no longer a producer, it was
converted to a water well and used to fill stock tanks. Oil has been

a considerate guest. Pumps, rigs, gas lines, and equipment are kept up to the standard of appearance of the ranch, which, not so incidentally, got with its royalties a free system of roads and free natural gas.

The free gas eventually became something of a headache for Humble. On one memorable occasion, the top executives of Standard Oil, Humble, and other oil companies were houseguests of Henrietta Larkin Armstrong, Bob's sister. Henrietta was an enthusiastic gardener. That night, a blue norther sent the temperature in South Texas into the twenties, so Henrietta set out dozens of gas stoves to keep her plants from freezing. Sometime after midnight, the stoves stopped working. With an undeniable logic, she rousted all the oil company presidents and board chairmen out of their beds with the command, "You all know everything about gas—get up and fix my stoves!" They did, and not long after that, they gave up supplying the ranch with free gas from their wells and installed propane tanks instead.

An Artist of Genetics

Bob Kleberg not only saved the ranch but also transformed it. Like Henry Ford, with whom he had a great deal in common, he loved to tinker. Were the mesquite thickets getting worse? He invented a root plow driven by a massive bulldozer that could clear four acres an hour. Were the native grasses thin and unnourishing? He developed his own grasses, some of which are now used around the world. Was the grass deficient in nutrients? He devised a phosphorus supplement that made cattle healthier. Was it difficult to move cattle into pens? He invented the cattle prod, based on the design for a fly electrocutor he was experimenting with. The list goes on and on. But his most inventive work was in breeding.

By World War I, the Longhorn, like the buffalo, had vanished from the frontier. But the English breeds that replaced it suffered mightily in the South Texas heat. For most of the year, they ran a fever just from standing in the sun. Their skin was too tight to allow much evaporation and too thin to resist screwworms, ticks, and other insects. They gained weight poorly when fed just grass, yet grass was what the King Ranch had in abundance. With the help of his brother, Richard, Bob Kleberg set out to invent his own cow. He brought in Brahmans and crossed them with his English Shorthorns, patiently working down through generations of cattle, until one day a bull calf was born that seemed *different*. He was so good-natured and playful that they called him Monkey.

Monkey was what Bob Kleberg had been looking for, and from Monkey he engineered a whole new race of cattle. To breed out undesirable characteristics, he repeatedly mated Monkey to a handpicked selection of other crossbreeds, then to the best off-spring from those matings and to their offspring. He would look at young bulls and heifers and announce that they would "nick well together"—would produce calves that would continue the progress toward his goal: an animal that would thrive on heat and grass and would repel insects, an animal that had the hardiness of the Brahman and the temperament and marketable beef of the fat and docile English cattle.

His invention was the world's first new breed of beef cattle in more than a century, and in 1940 (thanks largely to Richard Kleberg's skilled lobbying in Washington), it was officially named the first American breed. Bob Kleberg called the new breed the Santa Gertrudis, after the little creek that marked the spot of King's first rancho. The breed reflects Bob's practical genius, but it also confirms his artistic sense. It is an animal of beauty—deep russet in color, long and well proportioned. Like great art, the Santa Gertrudis appears simple but could only be re-created from scratch with incredible difficulty and a great deal of luck. Technically, it is three-eighths Brahman and five-eighths Shorthorn, but as one geneticist puts it, "You could cross Shorthorns and Brahmans all your life and not come up with a Santa Gertrudis."

Bob Kleberg's artistry in genetics wasn't limited to beef cattle. His father had crossed range horses with Thoroughbreds and standard breeds, but their descendants were too clumsy for ranch work. Bob set about to create a ranch horse that would be, in his words, "a joy to ride." The Quarter Horse he developed, known as the Old Sorrel (from the stallion that was the equine counterpart of Monkey), is a deep red like the Santa Gertrudis. Ringling Bros. bought King Ranch Quarter Horses for their circus acts, and when the American Quarter Horse Association was founded, a King Ranch stallion, Wimpy, was given the first number in the stud book. In the late 1930s, Bob devoted the same interest to Thoroughbreds, breeding racehorses that won the Kentucky Derby twice and, with Assault, the Triple Crown. In each case, he pushed out into the forefront of the geneticist's art and science.

Outside the Fences

Bob Kleberg was the first leader of the King Ranch born and bred to ranching. He did not share his father's interest in development and growth; if anything, the town of Kingsville—his father's personal creation—was an irritant to him. Still, he did not want to let Kingsville leave the ranch's paternal control. The family was proud of the land and money it donated for schools, churches, and social work, not to mention the leadership of generations of ranch women in charitable causes throughout South Texas. Bob Kleberg was squarely in that tradition. He saw himself as a *patrón;* in that role, he donated buildings and money for schools but fought any effort to let the school board tax the ranch to pay for the same improvements.

The arrival of a naval air station, Humble, and then the Celanese Chemical Company, combined with the social upheavals that began in earnest after World War II, changed forever the ranch's relationship to Robert Kleberg's town. Like a son who had grown to manhood, Kingsville wanted independence from its parents. First Richard Kleberg was defeated for Congress. Then, in the late 1940s, Kingsville voted in an anti-ranch school board. But today the town and the ranch coexist comfortably. The ranch pays about $336,000 in taxes, less than either Celanese or Humble. The streets bear the names of the family, and the ranch still owns the newspaper, the largest bank, a lumberyard, and a boot and saddle shop. But Kingsville and its 29,000 people have grown beyond the ranch, just as the ranch, in its worldwide activities, has grown beyond Kingsville.

The family, of course, did not drop out of politics. After Richard broke with Democrats over the New Deal, the Klebergs gradually became strong Republicans. In 1962, John Armstrong, now the ranch's executive vice president, modernized the Kleberg County Republican Party organization and personally helped canvass the whole county. Both Bob Kleberg and his nephews Belton Kleberg "B" Johnson and Dick Kleberg strongly supported Richard Nixon. Dick contributed $100,000 to Nixon's 1972 campaign. And when Nixon resigned from the presidency in 1974, a stunned and very distressed Bob Kleberg—only two months away from death—called one of his relatives to talk for hours about the fate of leaders, about how no man can hold power forever. But in local politics, the ranch takes a lower profile; for many Chicano activists, the ranch is too potent a symbol of how Anglo ranchers once controlled the county's destiny. Some individual family members still get involved in city and school elections, and the family-owned newspaper is fairly outspoken on local affairs, but no one in either the town or the family believes that the ranch calls the shots in Kingsville anymore.

Taxes weren't the only trappings of civilization that Bob resisted. The boom in the valley and South Texas, brought on in part by the success of his father's farming experiments, was attracting too many people, crowding out cattle, eating away at perfectly good ranchland. He ruthlessly set out to stop this encroachment, once calling one of the elder Kleberg's farming proposals "a dam-fool idea" to his face. For almost ten years, he and Johnny Kenedy, Mifflin Kenedy's grandson, blocked the completion of Highway 77, the main artery between Corpus Christi and Brownsville, because it would pass through their ranches. His opposition to progress earned the ranch its fame as "the walled kingdom."

Miles to Go Before He Slept

When Bob Kleberg went to Australia in 1952, he was fifty-six. The ranch he had run since 1918, when he was twenty-two years old, was doing well. At a time in his life when many men would have looked back on their accomplishments, he was ready for new challenges. He was irascible, magnetic, imperious, opinionated, able to mix with vaqueros and Rockefellers alike, and quite often absolutely impossible. "I've been out with him when he didn't put head to pillow all night," recalls John Armstrong.

> Then he'd saddle up his horse and work cattle until the sun went down the next day, and never slow down. I never knew when he slept, but I started to notice that he would sleep at the dinner table—sometimes over coffee, sometimes through the main course. And then he'd look up with a start and be ready to go again. When you were with him you were always drinking, laughing, and shooting rabbits. I went with him to South America, and when I came home I had to see my doctor. I was almost twenty-five years younger, but he'd worn me out.

When he went to the East, to the best boxes at Saratoga, to the suite at the Pierre, to "21," he arrived as the conquering provincial. During the horse-racing season, he customarily dressed in a silk hat and a serape and, thus outfitted, went calling on the Whitneys and the Vanderbilts. There was always something fabulous about him, almost as if he had just ridden up to the

Pierre Hotel surrounded by mounted and armed Kineños.

What Bob saw, he saw clearly; what Bob wanted done, he got done. He was not plagued by self-doubts or hampered by lack of confidence. He did as he pleased all his life. He knew his own mind, and he knew who he was. Faced with a world in which paperwork, bureaucrats, and "experts" assumed more importance every day, he became less and less patient with dissent, incompetence, and routine. A lifelong friend casually refers to him as "the old dictator." He wanted things done *his* way. "When he said 'frog,'" one crusty South Texas rancher and oilman recalls, "everybody jumped."

Instinct was as important to Bob Kleberg as organization. The management tools used in sedentary pursuits such as insurance and steel manufacturing were to be tolerated but certainly not encouraged. When he went to Venezuela to look into buying a ranch with his partner there, he was presented with a wealth of statistics, charts, and cost-benefit analyses. He brushed them aside, looked around at the land, opened a bottle, and made the deal. After all, his partner in Venezuela was a man he trusted, a *rancher*. That bond of respect was worth more than any economic analysis.

The partner, Gustavo de los Reyes, had owned a ranch in Cuba neighboring Bob Kleberg's first foreign venture. After Castro came to power in 1959, de los Reyes was imprisoned and the King Ranch's property and cattle were expropriated. (For years afterward, there were reports of Santa Gertrudis herds in Russia, the older cattle still bearing the ranch's Running W brand.) Kleberg had promised de los Reyes to set him up anywhere in the world when he got out of prison, and Kleberg kept the promise.

In 1966, Bob was visiting the Venezuela ranch. Terrorists had been attacking ranches nearby, and the Venezuelan government seemed powerless to stop them. As de los Reyes recounted the story to Charles Murphy, a *Fortune* writer, he turned to Kleberg and told him he wouldn't blame Kleberg if he wanted to pull out of Venezuela to avoid a repeat of the Cuban affair.

Kleberg thought about that. "You ever run away from anything?" he asked.

"Nothing that I can remember," the Cuban answered.

"Neither have I," said Captain King's grandson. Bob Kleberg then stood up, took off his King Ranch cowboy hat, and hung it on a hook in the ranch office, where it remained until his death. "I'll need this," he said, "when I come back."

That was how Bob Kleberg worked, in ranching, in oil, in everything. He had an actor's instinct for the dramatic gesture, particularly the one that would make him seem larger than life. But if he postured, as he did with his hat in Venezuela, he was also willing to back that posturing up. He might, for example, trot out some obscure fact about the Irish rebellion of 1797 to make a point, but if he was challenged, the chances were very good that he really knew what he was talking about. He did a great deal for effect, but he hardly ever did anything simply for show.

A sophisticated businessman, he was a determined foe of what passed for sophisticated business. After he made a deal, he had his lawyers and accountants come in and make sure it was right, but until then they made themselves scarce. He had a healthy respect for such professionals—his father and brother were both lawyers, and the ranch's main attorneys, Leroy Denman, Sr., and Leroy Denman, Jr., were two of his closest friends and advisers. But he knew also that a rancher was not a lawyer and that to be a rancher you had to know when not to return your lawyer's urgent phone calls.

A Woman's Touch

For the last two decades of his life, Bob Kleberg spent most of his time on his foreign empire. His nephew Dick Kleberg stayed in Texas and ran the original ranch. When Bob was at the ranch, his days almost always followed the same pattern: he was awakened with a steaming cup of black coffee at five or six, talked to all his foremen by phone, and then drove out onto the ranch in one of the special hunting cars he had designed. He never left without his pistols and his Mannlicher rifles. There was always the possibility that some hapless coyote—or, during hunting season, quail, turkey, or deer—might cross his path. Throughout the day, he would work on horseback with the Kineños. At lunch, they would break for barbecue, frijoles, and camp bread cooked in Dutch ovens over an open fire and smeared with molasses. It was a rugged, hardy, outdoor life; it kept Bob Kleberg in touch with his roots and with the frontier traditions of ranching; and it had almost nothing to do with how the ranch really made its money.

When he returned from his sojourns in Australia or South America, Bob made it a point to tour the ranch. His tours were legendary. Often he would take his nephew B Johnson along. "We'd leave at dawn and drive all day long," B remembers.

> We'd do two and sometimes three divisions in a day. He'd get to a pasture, take one look, and say, "I told you three years ago to do so and so. You didn't do it. See what happened?" He would work with the Kineños, straight through until we finished—no breaks for coffee, lunch, bad weather, anything. He did everything the hard way— he rode the hard way, with his stirrups fully extended; he roped the hard way, just using his shoulders; he studied the hard way, always poring over scientific journals. He hated the office. His life was outside.

Bob and his brother and their few close friends entertained themselves much as Captain King had. They hunted, of course—alone, with each other, and on a grand social scale at Christmastime. Both Bob and Richard were superb shots with rifle, pistol, or shotgun. Once Bob and a family friend shot out the streetlights of the nation's capital with wild abandon and great accuracy. Bob and Richard often bet on horses and sneaked away from the respectable life of the family compound to the more plebeian pleasures of cockfighting.

Their mother, Alice, the last link with the old ranch of Captain King, viewed their excesses with the same blinders her mother had worn. When someone mentioned that her son Richard was spending a good deal of time with fighting cocks, she replied, "How nice. He's the first member of the family to be interested in poultry." But at home the brothers made the same concessions to respectability that their grandfather had. They would, for example, hide liquor in the bathroom and answer a truly prodigious number of calls of nature during parties or in the long evenings they spent at home. Outside the house, they were their own men; inside, they played by women's rules.

But Alice King Kleberg was the last woman of the family to embody the struggle of gentility against reality. The next generation of women was different, as likely to sip bourbon as the men were, as eager to go out on roundups, as proficient at riding and shooting. The key woman of that generation was Bob's wife, Helen, the model for Leslie Benedict in *Giant*. If oil opened the world up to the ranch, it was Helen who pushed and prodded her reluctant husband out into it.

The daughter of a congressman from Kansas, she met Bob Kleberg at a party in 1926. Only seventeen days later, they were married. Helen threw herself into the romantic and varied wonders of the ranch but always—always—tried to awaken her provincial husband to what lay beyond its fences. She encouraged him to enter the world of Thoroughbred racing, which led them into friendships with the old families of the East. She bought her cowboy husband pinstripe suits, which he wore with good humor, even if they never quite seemed to fit. She carried her Episcopalian faith into the Presbyterian stronghold. And, determined that her daughter, Helenita, and other promising young Klebergs would be exposed to a wider world, she saw that they went east to prep school. She labored to keep up a sense of standards within the fairly rough-edged family she had joined; she even included the Queen of England on the family's wedding-invitation list, a reminder to everyone of exactly where she pegged the Klebergs' social position.

Every January at roundup time, Bob and Helen Kleberg worked cattle together. Everyone pitched in, for a veritable orgy of work and a hell of a good time. It was as if twice a year John D. Rockefeller went down to the oil field and drilled for oil. Few people of the Klebergs' station remained so in touch with the work on which their fortunes were built, and few people of their station could perform the roughest and most challenging tasks as well as their best workers.

Holding the Family Together

The stock of the King Ranch corporation was distributed to the family in 1954. For the first time, the five children of Alice King and Robert Kleberg were free to dispose of their shares as they wished. It was like the partition after Henrietta's death on a smaller scale, though this time four of the five branches chose to stay in. But Bob's sister Alice Kleberg East, even more of a fundamentalist rancher than her brother, decided to exchange her shares for part of the ranch. To her and her children, the King Ranch had become too civilized under Bob Kleberg; as they put it, there were "too many flowerpots to water." They had little patience with the Thoroughbred program and with Bob's foreign ventures. The Easts wanted to run their own affairs.

But Bob Kleberg had not taken over Captain King's ranch to preside over its dissolution. He was adamant. He would not give up part of the ranch. Luckily, his cousin Richard King and his family were ready to stop ranching and devote their attention to banking and other urban interests. So Bob engineered a trade that gave Richard King's Santa Fe property to the King Ranch in return for 10 percent of the ranch's oil royalties. Bob then traded the Santa Fe to Alice for her stock. Once again, he had used oil to hold the ranch together.

In 1958, with the original lease running out, the ranch and Humble negotiated an agreement that would change the course of the ranch's history and, in the 1970s, become a bitter bone of contention. The new agreement extended the Humble lease and granted Humble the right to build on the ranch (only eight miles west of the Santa Gertrudis headquarters) what was then the world's largest natural gas processing plant. In return, Humble agreed to pay the ranch a one-sixth royalty on all gas and oil, instead of the customary one-eighth. By 1969, the ranch was producing, *Fortune* magazine estimated, $120 million a year in oil and gas, making its one-sixth share worth $20 million, or about fifteen times the profits from the entire ranching operation.

Wealth in those proportions could have turned the Klebergs into stereotypical Texas oilmen, the Jett Rinks whose roots were swept away in the flood of oil. They could have become mad eccentrics or idle rich who frittered away their birthright. Instead, Bob Kleberg took the oil money and sank it into what the family knew best—more ranching. Millions of dollars went into Australia, Africa, and South America. He was consumed with the idea of claiming as productive ranchland the deserts and jungles of the tropics and claiming them using his own invention, Santa Gertrudis cattle. Bob Kleberg was convinced that with proper management the Santa Gertrudis could feed the poor people of the tropics.

In the space of twenty years, with an intense expenditure of energy, will, ingenuity, and money, he added eight million acres to the ranch, mostly under long-term leases. He never stopped acquiring new pastures. In his late seventies, he was absorbed with Spain and Morocco, and when he died, he was obsessed with winning for ranching the world's biggest wilderness—the Amazon. It was one of the most impressive bursts of creative energy in the history of American enterprise, and it made him a world figure, the confidant of presidents and kings.

Bob Kleberg took over the ranch during World War I and gave it up as the last troops left Vietnam; he came in with the Model T and went out after the final Apollo mission to the moon. "It's not hard to see why he might have seemed intolerant of suggestions from the younger members of the family," his daughter, Helenita, says. "After all, even if they were fifty years old, he had been running the ranch since before they were born."

In the last years of his life, he took his grandchildren on tours of the foreign ranches. They rode horseback all day and spent a good many evenings around the campfire. Bob Kleberg wanted more than anything to give his grandchildren a sense of who they were, wanted them to see the vastness of what their family had wrought. And he had decided to charge them with a weighty responsibility, just as Captain King, on his deathbed, had made his family swear never to sell a foot of the old Santa Gertrudis. One night, as the campfire flickered, he gave them their mission: "Do what you can with the ranch," he said, "but, above all, keep the family together." In 1974, scarcely a month after he had been working cattle in the saddle, he died.

The Hard Worker

Though Bob Kleberg transformed the ranch, he did not have the same effect on the family. As Bob grew beyond the ranch, many members of the family found him increasingly remote. The man who most influenced the family was not Bob but his nephew Dick, Richard's son. Dick was not the brilliant rancher Bob was. He did not seek new empires or command the center stage or extend the frontiers of ranching. He dedicated himself instead to husbanding what his forebears had built. Some members of the family were most inspired by Bob's vision and dominating presence; others believed in Dick's loyalty and sense of teamwork. Dick's protégés, and not Bob's, would end up running the ranch.

Dick was born out on the Laureles Division in 1916. Even before his father died in 1955, he had become his uncle's right-hand man. Dick was the first person Bob thought he could trust with the ranch, and he laid the weight of its responsibility on Dick's shoulders while he embarked on the worldwide expansion that occupied the last twenty years of his life.

There was never any doubt that Bob Kleberg was the boss, but it was Dick who kept the ranch going. He worked long hours every day, sweating, sunburned, choking with allergies. He chain-smoked and drank rivers of coffee and, like many of the other men in the family, too much whiskey. He worked the ranch's 825,000 acres as if he were the only hand on a family farm—no detail escaped him, no job was too small to take him out to the ranch. He never took a vacation with his family. Like Richard Kleberg, Sr., Dick subordinated himself to Bob.

Richard had been content to let his younger brother, Bob, have the attention, the acclaim, and the power. And he did that because he knew Bob was better at running the ranch than he was. That pride in putting personal ambition and fame aside for the best interests of the family sustained Dick also and won him the hearts of his family and of the vaqueros, who loved him, perhaps more than any other Kleberg before or since. They loved him in the vigor of his youth for his humor and his cowboy skills; and they loved him later, when he lay helpless with emphysema, with instinctive empathy for his suffering.

For in the end, Dick Kleberg's body was not up to the burden he placed upon it. Living and working at the pace set by Bob Kleberg could not have helped his health. And South Texas is one of the most hostile climates known to man. Its heat is more enervating than Death Valley's. The air is heavy with humidity,

laden with dust, and filled with pollen. Almost all of the Klebergs
are fair, with delicate skin that burns easily and is prone to cancer.
They are plagued with allergies and asthma. They cough, wheeze,
and sneeze, and they broil in the inescapable sun.

For Dick Kleberg, the dust, the pollen, and the cigarettes were
too much. He developed emphysema, and his lungs began to fill
with fluid. At first, he was only a step or two slower than in his
prime. But then there came hours at a time when he could not
even go outside. A man who hated to be indoors, he was confined
to his room, battling the disease that was smothering him. And
then the hours became days, and the walls of his room became
his world.

When Bob Kleberg died, Dick should at last have been able
to turn the daily grind of the ranch over to one of his cousins or
sons and enjoy the status on which Bob had thrived. But his body
would not let him. Several times he went into the intensive care
unit at Spohn Hospital in Corpus Christi, and his family was told
he was dying. But he rallied, returned home, and tried to work,
only to become an invalid again. In the late spring of 1979, his
favorite horse died, a mare named Anita Chica. "It was like an
omen," a member of the family recalled. A few weeks later, Dick
Kleberg, at sixty-two years old, was dead.

The Burial of the Dead

It rained most of the morning, a rancher's dream. In Santa
Gertrudis Creek, the narrow channel, scarcely a trickle, swelled
slowly out toward the muddy banks. Along the wire-mesh fences,
lantanas, horsemint, and ebony were beginning to bloom. The
ranch's 563 employees—foremen, vaqueros, cooks, blacksmiths,
farmers, secretaries, heavy-equipment men, veterinarians, accountants, maids, stableboys, pilots—had gathered on the banks
of Santa Gertrudis. A festive tent had been erected for a family
wedding scheduled the next day, but the crowds converging on

the King Ranch headquarters on this day were there for a more solemn purpose. They were there to bury Dick Kleberg. The accidental conjunction of wedding and funeral seemed appropriate for such a cohesive family: one generation was passing, and another was beginning. As the rain was bringing new life to the dry prairie, so too would the wedding bring new life to the ranch.

The memorial service convened in the courtyard of Dick's house, a rambling contemporary-style building laid out like one of the ranch's cow camp shelters. It nestles in a live oak grove next to the Big House. The gentle, steady rain had turned the grass green and rich. Across Santa Gertrudis Creek, cattle grazed; inside the courtyard, mariachis played the music of the border. The children perched on folding chairs, the girls in Easter dresses, the boys in neatly pressed suits. In the crowd were ranchers, Houston lawyers, South American diplomats, and New York bankers; on the outskirts stood the ranch executives and foremen. Beyond them, hats in hand, the Kineños stood awkwardly but proudly in their Sunday best. From behind the house emerged a procession of fourteen Kineños, each in khaki, each mounted on a rusty red King Ranch Quarter Horse. They lined up behind the swimming pool, their hats held over their hearts. In the center of this honor guard pranced a restless horse without a rider, a yellow poncho draped over its saddle. The saddle was Dick's, made in the King Ranch saddle shop. Tied over it on either side were his boots. The sunlight flickering through the clouds reflected off the mother-of-pearl inlays in the handmade spurs.

A plaintive trumpet solo signaled the beginning of the service. The rain had stopped, but the wind blew drops of water from the mesquite and live oak trees down onto the crowd. A young Episcopal priest spoke of how Dick had "loved the land, had felt the promise of it, had worked it and suffered on it." Then the Kineños' priest gave a eulogy in Spanish. He talked about how the ranch people were workers and the Klebergs were *patrones* but in death all were equal. The ranch workers, he added, addressing the family, had shared the family's joys and laugher and today shared their sorrow and their tears.

The mariachis played a polka, and the mounted Kineños turned their horses and filed away, holding their hats to their sides in respect. The mourners began breaking up into smaller groups to tell stories far into the night about Dick, about the ranch, and about the other members of its family, like a Greek chorus telling tales of the deaths of kings. The family had been given much by the chance of birth—fame, riches, a vast ranch. But the funeral of Dick Kleberg was, above all, a reminder that they had also been given a ration of suffering.

Two Brothers

In the five years between the deaths of Bob and Dick Kleberg, the family endured more tumult, change, and confrontation than it had seen since the ranch partition in the 1930s, if then. With Dick ill, the two most obvious heirs to the ranch were Dick's cousins B Johnson and Robert Shelton. They were the sons of Bob Kleberg's star-crossed younger sister, Sarah. Sarah was one of the new breed of ranch women who were not content to stay primly indoors. She was most at home on the ranch, and when she married in 1928, she chose a young cowboy named Henry Belton Johnson. Before their first child, B, was two, his father was dead of a brain tumor. Sarah remarried the next year, this time to a Kingsville physician named Joseph Shelton. They had one son, Robert Richard, who was six years younger than his half brother. In 1939 Dr. Shelton died, and in 1942 Sarah was killed in an automobile accident. Her two orphaned sons went to live with their grandmother Alice King Kleberg on the ranch. When she died in 1944 at the age of eighty-two, they moved in with their uncle Bob.

Bob and Helen Kleberg raised B and Bobby like they were the sons the couple never had. Their daughter, Helenita, grew up with the two boys in that odd combination of wealth and simplicity typical of the ranch. All of them had their own Kineño servant, their own horses, their own cowboy suits, and their own guns; they knew the significance of who they were. Yet they worked the roundups with the young Kineños, played with them, and rode with them.

"Most ranch kids of our generation lived in town," Helenita recalls.

> We three grew up on the ranch. We spent our youth playing with Kineños. This was all pre-oil. The porch was screened then—there wasn't any air conditioning. We didn't have a pool, and I can remember my father's spraying us with the hose in the summers while we jumped up and down and squealed. We didn't have cars or radios or television the way kids do today. We had to entertain ourselves. The ranch was our playground. The old Kineños always had time to talk, and they would show us things. We'd walk down a path and they'd know a use for every bush—this one would heal a wound, that one cure a toothache, this one over here would make tea, another one would make soap. My father was always telling us to become close observers, to notice details and to draw conclusions from what we saw.

B and Bobby grew up to be opposites, both in appearance and in personality. Bobby is short and scrappy, an endearing good old boy. After dabbling in college at Texas A&M and the University of Texas, he went to work at the ranch in 1958. He helped with the breeding programs in South America, ran the Laureles Division, then became executive vice president of the ranch after Bob's death and oversaw all of the domestic ranching operations. He is brash, opinionated, loyal, and uncomplicated. "I love the ranch," he said back in 1969. "I like to play cowboy and I don't mind working." A man of tremendous energies and a natural salesman, he would boast that he "could sell anybody anything." He owned a Buick dealership in Kingsville, and when things got slow on the ranch he would go down and sell a few cars, just to keep in shape.

B is tall and graceful, with the rosy complexion of an English beefeater. He was a young man of inner strength and drive, serious about his ambitions, and willing to challenge his uncle on his own ground. After prep school, he studied agricultural economics at Cornell. He entered the army at the end of the Korean War, then returned to attend the Stanford business school.

Bob Kleberg wanted nothing so much as for B to come back to the ranch and work with him. He took B along, for example, on his initial trip to Australia. When the ranch's first board of directors was formed in 1954, B, at twenty-five, was by far the youngest member, just as Bob had been the youngest trustee following Mrs. King's death thirty years before. Bob put B in charge of the Santa Gertrudis Division, the showplace of the ranch. But to B, being in charge meant *being in charge*. When Bob and Dick traveled around the Santa Gertrudis and gave orders to the foremen and the Kineños as was their custom, B considered that they had broken the chain of command. He had learned from the army how a successful organization worked, and he never forgot his military lessons. If you gave a man responsibility, you had to give him authority. How could he run the ranch unless Bob or Dick went through him?

But Bob Kleberg was not about to give up the absolute power he had always wielded. So in 1956, convinced that he could not continue to work in his uncle's shadow, B Johnson, then twenty-seven, took his financial statement to the bank and borrowed enough money to buy the 70,000-acre Chaparrosa Ranch southwest of Uvalde. No one since Captain King had ever done such a thing on his own. Bob saw this independence two ways: first, as a commendable sign of strength, confidence, and character; and second, as a direct challenge to his authority as head of the ranch and surrogate father. B remained an active member of the ranch's board, but he devoted the lion's share of his time to his own affairs.

More than any other member of the family, B was the logical person to take over Bob's role after Dick became ill. He was the oldest male in the bloodline; he had studied at his uncle's knee and knew everything about ranching and the ranch; and he was educated, diplomatic, and polished. He even inherited the old man's boots, which he wears just as Bob did, with the trouser legs of the ubiquitous King Ranch tan twills tucked inside. Yet when it came time to pick a successor to Bob Kleberg, the family did not call on B Johnson to fill his boots. Nor did they call on Bobby Shelton. Instead, they turned, as Captain King had almost a hundred years before, to an outsider.

The Outsider

In 1943, during the dark days of World War II, a tall and elegant young army captain from Pennsylvania named James Clement married Ida Larkin, the daughter of Bob Kleberg's sister Henrietta. The young man, a Princeton graduate, was from a prominent eastern family; his father was the chairman of the Pennsylvania Railroad. Not long after the marriage, James Clement went back to the war and was badly wounded in Normandy. After the war, the couple settled in New York. Clement's wounds were complicated by diabetes, and his physical weakness made him less than enthusiastic about the bitter labor battles that plagued the coal and railroad industries in the late 1940s. With Bob's encouragement, he and Ida (who is known as Illa) moved to Kingsville in 1947.

Jim Clement of Princeton and Philadelphia's Main Line went to work in the King Ranch office as the assistant office manager. His main duty was managing the inventories at the ranch's dry goods store and lumberyard. He was happy as could be, although Illa missed New York. They moved into the Big House and became occupied with the world of Kingsville and the ranch.

Clement did not immediately make the transition to the relaxed style of the South Texas ranching aristocracy. One family member recalls that his somewhat stiff urbanity, while appropriate for New York City clubs and boardrooms, seemed "a little out of place in the mesquite brush." The young Clement started out to bring a bit of eastern professionalism to the frontier informality of the ranch's operations. "You couldn't see anybody without an appointment for the first few days," remembers a former ranch employee, "but that didn't last long." Soon Jim Clement was having coffee every morning at Harrell's drugstore with the locals, soaking up gossip and being a part of things.

But though he adapted to the rough, masculine casualness of the ranch, Jim Clement has never pretended to be what he is not. He is not at home in the saddle, and he can't look at a bull calf and pick out its breed type or use cowman's jargon to describe its beef conformation. He is more likely to wear topsiders and a porkpie hat than boots and cowboy hat.

He is a businessman rather than a rancher. And by being so different, he carved out a place for himself at the ranch that no one else in the family wanted. "We can leave that to Jim," they said as they saddled up to go out and work cattle. "Jim understands all that," they said as they loaded up to go hunting. "Ask Jim about the figures," they said as they went off to pick out breeding calves. In other words, Jim Clement became indispensable.

Bob Kleberg had kept the ranch running as a ranch. By sheer force of personality, he had given the impression that it could be run from the saddle, that running it was an art, an insight, a way of life. But during Bob's lifetime, the ranch became an increasingly complex business stretching all over the world. When Bob Kleberg would not return the lawyers' and accountants' phone calls, they talked to Jim Clement. And so did the family members who had moved away and had questions or needed help. Unlike his more robust relatives, to whom the indoors was almost a prison, Jim Clement was always in the office. It was not calculated. It was just that business was what Jim Clement did best.

Who Runs the Ranch?

The beginning of the ranch's recent history dates from the board meeting in 1974 to pick Bob Kleberg's successor. Dick Kleberg should have taken over, but even then, his failing health would not let him. The board of directors was composed of two members from each branch of the family (the descendants of Bob and Richard Kleberg and their sisters Henrietta and Sarah): Bob's daughter, Helenita, and her daughter Helencita; Richard's son Dick and Dick's son Tio; Henrietta's sons-in-law, Jim Clement and John Armstrong; and Sarah's sons, B Johnson and Bobby Shelton.

On the day of the board meeting in 1974, Bobby and B each made a strong case that he should be named to head the ranch. Bobby based his claim on his determination to seek out better marketing approaches for the Santa Gertrudis breed, his plans for expanded oil and gas exploration, and his ability to come up with a reorganization of the ranch that would help the family's estate planning. B based his case upon his proven record and his commitment to maintaining the ranch's traditions. He was, he said, experienced and qualified—the logical choice.

The magnitude of the decision was not lost on the board members. Not one of them had been alive the last time the family had picked a man to head the ranch, and now they would be deciding its future. The initial choice was basically either B or not B. Some of the directors resented the time and energy B had devoted to his own projects and the distance he had kept between himself and the ranch for the past few years. But the crucial factor was that he was a chip off the old block. If they picked B, they would be continuing the ranch as it was. They would be turning it over to a vigorous, confident man in the prime of his life, a man who was certain to give them, in his own words, "exactly what they had with Uncle Bob, and more of it." The directors weren't at all sure that was what they wanted. As great a man as Bob Kleberg was, the longevity of his rule had stunted the growth of many members of the family. Perhaps, they thought, it would be better to have someone more like Dick, someone self-effacing and not so dominating.

After a night of painful soul-searching, the question became if not B, then who? Bobby had some support, but there was one man whom everybody trusted, a man who had not sought the leadership of the ranch and did not expect to get it. His integrity was unquestioned, and as everyone knew, he did not have any personal ambition. He was a man who could be counted on to serve the ranch selflessly for as long as necessary and then to step aside, a man who, although he was not of the family, exemplified the seriousness and sobriety of Henrietta King and Robert Kleberg, Sr., without the flamboyance or charisma of Richard King or Bob Kleberg.

When the nominations were taken, John Armstrong immediately nominated Jim Clement. And then, to everyone's surprise, Dick Kleberg, who had kept his own counsel, seconded the nomination. Dick was the chairman of the board of the King Ranch and, with Bob gone, the titular head of the family. If he wanted Jim Clement, then Jim Clement it would be. There were no other nominations. Jim Clement was elected unanimously. To everyone's recollection, he had not said a single word throughout the two days. He simply accepted what had been given to him and went back to his office.

"There was a feeling," one family member says, "that perhaps B would stay and mellow a little, or that Bobby would come along, and that one of them would take over from Jim." B Johnson knew, however, that it was one thing to be part of a ranch run by a brilliant, world-renowned rancher like Bob Kleberg and another thing entirely to be part of a ranch run by a laconic businessman like Jim Clement. B decided to sell out and go his own way, as the

Easts had done two decades before.

The irony, of course, is that B Johnson could have done well as the head of the ranch. All his life had been spent preparing for it. But if his ability to run the ranch was not questioned, his willingness to allow the rest of the family to get their hands on it certainly was. That the rest of the family thought him too much like Bob Kleberg is understandable—B *was* a good deal like his uncle. But Bob Kleberg at twenty-two got the chance to run the big ranch, and once he got hold of it, he didn't let go for fifty-six years. B Johnson never had the same chance.

Paying the Piper

B Johnson's departure was the first important test for the new regime. As is the case with matters at this lofty financial level, the U.S. tax code defined the limits of choice. A cash settlement would have an unfortunate impact on the estate taxes of several key family members, since it would establish a high cash value for their holdings. But it would also wipe out a great deal of the ranch's accumulated earnings and thus help reduce the family's taxes when the oil royalties were distributed. Still, that was easier to contemplate than giving up the ranch's status as a private corporation or, worse, disturbing the ghosts of Richard King and Bob Kleberg by giving up part of the ranch. In a tense strategy session, Bobby Shelton, Leroy Denman, Jr., and John Armstrong decided to offer B a cash deal. Not since Henrietta King died in 1925 had a price tag been put on the whole ranch—oil, cattle, and all. There was one thing the ranch's negotiators did not want to do: haggle. They went with their best offer—$70 million (which meant that the whole ranch was then worth about $600 million). B caucused with his advisers for five minutes, then came back in. "I'll take it," he said.

To get the money, the ranch went to Texas Commerce Bank in Houston. Instead of borrowing only enough to buy B's stock, the ranch made the amount a round $100 million, with the extra money going to finance new drilling ventures with Shell, Chevron, and other oil companies. The debt was transferred into long-term loans with two insurance companies. Those loans had as collateral a portion of the ranch's oil royalties and also the ranch itself. For the first time since 1933, the 825,000 acres of the ranch—its windmills, stock pens, swimming pools, Kineños' cottages, and even the Big House—were mortgaged.

While all these negotiations were going on, the price of natural gas—and oil—was skyrocketing. In 1972, a thousand cubic feet of natural gas had brought 30 cents; in 1976, the price was over $2. The ranch's great reserves of oil and gas, however, were running out—petroleum experts predicted that the flow would slow to a trickle by the 1990s. But before the ranch's fields dried up, they entered a period of great production called a "blowdown." This surge, coupled with the high prices, meant that suddenly the ranch was swimming in money. Royalties shot up from $20 million in 1970 to $100 million or so in 1979.

In theory, the ranch could have followed Bob Kleberg's gospel and plowed the oil money back into ranching. Not everyone was for that approach, however. For years, some family members had fought a futile battle to get Bob Kleberg to pay out more of the ranch's royalties in dividends. He always refused, saying, "You've got too much already." One veteran of those skirmishes recalls, "He wanted us to stay tough and hardy, like our cattle. He didn't want us to have it easy and become soft. I think he was more afraid, deep down, of what the oil money could do to us than he was of drouth."

But not even Bob Kleberg could have easily diverted so much wealth into cattle. And after his death, the foreign operations no longer had a strong champion. There was no one looking for new empires. Then, too, the gusher of money created serious tax problems. The wealth of the family was locked up in the ranch.

On paper they were well-off, but actually if one of them died, the heirs would be hard pressed to pay the estate taxes. So in 1977 the ranch decided to distribute 75 percent of its oil and gas royalties to the individual family members, thus allowing each to invest his or her own share, while the money lasted, without having to account to anyone.

At the same time, without the responsibility of having to manage so much royalty income, the ranch's leadership could concentrate on what it did best—ranching. No longer would the oil money cover up any mistakes, so the pressure to make ranching pay would be intense. As a far-flung business, the King Ranch is no longer the simple agricultural operation Captain King handled with his own ledger books. It needs a man like Jim Clement, with his legions of lawyers, accountants, and management consultants. More and more, the real work of the ranch is not done on horseback. It's done where Jim Clement works—behind a desk.

Clement is the ranch's president and runs the larger corporate affairs of the ranch. Next in command, with primary responsibility for the foreign operations and for the ranch's larger public role, is John B. Armstrong. Armstrong and Clement married sisters, the daughters of Bob Kleberg's sister Henrietta. Armstrong, a vigorous sixty, is still a world-class polo player. He comes from a neighboring ranching family whose roots run as deep in South Texas as the Klebergs'. His grandfather was first sergeant with the small band of McNelly's Rangers that won the cattle wars and saved Captain King's cattle empire. A few years later, his grandfather captured John Wesley Hardin and invested the reward in a ranch wedged between the Norias and Encino divisions of the King Ranch. John Armstrong's brother Tobin (who is married to former ambassador Anne Armstrong) runs the Armstrong Ranch.

As chairman of the Texas Animal Health Commission, Armstrong recently won acceptance from both government and cattlemen of the most controversial program in modern ranching history, the campaign to rid the state of a cattle disease called brucellosis, a campaign as far-reaching—and as unpopular to cattlemen—as was Robert Kleberg's drive to wipe out Texas fever.

The oil operations are handled by W. B. Yarborough, the husband of Dick's sister Katherine. He and Tio Kleberg are the ranch's two vice presidents. Tio oversees the four Texas divisions, the original ranch. Other family members have their own duties and serve on the management committee that monitors ranch policy, but these four men are in charge. Almost a three-decade span in ages separates Clement, Armstrong, and Yarborough from Tio's generation, palpable evidence of the gap in leadership left when Dick died and B and Bobby departed.

The Younger Brother

Unlike B, Bobby stayed with the ranch awhile, helping to negotiate the ranch's financing and its new drilling projects. But it soon became apparent that Bobby, who was a fountain of ideas, wasn't selling his family on very many of them. He wanted to set up the ranch as a limited partnership, with himself as the leader of a small group of general partners. He opposed the royalty distribution. He pushed for Santa Gertrudis "dealerships" near the major population centers to market cattle like cars. To Bobby, the family was maddeningly difficult to push to a decision. And it appeared that Jim Clement, far from being an interregnum "Pope John," as he refers to himself, would be in charge indefinitely.

And so, in June 1977, Bobby decided to leave the ranch. It could not have been an easy decision. He had spent years building a sprawling house for himself and his growing family on a rise opposite the Big House, right next to Highway 141. It was a symbol, clear and unmistakable, that he was at the ranch to stay. Today that house stands empty, a monument to the frailty of human ambition. When he left, Bobby moved his own ranching empire to a ranch near Kerrville that he bought as his headquarters. He's building another house there. "He's the biggest thing to come through Kerrville since the Guadalupe," one local ranger says.

His departure, however, was on somewhat different terms than that of his half brother. Instead of getting cash, Bobby got land and other assets in Texas and Florida. When that deal was settled, it appeared that the ranch had concluded a fairly difficult passage, the equivalent of the partitioning of 1935 and the Easts' departure in 1958. But when B learned what Bobby had gotten, something didn't seem quite right. There was in Bobby's deal a reference to an "Exxon claim." There had been no mention of that during *his* negotiations. When he realized what was at stake, Johnson was thunderstruck. It appeared to him that the ranch—his *family*—had concealed the possibility that Exxon underpaid the ranch by as much as $300 million between 1973 and 1976, a period when gas prices sextupled. If Exxon really did owe the ranch that money, B believed that he had been denied his fair share of the income from it, as much as $35 million.

After some negotiating with the ranch, B filed suit in federal court in San Antonio in June 1979. He charged that the ranch had told him nothing of the Exxon claim, which he says it was investigating at the same time it was negotiating a settlement with him. He also charged that once the ranch realized how much money might be involved, it changed its negotiating strategy and offered to buy him out for cash, depriving him of any portion of a future settlement with Exxon.

With the exception of a tersely worded response to B's allegations that denied virtually every charge, the ranch's testimony has been sealed by the court. The case was still pending at the time of this writing; Jim Clement gave his deposition in April 1980. As far as anyone can tell, the ranch's position is that B was much too closely involved in the ranch not to know about the Exxon claim. In any case, the ranch believes that B forfeited his claim on any future income from the ranch when he sold his stock. That B's deal did not include a future interest in the Exxon claim while Bobby's did only showed how different the two deals were. Bobby got assets, B got cash. A deal is a deal. Dick's sister, Alice Meyer, who sold out for cash a year after B did, isn't suing the ranch over the Exxon claim. Why should B?

In late October 1979, when the statute of limitations on the Exxon claim was about to expire, Bobby Shelton, who still owns 11.2 percent of the ranch's royalty income, stepped in and sued the ranch and Exxon. But while B's suit alleges deception, Bobby's accuses the ranch of mismanagement. He claims that the ranch has botched the Exxon claim and therefore has failed to fulfill its responsibilities to the royalty owners, who since 1977 have been the family members. His patience with what was, to his mind, the plodding, indecisive, and timid style of the new management was exhausted. If the ranch wasn't going to get after the Exxon claim, then by God *he* would!

Through all this heat and smoke, the ranch continued to negotiate quietly with Exxon. It rejected a $33 million settlement and proposed instead that Exxon increase the ranch's royalties on future gas sales from a sixth to a fifth. The ranch basically believes that such matters are nothing that gentlemen can't solve. After all, Bob Kleberg always insisted on treating Humble executives with the same trust, deference, and neighborly spirit that the ranch showed its fellow ranchers—and to sue a neighbor would be unthinkable. When Bobby left, he agreed that the ranch would handle the Humble lease—and the ranch contends that it is doing so, at its own speed. In fact, in the summer of 1980, the ranch and Exxon compromised on a higher royalty payment, a large step toward settling the Exxon claim. But the value of that settlement is considerably less than B and Bobby contend it should be and will likely not end their suits. Not since the Atwood suits has the ranch had so many legal entanglements.

The Crown Prince in Exile

B Johnson's Chaparrosa Ranch lies near Uvalde, 160 miles north-west of the King Ranch. It is a rugged, functional, but drouth-ridden place. Everything B learned from Bob he has put into practice there. Since he left the King Ranch, B has devoted his considerable talents and energies to his own affairs. He is on the boards of numerous companies, including AT&T, U.S. Trust, Tenneco, and First City Bancorporation. He is developing the landmark Hyatt Regency Hotel a block away from the Alamo in San Antonio, a stone's throw from where his great-grandfather died a century earlier.

He is also probably the single most talented breeder of Santa Gertrudis show cattle in the world. Starting from scratch, he has built a string of animals that sweep many major shows. (He has won grand champion at Houston, for example, five years in a row.) In fact, many people believe that B's cattle would give the King Ranch's foundation herd a good run for its money if the ranch were to drop its policy of not competing (it feels there are better standards by which to judge good cattle). His Santa Gertrudis auction now rivals the King Ranch's.

B still has a strong sense of belonging to the King Ranch family. In 1964, he and his wife, Patsy, began an annual summer camp, a tradition that, more than any single thing, could keep that family together. "The thirteen of us in my generation were all close," he recalls, "but the next generation just didn't know each other. Bob's wife, Helen, had done more than anyone else to sustain the family. When she died in 1963 there was a vacuum. So we started a sum-mer camp to bring the next generation together and to make the traditions of the ranch real. Tio's generation, the ones taking over the ranch now, were our first campers, and today they're running the camp themselves. If you ask them where they first learned how strong their family really is, they'll tell you it was at summer camp."

The ranch is still in his blood. B has acquired—through his

purchase of La Puerta de Agua Dulce Ranch from the King family—Captain King's original brand, the HK, for Henrietta King. His loyalty to the ranch and his family is unwavering. In spite of the separation and the lawsuit that followed it, he will not make a single negative statement about any of them. "They are my family," he says. "They mean a great deal to me, no matter what happens."

Something about B, however, is slightly out of scale. In spite of the magnitude and complexity of his projects, he seems somehow to be playing on too small a stage. Perhaps the family *did* make a mistake, for both his and their sake, when they did not choose him to succeed Bob Kleberg. Yet on his own, away from the family, B is free of the constant compromising and diplomacy that would have been necessary if he'd run the ranch. Most of the time, he believes he's better off.

But one day in the winter of 1979, flying high over his ranch in one of his airplanes, B Johnson, an immensely successful businessman in his own right, a man of intelligence, personality, and charisma, had the King Ranch on his mind. He unfolded a letter that Will Rogers had written to him when his father died, back when B was only one year old, and read it aloud to a friend. The letter reflects on what the ranch meant, who his parents were, and who B is. When he finished the letter, there were tears in his eyes.

Meanwhile, Back at the Ranch

Despite the squabbles, the oil wealth, and the lawsuits, the family survives, and so does the reality of 825,000 acres of South Texas. From the southernmost fences at Norias, which run right into the Laguna Madre just north of Port Mansfield, to the upper limits of the Laureles, on the outskirts of Corpus Christi ninety-three miles to the north, the King Ranch is still a *ranch*. In dollars, the ranching operations may be dwarfed by the oil income; in acres, the Texas land may be lost in the vastness of the foreign holdings.

But here, on land so flat and undistinguished that one can feel instantly disoriented and lost, here is where the heart of the family still lies.

The nuts and bolts of the four home ranching divisions—Santa Gertrudis, Norias, Laureles, and Encino—are Tio Kleberg's responsibility as a vice president of the ranch. Tio has worked full time at the ranch since 1971, when he and Janell moved back to Kingsville from El Paso, where Tio had been an army lieutenant at Fort Bliss. "I went to see Uncle Bob about a job," Tio recalls,

> and he told me I would be working for my dad. All my dad did was look at me and say, "Go to work." I got four hundred dollars a month and a Chevrolet Bel Air. I threw my saddle in the trunk and headed out to work cattle. We were in a tick quarantine, so we were moving herds all day, every day. We hadn't even moved into our house, and all our things were still in boxes. I spent my summers on the ranch growing up, so I had a good idea what to do. But it was hard at first, knowing that men who knew a lot more than I did would be watching me. But I couldn't have been happier. I've wanted to be a rancher since I was a kid. I've never wanted to do anything else.

What he wanted to become, he is. Today he drives a Chevrolet Suburban filled with ranching and hunting paraphernalia. He lives and breathes cattle and horses. Even at night and on weekends he is prepared for one of the ranch employees to show up on his doorstep with a problem. If anything goes wrong at the ranch, from a leaky pipe to a sick relative to a hurricane, Tio is off to fix it. Given the complexity and size of the business, much of his time is spent in the office. But like Bob and Dick Kleberg before him, Tio Kleberg is most at home outdoors. He is a determined, magnetic leader who works as hard as he expects the ranch's employees to work. He has developed, of necessity, a good sense of diplomacy. To run the ranching operations of the King Ranch requires different political skills than Bob Kleberg exercised. Bob owned 25 percent of the ranch. Tio has less than 2 percent of the stock, so he can't ride over the family like Bob did. He has to keep them happy.

Tio also has courage. "The traditions of the ranch are great," Joe Stiles says, "but they'll kill this place if you let them. Tio's got the vision and the guts to get rid of the ones that don't work." One such tradition was the Quarter Horse program, which had become the fiefdom of the division foremen, with each foreman controlling his own breeding program. The only problem was that the horses weren't good enough. When Tio set out to improve the ranch's horses, he centralized the whole breeding operation and gambled $125,000 to buy Mr. San Peppy and add his blood to the line. There were protests, difficult scenes, and mutterings of discontent, but the management problem was only the half of it. To change a breeding program is a serious risk, because the investment is great and results cannot be seen for years. The results are coming in now, and Tio has been vindicated: as they were forty years ago, the King Ranch Quarter Horses are today the envy of the business.

An Uncertain Future

The changes since the death of Bob Kleberg are subtle but significant. The current management's objective is an agricultural operation designed to be self-sufficient and to produce a profit (which it did last year), as if the oil money did not exist. The ranch raises cotton and milo on 37,400 acres of the Santa Gertrudis and the Laureles, tended by an array of machinery that would rival the Russian tank corps. The milo is processed at the ranch's own feed mill over on the Santa Gertrudis and is used in its huge feedlot. The farms were put in a year or so before Bob's death. "We'd just cross our fingers and hope that he wouldn't see them,"

Tio recalls. "I've got a hunch he knew what we were doing but had just decided not to say anything, to give us a shot at it, even though *he* knew *we* knew he hated farming."

The largest piece of Bob's Australian empire, the nearly 4-million-acre leasehold at Brunette Downs, was recently sold to an Australian syndicate. As a result, the ranch now runs about 4.3 million acres overseas, compared to 8.6 million in 1978. The rest of the foreign operations are barely to moderately profitable, but the family decided that the tremendous effort required to complete Bob Kleberg's plans for the Australian outback was simply not worth the candle. Very quietly, the new management of the ranch has announced the beginning of an era of limits, of pulling the fences back to what can be managed and afforded. It is a vision far less expansive than Bob's, but it is one that the management believes the ranch can handle.

It is too soon to tell whether they are right. They have already crossed some major hurdles: buying out B and Bobby, distributing the oil and gas royalties, selling off the largest foreign operation, and reinstituting farming. On the surface, the ranch appears to be headed for greener pastures. But the future may bring some thorny problems. One family member still with the ranch put it this way: "Sure, we're better off individually now that the oil money is coming out to us, but what about the ranch? What happens if we have a truly severe drouth, or if the bottom falls out of the cattle market? The oil money was the ranch's cushion, and it also gave it the capital to experiment and be innovative. That's how we've kept it going. Without the oil money I'm not at all sure we'll be so successful."

And although the family now seems unified, time may work against that. Jim Clement is not in the best of health, and no one knows how the ranch will be run when he and John Armstrong lay down the reins. Every twenty years since the 1930s—first with the Atwoods, then the Easts, and recently B and Bobby—the family has had to confront itself and its individual and collective ambitions before moving on. A decade from now, that confrontation will likely occur again. Everyone in the family seems very happy with Tio as the boss of the Texas ranches, but they have also grown too fond of their own roles to want anyone, at least for the present, to run the ranch single-handedly, the way Bob Kleberg did. And so a new era has begun, one of collective leadership, not as responsive, decisive, or visionary as one man could be but more representative of the family.

The people most prominent in that collective leadership are bullish on the ranch, but they are not without their doubts. "It's not at all a foregone conclusion that we'll make it," Tio Kleberg mused. "There's a lot working against a place like this." And there is. The modern world heads the list. It is hardly hospitable to a frontier institution with a paternalistic system, an aristocracy joined by tradition to loyal vaqueros who spring from the same piece of earth. The modern world lures those vaqueros off the land and into cities; it also tempts the family, seduces them away from the ranch with the endless possibilities for the use of their inheritance. "If the next generation is content to live off their income," John Armstrong says, "then we've lost it."

However, there is also a lot working *for* a place like this. The ranch has been through hard times before; ranchers expect that. The younger generation, although largely untested, could produce the visionaries and leaders the ranch's destiny will require. The family itself is the ranch's greatest resource: one of the children perched precariously on his first horse could be the next Bob Kleberg. History also is an ally. The ranch may survive into the next century because it survived into this one. No generation of the family wants to be the one that stood by and let the King Ranch fail. And at the core of that history is one simple, constant, endlessly repeated fact—on this day, as on every day, there is work to be done.

The Cattle Are Waiting

It is almost two o'clock at Norias, and the day's roundup is half over. Tio and Lavoyger make one last ride through the herd, checking to see if any barren cows or yearling calves have been missed. Then the whole crew breaks for lunch. In a grove of mesquite and ebony trees, some canvas has been stretched over rough wooden tables. A side of beef, slaughtered that morning, hangs over a limb. The other half gives off the pungent smell of barbecue as it cooks over an open fire. The tables are suddenly laden with plates of ribs and sausage and sliced tenderloin, bowls of rice and beans, and platters of thin camp bread to be washed down with sweet tea.

After lunch, the vaqueros bring the remainder of the herd out of the shade of the mesquites. The ground crew has dug a trench and built a fire of mesquite scraps in it. Branding irons have been stuck into the fire, and their ends are already white-hot. The family members loosen up their ropes and head into the herd to begin gathering the calves. Ed Durham, now seventy-two years old, ropes the first calf with a motion so simple as to escape the eye, and then drags it over to the fire.

In the next instant, Tio, Lavoyger, Scott, and Martín all have calves on their ropes and are dragging them to the fire. The calves jump around on the ends of the ropes like five-hundred-pound trout. The accuracy of the ropers on horseback is astonishing. They chase a loose calf at full speed through mesquite, twirling their ropes, then throw them deftly around the animal's hind foot or its head. Everyone is shouting in Spanish.

Some of the ground crew run wildly around the calves, twirling their ropes over their heads and then looping them toward the flailing hind legs of a roped calf. When they succeed, they are dragged along the ground, trailing plumes of dust from the heels of their boots, until the calf, now roped at both head and foot, can be thrown on its side and secured. The rest of the ground crew then run from calf to calf, applying three different brands—one for the pasture, one for the year, and one the Running W of the ranch. Another man notches the ear, another gives a shot, and still another paints the ear and the brands with white disinfectant, each in turn leaping over the calf he has just finished and heading for another one. Ropes attached to jumping calves sing through the air, sending the ground crew diving for the earth. The din is deafening. With each brand, a puff of smoke sizzles off the calf's hide. In the air is the smell of burning flesh, the same smell that seemed so appetizing at lunch.

By seven o'clock, the calves have been branded, and the most dangerous work begins. Very carefully, the men start roping the big bulls whose horns are starting to curl into their skulls and eyes. Then a vaquero with a hacksaw cuts off the horns. Halfway through, the saw turns red with blood. Finally, without warning or fanfare, there are no more cattle to be roped. The vaqueros prepare the herd for spraying with insecticide, and the Klebergs begin dismounting and loading the horses on trailers. Their faces look like those of Welsh coal miners, blackened with dust. Their chaps are damp with seat. The horses glisten.

The riders walk away with the tentative gait of people who have been on horseback for twelve hours, as if walking were an acquired and somewhat unfamiliar accomplishment. Off their horses, they look diminished; only when mounted do they assume their full personality and stature. The horses seem to relax too; they let out their urine in steaming streams. The paraphernalia of a cowboy's work—the spurs, the chaps, the bandannas, and the saddles, bridles, and blankets—are stowed away. Like props in a play, they no longer seem real.

Tio takes Mr. San Peppy back to his corral. Today, this horse that brings a $3,000 stud fee has worked like any cow pony. Tio brings him some hay, and the stallion rolls in the dust of his pen, cleaning himself.

"That was a good day's work," Tio says matter-of-factly.

At dinner in the Norias headquarters, the talk is dominated by good-natured kidding, particularly at the expense of Tio's younger brother, Scott. His horse, Show Boy, had spooked and, bucking and kicking, had carried Scott into the mesquite bushes.

"Where'd you get that horse, anyway?" Scott asks Joe Stiles, after he has endured as much teasing as he can.

"Aw, we just keep him around headquarters for the little girls to ride," Joe says.

"Hey, Scott," says Martín Clement, getting serious, "why didn't you help me bring the horses down?"

"I couldn't," Scott says. "I had to come down the night before."

"Well, heck," Martín says, "I brought the horses down this morning, and I was still out to the herd before you were."

Scott looks at his plate. This is exactly the sort of open criticism the family is constantly directing at each other. It wasn't a serious offense, coming to Norias early. But Martín wasn't going to let it pass. Then Lavoyger, who came late to dinner, has his turn. He looks at Martín and says, "You left."

"I what?"

"You left. We hadn't finished spraying the cattle, and you left."

Now Martín is on the defensive. "I just left when the boss did," he replies, gesturing at Tio.

"Yeah, I know. The boss left early, too."

Lavoyger has made his point. And as a group they have made another point: any and all of them are fair game if they relax their standards, even for a minute. These young men are in their twenties or thirties. They are sitting around a table that was dominated, until a year or two ago, by men in their fifties, sixties, and seventies. There are ghosts everywhere: the almost mythic presence of Captain King and Henrietta, the sober determination of Robert Kleberg, the commanding brilliance of Bob Kleberg, and the still-poignant memories of Dick Kleberg. All of those people who came before on this piece of earth shaped the destiny of the young men who now stand in their place. This new genera-tion *is* the ranch now; they know it, and they are determined to be worthy. There isn't any drinking, and everyone is in bed well before midnight.

In the morning, a new herd will be waiting.

Note

1.   Tom Lea, *The King Ranch* (Boston: Little, Brown, 1957).

8

Powder River Country
The Movies, the Wars, and the Teapot Dome

OAKLEY HALL

My wife and I are on the interstate, headed north toward Johnson County, Wyoming. Ten years ago, I prowled this country doing research for a novel that used material from the Johnson County War of 1892, when powerful cattlemen—in what is called "the Invasion"—attacked hardscrabble newcomers who were threatening their hegemony. Ten years ago, there was no interstate, and Highway 87 was the north–south artery, frequented by pickups with rifle racks in the rear windows, its blacktop notable for the amount of mashed wildlife displayed. When I asked the librarian in Buffalo, the county seat, for materials on the Invasion, she said she had none. Animosities still existed in the county.

The route of the Invaders, and ours, begins in Casper, a town that grew up around a crossing of the North Platte River. Half a million western emigrants passed this way in the mid-1800s, on the California, Oregon, and Mormon trails, and the Bozeman Trail struck north not far from here. Interstate 25 parallels the Bozeman, and just north of Casper we pass a hulking building emblazoned with the painted message MINING IS BASIC. This is southwestern terrain still, sagebrush and desert flora among rocky outcrops in gargoyle shapes, dull yellow buttes with

Originally published in *American Heritage* 40, no. 3 (April 1989): 43–51.
Reprinted by permission of *American Heritage* Magazine.

crenelated rimrock topped by piñon and dwarf juniper. Huge
mining trucks roar by, smoking like dragons. Silver mailboxes
perch on fence rails, and house trailers pimple the distance, as
though reluctant to cluster together in this vastness.

My wife remarks that there does seem to be enough land
here for everybody. She's thinking of the homeless, the refugees,
the crowded ghettos elsewhere. It's hard to believe that with all
this space, anyone would have ever had to fight for elbow room.
But violence has been basic to the Powder River Country. The
Crow Indians fought the encroaching Sioux, who then fought
the miners and cattlemen who were crowding in; the cattlemen
in turn fought to keep farmers and fences off the open range.
Later still, cattlemen and sheepmen fought each other in the
dirty wars of murder from ambush called dry-gulching.

Most dramatically, on the night of April 5, 1892, a special
train halted outside Casper, and a troop of heavily armed men
disembarked and prepared to ride north to Johnson County.
They called themselves Regulators, and they had been sent by
the cattle barons.

The Invasion by the Regulators is one of the infinitely expan-
sible legends of the West. It was the subject of the first western
novel, Owen Wister's *Virginian,* and a host of others, including
Jack Schaefer's *Shane,* Frederick Manfred's *Riders of Judgment,*
my own *Bad Lands,* and generations of pulp fiction and B films.
One of its latest appearances is in Michael Cimino's cinema epic
Heaven's Gate.

Bernard De Voto complained that the hero of the proto-
typical western served on the wrong side in the cattlemen's war,
for the Virginian is the loyal employee of cattle barons; he guns
down the rustler chief in the climactic shoot-out. *Shane* turns
this around, and the hero of the homesteaders blows away the
killer hired by the big cattlemen.

Many of the first cattlemen to settle in Johnson County were the scions of wealthy Scottish and English families who had come to Wyoming to hunt and had fallen in love with the land. Brits such as Moreton Frewen and Sir Horace Plunkett ranched in grand style, with servants, evening dress, and fine wine cellars in baronial dwellings. The Frewens' "Castle" overlooked one hundred thousand acres of the Powder River Cattle Company. Some of the more class-conscious among them sought to reduce proud cowboys to "cow servants," and one story tells of an English visitor inquiring of a cowhand, "Where can I find your master?" and receiving the response, "He ain't been born yet!"

Few of these overblown outfits survived the terrible winter of 1886–87, the "big die-ups," when cattle losses in northern Wyoming averaged 80 percent. They were succeeded by moneyed easterners, such as Teddy Roosevelt in the North Dakota badlands, and hard-boiled superintendents managing reorganized foreign corporations. Soon after the die-ups, these men faced an even greater threat to their way of life when newcomers—who did not consider the open range or another man's cattle inviolable—flooded the territory.

Johnson County's 1890s population consisted not of the European immigrants who people the film *Heaven's Gate* but of the homesteaders, squatters, small ranchers, and townsfolk who were the usual restless or busted Americans moving west from frontier to frontier. Certainly some of the small ranchers rustled stock on the side, just as rustlers ranched on the side. "The longest rope gets the maverick" was a cow-country expression, the "maverick" being unbranded range cattle. Settlers butchered cattle that wandered onto their homesteads or brought home steers as they might antelope. Worse, they strung barbed wire to keep out the cattle that trampled their crops. Cowboys knocked down the wire, which could make a mess of the steer or horse that blundered into it. At the same time, small ranchers were not allowed to participate in the Wyoming Stock Growers'

Association roundups, and the brands of newcomers were routinely rejected for the association's brand book.

Frank Canton, one of the leaders of the Invasion, might have been a model for Wister's Virginian, for he was born in that state. He was employed by the association as a stock detective. These men were the stock growers' security force, which gathered evidence of cattle thievery and turned it over to the local sheriffs for prosecution. But the system was failing; detectives such as Canton were no longer able to get convictions in Johnson County. The county seat, Buffalo, became known as the rustler capital.

That spring, when word reached them that the small ranchers had scheduled their own roundup in brazen competition with the association's official one, the junta of wealthy cattle barons headquartered in Cheyenne was filled with indignation. Now, it seemed to them, rustling was to be legitimized.

The Invasion was planned by the association in the Cheyenne Club. There would be a lightning march on Buffalo. The town was to be seized, and known rustlers rounded up. A "dead-list" of thirty men was compiled. The Invasion force consisted of twenty-one association members, six "civilians"—three teamsters, two newspaper correspondents, and a surgeon (Dr. Penrose, of Philadelphia, who went along for the adventure)—and twenty-two mercenary gunmen, recruited mainly from Texas. Major Frank Wolcott, who had served in the Union army, commanded the expedition.

North from Casper, the landscape subtly changes. The buttes become more rounded, and herds of cattle graze on a carpet of grass, usually with a few white-bottomed antelope alongside them. From the Johnson County line, the Bighorns are visible. Rumbling over a cattle guard, my wife and I veer off the interstate onto State 259 and cross the Powder River, which runs between banks stained with the white powder of its salinity. Downstream it is famous for being "too thick to drink and too thin to plow." The horses of the Regulators must have trodden through oil seepage in these bottoms, for this is salt-dome terrain, which petroleum prospectors learned early to search for.

Above a clean white cluster of ranch buildings rises Teapot Rock on its hillock. Having lost its spout in a storm some years ago, it now resembles an Easter Island head more than a teapot. North of Teapot Rock is Teapot Creek, and up Teapot Creek is Naval Petroleum Reserve No. 3, better known as Teapot Dome. In 1922, Albert B. Fall, Warren G. Harding's secretary of the interior, was convicted for illegally selling rights to this field to Harry Sinclair's Mammoth Oil Company. The reputation of the Harding administration was ruined in the scandal.

Sparse pumps dot the hillside of Naval Reserve No. 3, but just beyond it, in a rich stench of oil, the great Salt Creek Field is alive with pumps like iron praying mantises sucking the fine green oil from underground cavities. Beyond Salt Creek, the interstate winds through sullen malpais, with tiny trucks approaching on slants of highway out of vast distances. Among bony hills, we come upon the hamlet of Kaycee, named for the old KC Ranch, which once encompassed these parts. At a line camp just south of the present town, the Invaders encountered the first name on their dead-list.

He was Nate Champion, and he was to become a western legend because of the stand he made that day, which saved the necks of many of his neighbors, and because of the moving record of the fight he kept in his diary. The Regulators surrounded the cabin where Champion and a companion, Nick Ray, were sleeping. Ray was shot when he stepped outside at dawn to relieve himself. Champion dragged the dying man inside, and the siege began. It continued all day, with the Invaders infuriatingly delayed in their strike at Buffalo and Champion desperately hoping to make his break when night came. His diary entry reads,

> Shooting again. I think they will fire the house this time. It is not night yet. The house is all fired. Good-bye boys, if I never see you again.

They shot him down when he ran out of the blazing hut, and a card was pinned to his blood-soaked vest: "Cattle thieves, beware!" They neglected to destroy the diary in his pocket. Then they continued their interrupted march on Buffalo.

We knew we would have to make inquiries at Kaycee as to how to get to the legendary outlaw hideout of Hole-in-the-Wall. We stopped at the Invasion Bar, on the two-block main street, where Betty, the bartender, faced a counter lined with drinkers in tractor caps. There was a conference as to the best route into Hole-in-the-Wall. There were apt to be locked gates if we went by way of Burnham. Best to phone George Taylor, they decided, for Hole-in-the-Wall is on his property. I phoned and received directions to Willow Creek Ranch, where Taylor would give me further directions. An appointment was made for the next morning.

Betty informed us that at the community center that very night, as part of the Wyoming Centennial, a local group was performing a one-time-only production of an original melodrama, *The True Story of the Hole-in-the-Wall Gang*. So at eight o'clock we presented ourselves at an echoing metal barn of an auditorium, where, among basketball standards, a stage, a curtain, and sets had been erected. The hall was already crowded, but metal folding chairs were cheerfully emptied for us. The community center continued to fill and overfill, and beautiful, lanky local children sat on the floor before the stage. The lights went down.

There was no doubt that the cast was amateur, delivering

the dialogue with awkward pauses between the lines and with frequent anguished appeals to the prompter stationed behind the curtain. But the audience was enthusiastic, for the plot was cleverly devised. Six women who hoped to marry the confirmed bachelors of old-time Kaycee were running out of money and threatened with having to go to work for Belle, the local madam. The women perpetrated a bank robbery and rustling foray, and after their marriages, when a Pinkerton man came to investigate, their husbands were faced with covering up their crimes. They invented a gang, operating out of a place called Hole-in-the-Wall, upon which everything was to be blamed. Someone suggested that a fictional outlaw be called the Sundance Kid, named for a town in the northeastern part of the state. Another argued that that was a sissy moniker. What about a tough name like Butch—say, Butch Cassidy?

The final applause, in which we enthusiastically joined, for the heroic cast, for the playwright, Nancy Schiffer, and for Mrs. Joe Harlan, who had written the music, rattled the basketball backboards.

For half a century, the real Hole-in-the-Wall was an outlaw hideout, home to the Hole-in-the Wall Gang and the Wild Bunch. It was protected by the Red Wall, a sandstone scarp facing west and running north and south for thirty-five miles, with only the one easy western entrance, which a few armed men could defend. Hole-in-the-Wall was an important station on the Outlaw Trail, which led from Canada to Mexico; it served as the roost of such redoubtable figures as Flat Nose George Curry, Harvey Logan, Ben Kilpatrick ("the Tall Texan"), and, of course, Butch Cassidy and Sundance. In Sam Peckinpah's film *The Wild Bunch*, it was also the home base of the doomed and exhausted band that fled south to a violent apotheosis in the Mexican Revolution.

It is twenty-eight miles from the 3T freeway exit south of Kaycee over the Red Wall to Willow Creek Ranch. From there, we were directed north along the wall, eight or nine miles through six unlocked gates in the gray-green meadows that splashed up against red cliffs. Toward the end, I had to shift into four-wheel drive, churning up a rooster tail of red dust that poured over the car like liquid whenever we slowed for a difficult passage. The famous notch in the wall is located opposite some sheep pens. From here Butch and Sundance, fleeing the Union Pacific detectives, collected Etta Place and headed for South America and a violent end in Bolivia or maybe Patagonia. It is possible, however, that Butch slipped home again to live out his life as William T. Phillips in Spokane, Washington. Multiple sepulchers are the hallmark of the authentic hero. Billy the Kid is also rumored to have lived on under another name.

The actual Hole-in-the-Wall does not compare to the vision in the film *Butch Cassidy and the Sundance Kid*, where a clear-running, leafy creek winds back through cliffs to a verdant paradise; Hollywood's location hunters are tasked with providing sites more dramatic than the actual. The homesteads in the film *Shane*, for example, were in the shadow of the Tetons near Jackson, rather than near the less spectacular Bighorns, where the real action took place.

About noon of the day that Champion was killed, Jack Flagg, who was also on the Regulators' dead-list, passed by in his wagon, headed for Buffalo. He was fired upon but escaped, and so the news of the Invasion reached the "rustler" capital. Sheriff Red Angus began swearing in deputies, and Robert Foote, Buffalo's leading merchant, galloped from ranch to ranch on his black horse, with his black cape and white beard flying, to alert the citizenry. He opened his store to supply arms, ammunition, and tobacco to the settlers converging on the county seat. A Home

Defenders Corps was organized, and churches and schools turned into sanctuaries for women and children. The sheriff's posse rode south to do battle, and soon the Regulators were surrounded at the TA Ranch, fourteen miles south of Buffalo.

Already there had been desertions from the ranks of the Regulators: one man with painful piles, and a cattleman and Dr. Penrose with what the Texans called "gunnarrhea." Relations between the mercenaries and their employers became increasingly strained. In their haste to get behind makeshift fortifications at the ranch, they had lost their supply wagons to the settlers' army, which now numbered four hundred. Somehow a message of distress was sent to Governor Amos Barber, a friend to the cattlemen, whose ambiguous telegram to the president of the United States began, "An insurrection exists in Johnson County ... in the immediate vicinity of Fort McKinney, against the government."

The siege of the TA Ranch began on Monday, April 11, 1892. Tuesday was a long day for the Regulators, ducking bullets behind their barricades. Sorties were planned and abandoned. Everyone quarreled. It could be seen that the settlers' army was building the "Ark of Safety," a breastworks mounted on the running gear of a wagon. This was to be maneuvered close to the fortifications so that dynamite bombs could be lobbed inside.

In the fantastical *Heaven's Gate*, the Regulators, vaguely fascist in their uniform horsemen's dusters, are dismounted in a meadow while European immigrants in careening wagons, officered by good American gun toters, circle the coolly firing enemy, like some weird reversal of Indians attacking a wagon train.

In actuality, when Wednesday dawned, it was the settlers' "Ark of Safety" that lurched forward into a hail of lead. Just then a bugle sounded, and in as corny a deus ex machina as could be imagined, Colonel Van Horn and three troops of the Sixth Cavalry from Fort McKinney appeared upon the scene. The Invaders were more than happy to surrender to the U.S. Army.

Fictional versions of the final events of the Invasion have homesteaders and hired killers dying in storms of rifle fire. In fact, the only casualties were the Texan Jim Dudley, who contrived to shoot himself in a fall from his horse, and his fellow Alex Lowther, also a victim of a six-gun accident. With Nick Ray and Nate Champion dead at the KC, the final score stood at 2 to 2.

In custody in Cheyenne, the Regulators were among friends, with a properly functioning legal system. Reasons were found for excusing a number of the well-connected from trial, and with delay after delay, Johnson County faced bankruptcy from paying the expenses of the prisoners. Finally the Regulators' lawyer appealed for a dismissal of charges, and everybody went home. The war continued as a series of murders, and Tom Horn, a frontier hero turned mercenary-assassin (played by Steve McQueen in the film *Tom Horn*), began his dry-gulching operations, for which he was hanged in 1903.

The TA Ranch's weathered, patient log structures cluster beneath spreading shade trees. It is rather melancholy here and situated, like Nate Champion's last stand, between the interstate and the old road. This, State 196, becomes Buffalo's main street, a one-time cow trail curving between hills, with false-fronted buildings of wood, stone, and warm old brick springing up to bracket it. The saloon at which we thirstily stop is closed because today is Sunday. Farther along, the town's one traffic light is under repair.

The Bozeman Trail crossed Clear Creek at Buffalo, and to the north the Great Plains collide dramatically with the Rockies—sunny meadows sweeping up against the dark verticals of the Bighorns. The country from Buffalo to Fort Phil Kearny, seventeen miles farther along, was the scene of a hundred Indian fights in Red Cloud's War against the incursion of settlers on the Bozeman Trail, including the Fetterman Massacre and the Wagon Box Fight. Not far from here, General George Crook had his nose bloodied twice by the Sioux and their allies, first on the Powder River in March of 1876 and again on the Rosebud in June. From this last victory, Sitting Bull, Crazy Horse, and Chief Gall drifted north to the Little Bighorn and Custer's Last Stand, which was also the Last Stand of the Plains Indians.

The hundred miles from Casper to Buffalo, and another hundred north to the Custer Monument, cover a powerful span of western history. When we returned to San Francisco after our trip, a mechanic looked disapprovingly under the hood of the Subaru and suggested a steam cleaning to get rid of the caked dust. But I would not disturb it, for that fine red dust is the stuff not merely of history but of legend.

PART THREE

Battles Lost and Won

9

"It Was But a Small Affair"

The Battle of the Alamo

PAUL ANDREW HUTTON

As the sun rose over the smoking ruins of the Alamo on the frigid morning of March 6, 1836, it brought light but little warmth, finally revealing the true horror of the battleground. For some time, Mexican *soldados* had stumbled through the darkness, shooting at shadows and bayoneting both the dying and the already dead. Many of the Mexican officers were sickened. "The bodies, with their blackened and bloody faces disfigured by the desperate death, their hair and uniforms burning at once, presented a dreadful and truly hellish sight," noted Lieutenant José Enrique de la Peña. "The enemy could be identified by their whiteness, by their robust and bulky shapes. What a sad spectacle, that of the dead and dying!" The stench of burning flesh was unbearable. The lieutenant observed the arrival of his commander, General Antonio López de Santa Anna, once the firing had ceased. "He could see for himself," grumbled de la Peña, "the desolation among his battalions and that devastated area littered with corpses with scattered limbs and bullets, with weapons and torn uniforms."

The president of the Mexican republic, commander of the Army of the North and self-styled "Napoleon of the West," was not troubled. Santa Anna paced to and fro as officers reported

Originally published in *Wild West* (February 2004): 38–47, 72.
Reprinted by permission of Weider History Group.

their unit losses—nearly one-third of the attacking force, some six hundred total in killed and wounded. All two hundred of the enemy had been slain, most in the fort but some outside it. "Much blood has been shed but the battle is over," Santa Anna casually remarked to aide-de-camp Fernando Urriza. "It was but a small affair."

The general was wrong, as wrong as he would ever be in his long, delusional, megalomanic life. The fall of the Alamo would mark him as one of the great villains of North American history, even more so than his cold-blooded murder, a few weeks later, of over three hundred helpless Texan captives at Goliad. It would set great forces in motion, enabling Sam Houston to annihilate Santa Anna's army at San Jacinto on April 21, 1836, ensuring the independence of Texas and its eventual annexation to the United States in 1845. The Mexican-American War that followed led to the loss of all of northern Mexico and the creation of the conti-nental American nation. The fall of the Alamo was anything but "a small affair."

Texas had been nothing but trouble to both Spain and Mexico. Spanish efforts to colonize the province were haphazard and poorly supported. By the time Mexico threw off the Spanish yoke in 1821, there were fewer than three thousand settlers north of the Rio Grande in Texas. They had a scarce market for their produce, a barely functioning government, and no protection whatsoever from the haughty Comanches to the north who raided them at will. Desperate to see the province prosper yet unwilling to expend any resources on it, the struggling Mexican government, in 1825, offered generous land grants combined with exemptions from taxes and trade duties to induce foreign colonists to settle in Texas. Empresarios such as Stephen F. Austin received vast land grants in exchange for bringing settlers to Texas. The colonists had to swear allegiance to the Mexican republic and become nominal Catholics but were otherwise unburdened by the government far to the south. By 1830, the colonists, almost all of them from the United States, had come to outnumber the Mexican population ten to one. These settlers, while generally law-abiding, grew increasingly restless under the inefficient if benign rule of the unstable Mexican government. Almost all trade went northeast to the United States rather than south to Mexico, smuggling was habitual, religious and racial prejudice endemic, illegal slavery commonplace, and land speculation an absolute mania.

Government officials in Mexico City, increasingly worried that the situation north of the Rio Grande was slipping out of their hands, responded with a new colonization law in April 1830. All immigration from countries adjacent to Texas was banned (there was, of course, only one adjacent country), future colonization agreements were canceled, customs exemptions were ended and ports closed to outside trade, slavery was again banned, and all foreigners were required to carry passports signed by a Mexican government official. The Texans, including several prominent Mexican (or Tejano) leaders, were outraged at this abridgement of their rights under the Mexican constitution of 1824. They began to organize.

No one was more active in this political ferment than a young South Carolinian named William Barret Travis. Arriving in Texas in the spring of 1831, the twenty-two-year-old was a young man in a hurry, fleeing from a failed marriage while rushing toward an imagined grand future. Upon opening a law practice in San Felipe, he cut a dashing figure among the pioneer population, dressing stylishly, gambling incessantly, and courting the local ladies with passionate determination. When his wife appeared in 1834 in hopes of reconciliation, she got instead a divorce—he suspected her of infidelity—and Travis retained custody of their young son, Charles.

As soon as he arrived in Texas, Travis identified himself
with those opposed to Mexican role. His actions at Anáhuac in
May 1832 got him thrown into jail by the Mexican commander
of that port town. The colonists marched on Anáhuac to force
the release of Travis, and it seemed as if conflict might erupt,
but events in Mexico City solved their problem. General Santa
Anna, who had defeated a Spanish attempt to reconquer Mexico
at Tampico in 1829, deposed Conservative president Carlos
Bustamante and won election as president of the fledgling republic. The new Liberal government removed the commander at
Anáhuac, released Travis, and temporarily removed the customs
duties that had proved so repulsive to the Texans.

Stephen F. Austin, along with other advocates of negotia-
tion with the central government, prevailed over Travis and the
so-called war party in Texas. At a meeting in San Felipe in
April 1833, delegates drafted a state constitution for Texas and
prepared a petition requesting the separation of Texas from
Coahuila, tariff exemption, and the resumption of free immigration from the United States. Austin carried the petition and new
state constitution to Mexico City.

Austin met with some initial success (the immigration
restrictions were eventually rescinded), but he was arrested on
January 3, 1834. For nearly a year, Austin remained in prison
before winning release on bond on Christmas Day, but he was
still detained in Mexico City until July 1835. Santa Anna then
decided to tighten his control over Texas, ordering his brother-
in-law General Martín Perfecto de Cós northward with four
hundred troops to establish martial law.

The news swept Texas, and "committees of public safety"
were quickly organized. Travis was in the thick of the organizing.
"Although the Mexican or Tory party made a tremendous effort
to put us down," Travis wrote a friend on August 31, "principle
has triumphed over prejudice, passion, cowardice and knavery.

The people call now loudly for a convention in which their voices shall be heard." On September 1, Austin returned from Mexico, landing at Velasco. When a thousand Texans honored him at a banquet in Brazoria, he declared that all Texans needed to unite against the invading force and organize a government. By this time, Santa Anna had betrayed his Liberal supporters in Mexico, abolishing the federal constitution of 1824 and declaring himself dictator. When Liberal opponents in Zacatecas resisted his authority, the dictator made an object lesson of that unfortunate state, allowing his soldiers to pillage and loot the inhabitants while executing all foreigners serving in the Liberal militia. With the Liberals south of the Rio Grande cowed, Santa Anna prepared to deal with the last Liberal stronghold in Mexico—Texas.

When Mexican troops from San Antonio de Béxar attempted to confiscate an old 6-pounder cannon from nearby Gonzales on October 2, 1835, they were met by a defiant Texas militia force of 167 men led by Albert Martin and Almeron Dickinson. They taunted the Mexicans with a banner on which was emblazoned a cannon and the words "Come and Take It." Shots were fired, the Mexican troops retreated to Béxar, and the Texas rebellion was on.

After returning to Texas in September, Austin was elected commander of the militia forces gathered in Gonzales, and under him they advanced on Béxar. Although General Cós had twice as many troops as Austin, he was short on both supplies and fighting spirit. He retreated to a fortified mission, called simply the Alamo, on the outskirts of Béxar and on December 10, 1835, surrendered his thousand men. They were paroled and allowed to peacefully depart, promising never to return.

Travis had distinguished himself in several scouts and hit-and-run raids against the Mexicans but was absent when Béxar was finally assaulted. Austin was also gone, having been sent to the United States to seek aid. By this time, a convention had finally gathered in San Felipe and organized a state government for Texas under the Mexican federalist constitution of 1824—the Liberal charter that Santa Anna had overthrown. Henry Smith was selected as provisional governor, with a twelve-member council appointed to assist and advise him. Smith and the council immediately set to quarreling, much to the consternation of the newly appointed commander of the Texas army, General Sam Houston.

With the victory over Cós, the army disintegrated. Military stores left at Béxar by the defeated Mexicans were soon looted by men who proposed a strike south into Mexico against Matamoros. Houston bitterly opposed this scheme but was helpless to stop it. Colonel James Neill, in command at Béxar, gloomily reported that most of his men had joined the Matamoros venture. "We have 104 men and two distinct fortresses to garrison, and about 24 pieces of Artillery," he wrote Governor Smith on January 6, 1836. The governor, in response, ordered Travis, who had been commissioned a lieutenant colonel in December, to reinforce Neill. Travis, with 30 men, reported to Neill in Béxar on February 3. He was surprised to find Colonel James Bowie there.

There was hardly a man in Texas better known than the forty-year-old Bowie. Tall and big boned, this sandy-haired giant's imposing force of personality was as oversized as his physical presence. All across the Old Southwest, men recounted his deeds of daring—roping wild mustangs, riding alligators, smuggling slaves with the pirate Jean Lafitte, battling Indians, and searching for the lost San Saba silver mine. But mostly they spoke of his knife—a monstrous, double-edged blade—and of the men he had slain with it. As his fame spread, men began to ask blacksmiths to make them a knife "just like Bowie's," and the most peculiarly American of weapons was baptized.

Bowie had first journeyed to Texas in 1819 along with his brother Rezin. There he fell in with Lafitte, who was then running a lucrative smuggling operation in slaves off Galveston Island. The Bowie brothers worked for Lafitte and used their ill-gotten gains in wild land speculations. These "business transactions" engulfed Bowie in controversy, resulting in the Vidalia Sandbar duel on September 19, 1827, near Natchez, Mississippi. The duel left two men dead and three others badly wounded and made Bowie famous throughout the Old Southwest as a man-killer.

In 1828, Bowie headed again to Texas, this time moving easily in the elite circles of society. Austin disliked him, dismissing him as an adventurer, but Don Juan Martín de Veramendi, the vice governor of Texas-Coahuila, admired the big man from Louisiana. Even more impressed was the vice governor's seventeen-year-old daughter, Ursula, who quickly captured Bowie's heart. Bowie took up Mexican citizenship, was baptized into the Catholic Church, and was married to Ursula in Béxar's San Fernando Church on April 25, 1831. Because his new mother-in-law was a Navarro, Bowie found himself connected by marriage to the two most influential Hispanic families in Texas. He soon held title to nearly a million acres of prime Texas land.

In 1833, Bowie returned to the States on business, missing a cholera epidemic that claimed the lives of his wife and in-laws. Devastated, he was rarely sober thereafter. When Santa Anna abolished the corrupt Coahuila government, which was in the pocket of the American land speculators, he also ordered the arrest of Bowie and several other land jobbers. Bowie, sobering up, eluded arrest and joined the Texas war party.

Bowie had no better friend in Texas than Sam Houston. The former Tennessee governor, broken by marital scandal and the bottle, understood both the passions and the demons that drove a man like Bowie. Houston, supposedly in Texas as a representative for American land companies but actually the agent of President Andrew Jackson, had taken an immediate liking to Bowie when they had first met in 1833. "There is no man on whose forecast, prudence, and valor I place a higher estimate," Houston declared of Bowie. Little wonder, then, that in January 1836, as his army melted away, Houston ordered Bowie to Béxar to destroy the fortifications at the Alamo and withdraw Neill's men to Gonzales.

Bowie, upon reaching Béxar on January 19 with thirty men, promptly discarded his friend's orders. Learning that Santa Anna was on the march, he decided that Béxar was the key to the defense of Texas. Of course, it was also his home, where his family had lived, and where his Mexican friends still lived—he was not about to abandon it to an invading army. "The salvation of Texas depends in great measure on keeping Béxar out of the hands of the enemy," he wrote Governor Smith on February 2. "Colonel Neill and myself have come to the solemn resolution that we will rather die in these ditches than give it up to the enemy."

The ditches that Bowie was so determined to defend were hardly imposing. The mission San Antonio de Valero had been founded by the Franciscans in 1718 to Christianize the Indians, with construction finally completed during the 1750s. It was never successful as a mission, and the friars had abandoned the place in 1793. After 1801, it had been converted into a fort by Spanish troops. Some of the troops were from the company of the Alamo of Parras, Coahuila, and their name stuck to the old mission. It was similar in construction to other Spanish missions. There was a large rectangular plaza of about three acres, lined by high stone walls from nine to twelve feet high and up to three feet thick. The main entrance lay on the south side and ran through a single-story building now called the low barracks. Adobe dwellings lined the west wall and faced toward Béxar, some four hundred yards distant. The north wall was similar, while the east wall was composed of a two-story long barracks. This imposing structure was further fortified by a corral to its rear. Just south of the long barracks was the ruined Alamo church, with four-foot-thick walls, some twenty-two feet high. Its roof had collapsed in the 1760s, but several small rooms along its side wall were still covered. There was a fifty-yard gap between the church and the low barracks, and Bowie promptly set his engineering officer, Green Jameson, to constructing a low log-and-earthen wall to cover this gap. Cós had been unable to defend this sprawling compound with a thousand men, but numbers did not worry Jim Bowie.

The defenders, cheered by the arrival of Travis and his thirty men on February 3, had their spirits further bolstered five days later when Colonel David Crockett and more than a dozen companions—dubbed the Tennessee Mounted Volunteers—rode into Béxar. Word of Crockett's arrival spread quickly, and before long, most of the Alamo garrison and many of the citizens of Béxar were gathered in the main plaza, demanding a speech. Giving speeches was what the forty-nine-year-old politician did best. He had told his Tennessee constituents that if they did not reelect him to a fourth term in Congress, they could all go to hell, and he would go to Texas—and here he was in Béxar! "I have come to aid you all that I can in your noble cause," he informed the assembled crowd. "I shall identify myself with your interests, and all the honor I desire is that of defending as a high private, in common with my fellow citizens, the liberties of our common country." The speech promptly established him as a natural, democratic leader of the Alamo garrison.

Crockett was undeniably one of the most famous Americans in the world, but like his Tennessee political colleague Houston, he also saw Texas as a place to once again reinvent himself. Reinvention was becoming a forced habit—brought on by circumstances, failure, and an unbridled spirit of pure audacity. Bear hunter, Indian fighter, magistrate, congressman, humorist, author, presidential aspirant, and, above all, the living symbol of American democracy in all its crude glory—Crockett was all this and more.

After winning election to Congress in 1827, he had championed the rise of the West and Jacksonian democracy. His eccentric habits and backwoods humor quickly made him a celebrated and picturesque figure in Washington. Crockett eventually broke with Jackson in 1830 over the question of Indian removal—the policy of forcing Indians to resettle in the Indian Territory west of the Mississippi River. This stand for justice cost him his congressional seat in 1831, but he came back strong in 1833, clearly allied with the opponents of Jackson. This political reincarnation made him more famous than ever. Eastern audiences had been applauding James Paulding's play *The Lion of the West,* starring James Hackett as the Crockett-like Nimrod Wildfire, since its April 1831 New York premiere. A biography appeared in 1833, and Crockett responded the next year with his autobiography, in which he gave the world his motto: "Be always sure you're right—Then Go Ahead!" He promoted the book on a grand eastern tour, even riding on a train. His head was turned during the tour by Whig talk of running him for president in 1836. In 1835, he attached his name to two Whig ghost-written books—one on his tour and the other a bitter biography of Martin Van Buren—and associated himself with the first of fifty Crockett almanacs. Expanding on Crockett's autobiography, the almanacs presented him as a comic superman, riding alligators, wrestling bears, and wringing the tail off Halley's comet. Despite this fame, or perhaps because of it, the folks back in western Tennessee did not reelect him to Congress in 1835. Deeply embittered, he turned toward the West, departing Memphis on November 2, 1835, on a road that led him to the Alamo.

On February 10, 1836, a fandango was thrown in Crockett's honor, with drinking and dancing still going strong after midnight, when a scout galloped into Béxar with news that Santa Anna had reached the Rio Grande. A hurried officer's call followed, but after a quick meeting, everyone returned to the party, convinced that the Mexicans were nowhere near. Colonel Neill, however, was having second thoughts and the next morning departed on family business. Before leaving, Neill appointed Travis, the senior regular army officer in Béxar, to take command of the Alamo.

This did not please the volunteers, who demanded an election for commander. Jim Bowie was overwhelmingly elected to command the volunteers, while the humiliated Travis, who still commanded his regulars, retreated to his rooms to brood. Travis bitterly complained to Governor Smith that since Bowie's election, "he has been roaring drunk all the time; has assumed command. . . . I am unwilling to be responsible for the drunken irregularities of any man." By February 14, however, Bowie had sobered up enough to reach an agreement with Travis to share command.

While Travis and Bowie bickered, the Mexican army struggled toward Béxar. Santa Anna personally commanded the army, reinforced at Saltillo by Cós's retreating soldiers and on the Rio Grande by 1,541 men under General Joaquín Ramírez y Sesma. This force, some 5,500 strong with twenty cannons, crossed the river on February 16, 1836, the ghastly march from Saltillo to Béxar, some 365 miles, marked by both a blizzard and miles of dry desert. Many soldiers were felled along the trail by exposure or disease. Nevertheless, the Mexican advance guard was within striking distance of Béxar by February 23, halted only by a swollen river.

Travis had been receiving warnings for days that the enemy was near, but he had not believed the reports. Now he found many of the citizens of Béxar fleeing the town. Two volunteers, John Sutherland and John W. Smith, rode out of town to have a closer look. They had not gone far before they came upon the Mexican cavalry. Back toward Béxar they galloped. In the San Fernando Church tower, a sentry saw them coming and jerked the bell rope.

The defenders of the Alamo gathered together their possessions and hustled toward the old mission. "Poor fellows, you will all be killed," cried the Béxar ladies. Some had family to look after. Jim Bowie rushed to the Veramendi house to gather his two young sisters-in-law, while Almeron Dickinson of Gonzales hurried to his quarters to get his eighteen-year-old wife, Susannah, and their infant daughter. "Give me the baby," he cried. "Jump on behind and ask me no questions!" Soon they galloped through the south gate into the Alamo.

Gregorio Esparza told his wife, Ana, to take their four children away from Béxar, but she adamantly refused. "No, if you are going to die, I want to be near you," she proclaimed and then, after gathering her children and a few possessions, fled to the Alamo. Their eight-year-old son, Enrique, tarried long enough in Béxar's main plaza to witness the grand entry of the dictator himself. "Pennants were flying and swords sparkling in the bright winter sun," he later recalled. "Riding in front was Santa Anna, *el Presidente!* This man was every inch a leader. All the officers dismounted, but only the general tossed his reins to an aide with a flourish. I was very impressed."

Travis hurriedly scratched out messages requesting reinforcements. As he sent Sutherland off to Gonzales with one appeal, Davy Crockett reported to him. "Colonel, here am I. Assign me to a position, and I and my twelve boys will try to defend it," he declared. Travis assigned him to the rough palisade between the church and the south barracks, the weakest point in the fort.

Santa Anna had his band play as a blood-red flag was

raised over the San Fernando Church—a symbol of no quarter. Messengers soon ushered forth from the Alamo. Green Jameson came first, at the instigation of Bowie, to be followed a few minutes later by Captain Albert Martin, sent out by Travis in a startling display of disunity in command. Both men received the same response from the Mexicans—unconditional surrender. Travis sent an eloquently simple response with a blast from the Alamo's 18-pounder.

It was dawn on the 24th before the Mexican artillery responded. From the partial cover of the riverbank, some four hundred yards from the Alamo, two 9-pounders and a small howitzer bombarded the fort for the rest of the day. But the shells caused little damage, and none of the defenders were injured. There was, however, one great loss to the garrison that day: Bowie collapsed from a strange and terrible illness. Unable to even stand, he turned over command to Travis.

As dark approached, Travis dashed out another appeal for assistance, this one addressed "To the People of Texas and All Americans in the World." He ended the letter with a flourish: "If this call is neglected, I am determined to sustain myself as long as possible and die like a soldier who never forgets what is due to his honor and that of his country—Victory or Death." Travis handed the message to Albert Martin, with instructions to carry it to Gonzales. From Gonzales, other men carried Travis's words to the settlements in Texas and then across the Sabine and Red rivers into the United States and the rest of the world.

Santa Anna sent elements of the Matamoros and Jiménez battalions against the fort at midmorning on February 25, only to have them stopped short by Captain Dickinson's artillery. A small band of Texans then sallied forth and burned some nearby huts that had provided cover to the attackers. Again the Texans suffered no casualties, but Santa Anna tightened his ring around the Alamo, placing new batteries south and southeast of the fort.

That evening Travis dashed off a report of the day's fighting, lavishly praising Crockett and others for their gallantry in
repelling the Mexican attack and again appealing for assistance.
He reluctantly agreed that Juan Seguín should carry the letter
to Sam Houston. Travis hated to lose Seguín, for he might yet
prove invaluable in future negotiations with Santa Anna. Scion
of a wealthy and influential Hispanic family, Seguín had long
been a friend to the American settlers in Texas. In the early
days of the war, Seguín's company of Tejano cavalry had proven
invaluable as scouts.

After delivering his message, Seguín raised another company
of Tejanos, some twenty-five in number, several of whom had
been with him in the Alamo but had left after his departure.
Learning that Colonel James Fannin was marching toward the
Alamo with three hundred men, he halted at Cibolo Crossing
to await this larger force. Seguín was joined there by other small
bands of volunteers, but not Fannin.

Fannin had started for the Alamo on February 26 with more
than three hundred men and four cannons, but while still in
sight of the fort at Goliad, several of the wagons had broken
down. It soon became a comedy of errors—the oxen wandered
off while the wagons were being repaired. At a council of war,
the decision was made to return to Goliad. Fannin had abandoned the Alamo.

At Gonzales, however, George Kimball had assembled thirty
men and, guided by two of Travis's messengers (Albert Martin
and John Smith), headed for the Alamo. Carefully avoiding
Mexican patrols, they dashed safely into the fort at 3:00 A.M.
on March 1. Travis, ever optimistic, was certain that Fannin
would come. He had earlier sent his most trusted officer, James
Buffer Bonham, to Goliad. Like Travis, Bonham was a South
Carolina lawyer with soaring ambition and romantic sensibilities.

Commissioned a lieutenant in the cavalry, he quickly won the admiration of all who came into contact with him. "His influence in the army is great," Sam Houston noted, "more so than some who would be generals." Bonham found all his powers of influence wasted on Fannin, so he headed for Gonzales. There he met Robert Williamson, who gave him a dispatch for Travis. Bonham hurried back to the Alamo, entering the fort just before noon on Thursday, March 3. Williamson's letter assured Travis that he was awaiting the arrival of three hundred more men before advancing on Béxar. "For God's sake hold out until we can assist you," he declared.

At Goliad, many of Fannin's men were unhappy with their commander's decision. John Brooks, Fannin's adjutant, wrote home that "the Mexicans have made two successive attacks on the Alamo in both of which the gallant little garrison repulsed them with some loss. Probably Davy Crockett 'grinned' them off." Brooks also declared that two hundred men would soon ride to the relief of the Alamo from Goliad. A detachment of New Orleans Greys, perhaps fifty men, almost certainly did march to Béxar. Some of these men skirmished with Mexican forces outside Béxar late on March 3 and were driven back, while others probably made it into the fort, bringing the number of defenders to over two hundred.

Despite Williamson's letter and the arrival of the Gonzales men and other small reinforcements, the situation within the Alamo grew increasingly grim. Provisions were slim, and while weapons remained plentiful (many of them surplus British muskets taken from Cós's men), powder was limited, and there were not enough defenders to adequately man the walls or even properly service the artillery. The long days of siege began to take a toll. Even Crockett, who had so often cheered the men with his humorous tales and fiddle playing, gloomily noted to Susannah Dickinson that he wished to "march out and die in the open air.

I don't like to be hemmed up." Beyond the walls, Crockett could well see that Santa Anna was receiving more reinforcements. By March 4, the dictator had nearly three thousand men around the Alamo.

Late on March 4, John Smith again galloped out of the Alamo, heading east to Gonzales, carrying letters from Travis warning his countrymen, "I am determined to perish in the defense of this place, and my bones shall reproach my country for her neglect." Smith also carried a far more personal letter from Travis to David Ayers, who was caring for his son, Charles. "Take care of my little boy," Travis wrote. "If the country should be saved, I may make for him a splendid fortune, but if the country be lost and I should perish, he will have nothing but the proud recollection that he is the son of a man who died for his country."

On that same day, Santa Anna called his officers together for a war council. The council was contentious because General Manuel Fernandez Castrillón and others argued that the assault should be postponed until heavier artillery arrived. Castrillón and Colonel Juan Almonte also protested the red-flag declaration of no quarter, arguing that humanity dictated that prisoners must be taken if possible. Disgusted with himself for even calling a council, Santa Anna dismissed them with the orders to prepare an assault before dawn on March 6.

As the Mexican army made its preparations, there was a lull in the artillery bombardment of the fort. Travis took advantage of this momentary quiet, late on March 5, to call the garrison together. He spoke to them, as militia officers often had done to their democratic armies from the time of the American Revolution onward, of their duty, of their personal freedom, and of their possible fate. He wanted no man with him who did not fight willingly, and he offered any who chose the right to depart. Bowie, too sick to rise from his cot, asked to be carried to Travis's side. Susannah Dickinson watched as her husband and every

other man joined Travis, save one, who soon vanished into the
darkness beyond the Alamo's wall.

As the Alamo defenders slept, Santa Anna ordered his attack
columns into position. For the assault, he relied on his veteran
troops, with some 1,100 actually engaged. General Cós was to
attack from the northwest with 350 men. Colonel Francisco
Duque would lead 350 more in from the northeast. From the
east, Colonel José María Romero led 300 soldiers, while Colonel
Juan Morales was to assault Crockett's position at the southern stockade with 100 men. General Ramírez y Sesma's cavalry
moved out east of the Alamo to prevent any escape. Santa Anna
kept the crack *zapadores* and the infantry grenadiers in reserve
under his command.

By 4:00 A.M. on March 6, 1836, the troops were in position,
hidden from the moon's glow by clouds. For an hour, the soldiers
shivered in the cold. Suddenly a soldier shouted, "Viva Santa
Anna!" which quickly became a chorus. Santa Anna signaled his
bugler to sound the call for attack, signal rockets were fired, and
the columns rushed toward the Alamo.

Travis, awakened by his adjutant, sprang from his cot and
grabbed his sword and shotgun. Followed by his slave, Joe, he
rushed to a three-gun battery of 8-pounders at the center of the
north wall. The Mexicans, rushing from the darkness, were already dangerously close and were illuminated by the cannon fire
from the Alamo. The attacking columns reeled and hesitated in
the face of terrible blasts of grapeshot. One volley brought down
half the company of *cazadores* (light infantry) from Toluca, killing the captain and wounding the lieutenant. Colonel Duque,
commanding the north column, fell wounded as well. Some
soldados sought sanctuary directly under the walls of the fort,
where the defenders could not easily fire down on them, while
others fell back.

Santa Anna ordered in his four hundred reserve troops

and sent his staff officers to rally the other faltering columns.
Castrillón took command of Duque's column while General
Juan Amador inspired the soldados by becoming the first man
over the north wall. The few ladders had long since been lost, so
the men climbed over each other's backs to reach the top. They
were met with clubbed rifle and bowie knife, but the defenders
were stretched far too thin.

Travis, his cannon useless against the Mexicans massed directly below him, fired his shotgun down into them. Joe watched
in horror as his master was suddenly spun around by a bullet in
the head: Travis's little boy would have only a proud recollection
of his father.

Joe and the other Texans fell back from the wall, firing
as they retreated toward the long barracks, and the Mexicans
poured in. On the west wall, the defenders turned their cannons
around to fire into the plaza at the advancing enemy. Morales's
column, checked by Crockett's men at the stockade, veered to
the left and stormed the southwest corner while the defenders
were busy firing toward the enemy advancing across the plaza
from the north. Within minutes, the 18-pounder was captured
and turned against the Texans.

Inside the church sacristy, Susannah Dickinson clutched
Angelina to her breast as the sounds of combat grew louder.
Captain Dickinson suddenly burst into the room. "Great God,
Sue, the Mexicans are inside our walls," he cried, embracing her
for a final time. "All is lost! If they spare you, save my child!"
In an instant he was gone, climbing back to join Bonham and
Esparza manning the battery atop the church. Enemy fire raked
their position, and Esparza tumbled from the emplacement as
his family watched in horror.

Jim Bowie waited in his room in the low barracks, with a
brace of pistols and his knife at his side, attended by a Mexican
woman from Béxar. Pale and emaciated, he was not far from

death anyway. The door crashed open, and angry faces peered in at the bedridden man. He was tossed on enemy bayonets like so much hay.

In the long barracks, the Texans fought bitterly from room to room, contesting every inch of ground. General Amador ordered the captured cannons pulled up into the doorways and fired point-blank into the rooms. The stout doors of the church were also blasted open and the defenders there quickly overwhelmed.

As the Mexicans invested the fort, at least two bands of defenders tried to cut their way out. With Morales's column sweeping over the southwest wall, the way toward the cover of the alameda over the Gonzales Road lay open, and perhaps as many as fifty Texans broke out in that direction. In the darkness waited Ramírez y Sesma with four hundred lancers. A sharp fight followed as the Mexican cavalry slaughtered the Texans.

It was all over in about two hours. Santa Anna finally entered the Alamo at 6:30 A.M., as the final mopping up ended. He was between the church and long barracks when Castrillón approached with a handful of prisoners under guard. Lieutenant de la Peña was deeply impressed by one of the prisoners, "of great stature, well proportioned, with regular features, in whose face there was the imprint of adversity, but in whom one also noticed a degree of resignation and nobility that did him honor. He was the naturalist David Crockett, well known in North America for his unusual adventures." Santa Anna cut off Castrillón's intervention on behalf of the prisoners and ordered them immediately executed. When Castrillón refused to obey, several other officers fell upon the helpless prisoners with their swords.

Minutes later, the surviving noncombatants were brought out of the church. Besides Susannah Dickinson and her daughter and Ana Esparza and her children, there were at least a half-dozen Mexican women, along with Travis's slave Joe and Brigido Guerrero, who somehow convinced the Mexicans that he had been a prisoner in the Alamo. They were all set at liberty after questioning by Santa Anna.

Señora Esparza and her children faced the dictator with dread. He gave her two silver dollars and a blanket and asked her why her husband had fought his countrymen. "They are not our countrymen," she responded; "We are Texians." Enraged, Santa Anna threatened her and sent her away. Young Enrique, who studied the dictator as they left, later observed, "He had a hard and cruel look and his countenance was a very sinister one. It has haunted me ever since I last saw it and I will never forget the face or figure of Santa Anna."

Across the river, along the alameda, funeral pyres were by then consuming the bodies of the Alamo defenders. Travis, Bowie, Crockett, Bonham, Dickinson—all save Gregorio Esparza, whose body was retrieved by his brother, a soldier in Santa Anna's army, for burial—were stacked amid cordwood and slowly consumed by the flames. From that fire rose a new nation and a towering legend. Both were conceived in blood and sacrifice, for indeed the Alamo had been anything but "a small affair."

« **10** »

What Happened at
Mountain Meadows?

SALLY DENTON

On August 3, 1999, a backhoe operator powered his shovel into a
hard-packed mound of earth at a remote site in the southwestern
corner of Utah, and to the shock of those watching, the bucket
emerged with more than thirty pounds of human skeletons. The
excavation, part of a renovation of a crumbling monument, had
not only uncovered an old burial site but also exposed anew one of
the enduring controversies in American history.

Nearly a century and a half before in that spot, as many as
140 men, women, and children, traveling in one of the richest
California-bound wagon trains ever assembled, had been attacked, besieged for five days, persuaded to surrender under a
flag of truce and a pledge of safe passage, and then murdered.
According to contemporaneous accounts, including the evidence
presented at the trial of the one figure held legally responsible
for the murders, John Doyle Lee, the attack on the train and the
ensuing killings were carried out by a combined force of Paiute
Indians and members of a local militia of the Church of Jesus
Christ of Latter-day Saints, known as the Mormons. Lee was an
adopted son and longtime intimate and military commander of

the Mormons' leader, Brigham Young, and the atrocity he was
part of, known as the Mountain Meadows Massacre (after the
pastoral valley where the murders took place), was the worst in
the annals of the West. Now, as then, however, the full story
of what happened on September 11, 1857—who was responsible,
and why, how the tragedy unfolded, and, not least, its restless
legacy embroiling one of the richest and fastest-growing religious movements in the world—has remained one of history's
most stubborn mysteries.

Before the backhoe incident took place, the Mountain
Meadows Association, a group the *Salt Lake Tribune* has described as "an unusual mix of historians and descendants of
massacre victims and perpetrators," had expressed concern
about "the deplorable condition of the site" and appealed to
the owners of the land, the Mormon Church, to rebuild an old
memorial rock cairn. LDS officials had agreed in 1998 to restore
the gravesite. The church hired Shane Baker, an archaeologist
from Brigham Young University, to examine the area before any
earth-moving equipment was sent in. "There are a million different stories about how many victims there were and where their
bodies are buried," Christopher Smith, a *Tribune* journalist, later
explained, "and the last thing the church wanted was to dig up
any bones and set off a public controversy." Most experts believe
that the cairn marked the burial site of only some of the victims;
the remains of the rest have never been located, nor, strangely,
has any physical evidence of the event itself, such as bullets or
wagon parts.

In 1999, scientists working on behalf of the church used
aerial photographs, metal detectors, core soil sampling, and
ground-penetrating radar for a noninvasive study of the location.
Forensic geologists and geophysicists searched for anomalies in
the soil pattern: chemical concentrations of calcium, for instance,
that would indicate where burials had taken place. All the while,

church leaders went to great lengths to keep the renovation secret from the public and the press. Then, on August 3, church officials announced that the digging could go ahead without disturbance. Baker had found that "the archaeological evidence was 100 percent negative," as he told a reporter, so the excavation began.

On making their grim discovery, the men at the backhoe that August morning were first inclined, one of them admitted later, to dump the shovel's load right back in the hole and swear one another to secrecy. But after discovering that there were specific state laws about handling excavated remains, they eventually decided to call Washington County Sheriff Kirk Smith, who drove out to the cairn. "It was a very humbling, spiritual experience," Sheriff Smith recalled. "I saw buttons, some pottery, and bones of adults and children. But the children—that was what really hit me hard."

After a flurry of meetings, discussions, and phone conversations, the Utah state archaeologist, Kevin Jones, explained that state law required that any unidentified human remains found on private property be forensically examined and that failure to comply would be a criminal felony. Jones issued a permit to allow scientists to determine the age, sex, race, stature, health condition, and cause of death of those whose remains had been found and to segregate them for individual and proper reburial. Utah's governor, Mike Leavitt (a descendant of a participant in the massacre), was in the discussions and asked that the bones be quickly reburied, ordering state officials to find administrative or other means to do so.

Teams of anthropologists, archaeologists, and other scientists around Utah began working long hours, poring over the remains as fast as possible. They were intrigued by the discovery and well aware of what one newspaper editor called Utah's "unique church-state tango." "This [kind of work] is giving the dead a chance to speak," said Shannon Novak, a University of Utah forensic anthropologist whose analysis of a mass grave in Croatia had helped lead to the prosecution of Serbian war criminals. But neither Novak nor her colleagues were prepared for what they would find among the victims at Mountain Meadows.

Reconstructing some eighteen different skulls from 2,605 pieces of bone from twenty-eight victims, including women and children, the scientists produced the first physical evidence in a long and disputed history. The investigation indicated that "the killing of women and children may have been more complicated than [previous] accounts" had suggested, Dr. Novak wrote in her final study, presented in October 2000 to the Midwest Bioarchaeology and Forensic Anthropology Association. Among other revelations, the examinations disclosed that some of the victims, including several women and at least one child, had been killed while facing their executioners head-on, by point-blank gunshots between their eyes, rather than by being shot in the back while fleeing, as earlier accounts had claimed.

Further, it became evident that the murders had been committed by whites rather than by the Paiute Indians who were commonly blamed for all the attacks on the women and children. And it was especially clear that John D. Lee, the one man ever held accountable for the crime, could not possibly have acted alone in a mass murder of this magnitude. Paiute leaders say that the new forensic evidence supports their own oral histories in showing that the tribe has been wrongfully blamed.

Novak's examination was still not completed in crucial aspects, including DNA testing, when the bones were reburied, under orders from Governor Leavitt. Marian Jacklin, a U.S. Forest Service archaeologist, was one of the many who fought the state's decision to halt the inquiry. "Those bones could tell the story and this was their one opportunity," she said. "I would allow my own mother's bones to be studied in a respectful way if it would benefit medicine or history."

The brief episode of revelation and suppression sparked heated charges and countercharges. Hundreds of victims' relatives around the country petitioned the state of Utah to retrieve the remains of their ancestors; some demanded DNA testing. More than 28,000 hits were recorded on a once-obscure Internet Web site about the massacre. The governor of Arkansas, Mike Huckabee, speaking for descendants living in his state, requested federal stewardship of the site, which would remove it from church control. "It's like having Lee Harvey Oswald in charge of JFK's tomb," said Scott Fancher, a descendant of one of the leaders of the wagon train.

The contemporary conflict is only the latest episode in the often stormy 150-plus-year aftermath of the massacre. It all comes down to a still-unfinished search for meaning and responsibility. Brevet Major James H. Carleton summed up the problem in a special report to Congress in 1859: "In pursuing the bloody thread which runs throughout this picture of sad realities, the question [of] how this crime, that for hellish atrocity has no parallel in our history, can be adequately punished often comes up and seeks in vain for an answer."

Carleton, commanding a troop of U.S. dragoons from California, had been among the first federal officers to investigate the incident, two years after it happened. According to his official report, his men found thirty-four exposed skeletons and buried them in a grave marked with a rough stone cairn. They placed a twenty-four-foot cedar cross on top with the defiant inscription "Vengeance is mine: I will repay, saith the Lord."

Carleton's epithet set off a checkered history of monuments. When Mormon Church leader Brigham Young visited the site two years later, he pronounced his own imprecation: "Vengeance is mine, and I have taken a little." He then lifted his right arm, according to Mormon histories of the event, and a band of

Mormon men, including Governor Leavitt's ancestor, destroyed the cairn and the cross and scattered the rocks. U.S. Army soldiers rebuilt the monument a year later, and once more, Mormons tore it down. In 1932, the Utah Pioneer Trails and Landmarks Association erected a nearly inaccessible stone marker two miles off the highway and atop a steep climb; it survived until 1990, though the church removed every road sign indicating it.

In the late 1980s, a group of John D. Lee's descendants, including former U.S. secretary of the interior Stewart Udall, began working to clear their ancestor's name. Simultaneously, descendants of the Fanchers and Bakers—two of the families on the wagon train—began pressing the federal government for a new memorial. Responding to the descendants of both the victims and the perpetrators, the state of Utah built a granite wall on Dan Sill Hill, overlooking the site and bearing the etched names of 120 of the slaughtered pioneers and an inscription that read "In Memoriam: In the valley below, between September 7 and 11, 1857, a company of more than 120 Arkansas emigrants led by Capt. John T. Baker and Capt. Alexander Fancher was attacked while en route to California. This event is known in history as the Mountain Meadows Massacre."

The wall soon fell into disrepair, and within a decade, descendants were once again pushing for a new monument. When plans for one got under way, they led to the accidental uncovering of the bones in the summer of 1999. Those examined bones were reburied a little more than a month later, on September 10, 1999, near yet another plaque installed by the church, which reads, in part, "In the early morning hours of September 7, [1857,] a party of local Mormon settlers and Indians attacked and laid siege to the encampment. For reasons not fully understood, a contingent of territorial militia joined the attackers. This Iron County Militia consisted of local Latter-day Saints acting on orders from their local religious leaders and military commanders headquartered thirty-five miles to the northeast in Cedar City."

Through every successive version of the monument, the church has denied any responsibility for the massacre on the part of any of its headquarters authorities in Salt Lake City, including Brigham Young. The original official church version of the incident was that local Paiutes, provoked by depredations by members of the wagon train, had led the attack and carried out the executions. Mormon historians eventually included renegade zealots operating outside the control of the church as participants with the Paiutes, attributing their fanaticism to Utah's pioneer theocratic distrust of government and fear of an impending invasion by American forces. "That which we the church have done here must never be construed as an acknowledgment on the part of the church of any complicity in the occurrences of that fateful day," church president Gordon B. Hinckley declared at the dedication of the 1999 marker.

All along, the explanatory inscriptions at the site have tended to be cast in a vague passive voice, avoiding any indication of who attacked the train, who did the killings, or what came before or after. "The difficulty," according to Utah historian Will Bagley, "is how to tell the truth about it without it becoming a divisive and inflammatory issue." The current monument, he says, "perpetuates an injustice by saying nothing of how these people died." *New York Times* correspondent Timothy Egan has called it "the most cryptic historical marker in the West." In his 1999 book about the West, *Lasso the Wind,* Egan observes, "The most pedestrian of roadside historical markers in Utah is crammed with numbing detail about a simple crossing of a river, a first planting of a peach orchard. . . . But here, [at the] site of what was the worst carnage ever inflicted on a single band of overland emigrants in the entire nineteenth century expansion of the West, the stone has nothing to satisfy these questions." For its part, the state of Utah "is not going to pursue any more interpretation of the site," according to a State Parks official. "We're not interested in stirring the pot."

What really happened? "There is no politically correct way," a *Salt Lake Tribune* reporter wrote in 1998, "to spin historical fact to hide the ugly truth that God-fearing Utah Mormon pioneers, pitched into a religious and military frenzy, posed as rescuers of the wagon train only to summarily execute the emigrants." As most versions agree, it was the worst butchery of white pioneers by other white pioneers in the whole colonization of America, and it was by definition an elaborate criminal conspiracy of planners, participants, and protectors. The murders were carried out with a grisly swiftness and precision that foreshadowed European and African atrocities of the next century. One of the participants, Nephi Johnson, remembered that the slaughter took no more than five minutes.

To comprehend what happened in those few minutes, one must understand something of the extraordinary emergence of the Mormons. Mormonism, born of one man's vision and fueled by passions of persecution, was unlike any other creed in the United States. The religion's founder was Joseph Smith, a farmer from Palmyra, New York, who was twenty-one when he began writing the Book of Mormon in 1827. His texts were derived, he said, from golden plates he had unearthed by angelic inspiration. In the early-nineteenth-century fervor of evangelical revivals, such supernatural visions were not unusual. According to his, Smith had been designated by God to lead the world's "only true church," which he called the Church of Jesus Christ, soon appending "of Latter-day Saints." His followers became known as Mormons, and Smith himself as a Prophet.

"Joseph Smith's was no mere dissenting sect," historian Fawn Brodie writes. "It was a real religious creation, one intended to be to Christianity as Christianity was to Judaism." Prophet Smith would lead the "chosen people" with direct and continual revelations from God; they would follow with a highly disciplined and unquestioning submission. The movement's clannishness and radical theology were both its strength and its curse, drawing the Mormons into a prosperous and cohesive community while arousing the political, economic, and social fears and resentments of those they called Gentiles. When Smith's followers still numbered only forty, an angry mob destroyed his baptism pool near Palmyra, prompting Smith to set his sights on the western frontier. By the summer of 1831, his missionaries had converted two thousand souls and migrated to Kirtland, Ohio. There, he was tarred and feathered, so they moved on to western Missouri—the original site, according to the Prophet, of the Garden of Eden—where they were met by a settlement of Mormon missionaries and converts and took on thousands more new converts, as well as the recurring enmity of local settlers. In October 1838, Governor Lilburn Boggs called for the Mormons' extermination, prompting Smith and his followers to move in a mass migration to Nauvoo, Illinois.

Adding polygamy to their controversial doctrine, the Mormons fared little better with their new Illinois neighbors. The church at that time claimed to have as many as two hundred thousand members, with Smith the general of a four-thousand-man army and commander of an elite military unit. As a presidential candidate in 1844, he advocated the polemical policies of abolishing slavery and putting the entire nation under theocratic rule. In June of that year, he was shot to death by anti-Mormon militiamen in Carthage, Illinois. The atmosphere of persecution and insularity, piety and spiritual supremacy, and zealotry and vengeance that Smith's death and martyrdom heated up would culminate in the Mountain Meadows Massacre.

Brigham Young, an uneducated but charismatic New York carpenter, succeeded Smith as the new Prophet and led the growing congregation for the next three decades. George Bernard

Shaw called Young the American Moses; his exodus ended in
July 1847 in the Great Salt Lake Valley. Young and his followers
waged over the next decades a bitter struggle with the U.S. government to establish a theocracy apart from the rest of the nation.

With the 1849 California gold rush, Salt Lake City became
a busy stopping-off point for wagon trains heading west. Utah's
Mormons at first welcomed the migrants, trading livestock and
provisions for coveted household furnishings and other luxuries.
But as the traffic thickened, in the early 1850s, the frictions between the Mormons and the "Gentile" world, especially the U.S.
government, grew steadily.

President Zachary Taylor, the Mexican War hero elected in
1848, was avowedly hostile to the Mormons as both religious
fanatics and a rival power center in the West. But after he died
in 1850, his successor, Millard Fillmore, legitimized the Mormon
theocracy, naming Young governor of the new Utah Territory.
Following Fillmore, Franklin Pierce's administration let the
Mormon regime fasten its hold still tighter on Utah politics and
society. By the time James Buchanan was elected, in 1856, the
Mormons were defying every federal authority, from judges and
U.S. marshals to Indian agents. Territorial officers were fleeing
Utah. There followed increasing reports of Mormon clashes
with emigrant parties headed to California, as well as with the
government surveyor Captain John W. Gunnison, who (along
with members of his party) was massacred in south-central Utah
while mapping a route for the transcontinental railroad. Church
militia—"blue-eyed, white-faced Indians"—were said to be
masquerading as Paiutes in these confrontations. As the attacks
became widespread, pressure mounted in Washington to take
some action. At the same time, the emerging Republican Party
designated Mormon polygamy a "relic of barbarism," equated
with slavery in the party's first national platform.

But perhaps even more relevant to the later events at

Mountain Meadows was the role of a church doctrine more secret, sacred, and controversial than polygamy. The belief in "blood
atonement"—that there are certain sins that can be forgiven
only when the sinner's blood spills on the ground—was a reality
not even the most sympathetic chroniclers of the church have
been able to deny. "It would be bad history to pretend that there
were no holy murders in Utah," Wallace Stegner wrote gingerly
but candidly in his classic book *Mormon Country*, "that there was
no saving of the souls of sinners by the shedding of their blood
during the 'blood atonement' revival of 1856, that there were no
mysterious disappearances of apostates and offensive Gentiles."

By the winter of 1856–57, Young was tormented by defections
in his ranks. Responding with his "Mormon Reformation," he
had his church elders sweep through the communities of the territory "in an orgy of recrimination and rebaptism." He instructed
that backsliders were to be "hewn down." His enforcement arm,
called the Danites, for Sons of Dan, and commonly referred to
as the Avenging Angels, gained especial notoriety.

By the spring of 1857, Young was flaunting his secessionist
leanings, often whipping his audiences into an antigovernment
frenzy as fervid as anything in the pre–Civil War South. Only
a few months after taking office, Buchanan responded to the
mass exodus of government agents—the "runaway officials," as
Washington called them—by ordering a punitive expedition to
enforce the federal writ in Utah. By late that summer, troops
under the command of U.S. Brevet Brigadier General Albert
Sidney Johnston were marching from Fort Leavenworth toward
the remnants of Fort Bridger near the Wyoming-Utah border, a
post the Mormon militia had burned down. Young prepared his
followers for what was being called the Utah War. "We are in-
vaded by a hostile force who are evidently assailing us to accomplish our overthrow and destruction," he declared in a broadside
proclamation on August 5, 1857.

"Into this cauldron of suspicion," a historian later wrote, "came the unfortunate Fancher party en route from Arkansas to California." A few on the train were affluent, some even wealthy—"livestock growers, drovers, and traders," as one descendant described them. Others were cattlemen and Thoroughbred horse breeders from northwestern Arkansas. Most of the party were members of large families, the Bakers and Fanchers, heading to join relatives who had migrated the previous year to California's Central Valley, where the range was free and land grants were available for men with prior military service. Most were newly married young couples; several had newborn infants and toddlers, and some wives were pregnant and destined to give birth on the trail. There were also many unmarried young men and women in their twenties, mostly cousins and childhood friends, and adults in their thirties with older children, along with a handful of aunts and uncles in their late forties. Accompanying them for security were at least twenty hired riflemen. Most of those not related by blood were old friends and longtime neighbors.

The company's Thoroughbred mare, One Eyed Blaze, was conspicuous. Another, a "black satin stallion," as one account described him, was worth almost a million dollars in today's value. The families were famous for their livestock, the best of which they were bringing with them: a thousand prize beef cattle, dairy cows providing fresh cream, butter, and milk along the way, and a choice herd of Kentucky racehorses. Among the valuables hidden in the floorboards of the wagons or in the ticking of the feather beds was as much as one hundred thousand dollars in gold coins and other currency. The group carried quality weapons, mostly Kentucky muzzleloaders, and a stockpile of expensive ammunition and had along three elegant carriages, emblazoned with stag's heads, for women to ride in.

Leading the train was Captain Alexander Fancher, born the

second of three boys in 1812. His elder brother, John, had moved from Arkansas to California in 1856 and urged Alexander and the younger brother, Richard, to join him. Although Richard declined, Alexander eagerly prepared to take his wife, Eliza, and their nine children, four boys and five girls ranging in age from eighteen months to nineteen years. John and Alexander Fancher persuaded their friend John T. Baker, the fifty-two-year-old patriarch of a close-knit clan of around twenty-five, to join them. Baker's eldest son, Jack, was a superior horseman who would play a key role in leading the train. Joining the Bakers and Fanchers would be the Dunlaps from Marion County: Jesse and his wife, Mary, and their six children; and Lorenzo and Nancy and their five children. One man, William Eaton, joined the group as a friend, with no blood relations. Among the many mysteries of the event are the identities of the dozens of others who left Arkansas with the Bakers, Fanchers, and Dunlaps. There was said to be a sheriff, a Methodist minister who performed services each morning and evening, a physician, two dozen horsemen who handled the livestock, some fifty marksmen, and at least three other families. It was to be Captain Fancher's third trip to the coast, where he had already staked out a ranch for himself and expected to make a 500 percent profit on the cattle he trailed across the plains, as he had done before.

On March 29, 1857, some forty wagons carrying approximately fifty men, forty women, and fifty children rolled out of Arkansas with their thousand cattle and two hundred horses. They planned to rest their livestock and stock up on provisions in Salt Lake City. The party got there on August 3 and set up camp. But although the fields were obviously brimming, the Mormons refused to sell them any food.

A Mormon emissary approached them and urged them to turn the train south, where there was good pasture and food

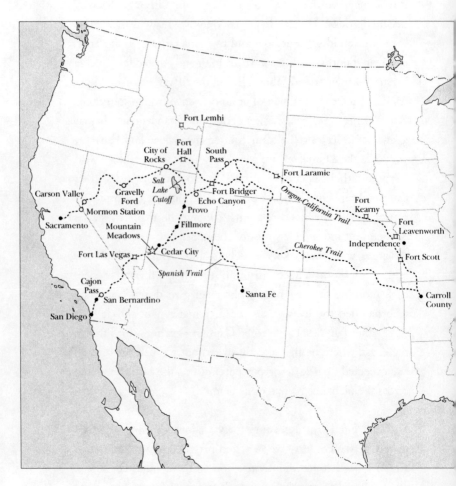

The Fancher family's trails west, 1850–1857.

along the way. The train's leaders discussed the routes and fell into a disagreement, after which the families in four wagons split off to head west along the well-mapped northern route. The rest of the party pulled out of Salt Lake City on August 5. Eaton, the Fanchers' Arkansas friend, wrote a cheerful letter to his wife in Indiana before leaving the Utah capital. It would be the last communication from the group.

Seeing bountiful crops under cultivation, the emigrants sought to buy supplies in the town of Lehi. Again, all the farmers refused to sell to them. Later evidence revealed that church leaders had issued orders to the Mormons living in the small communities along the trail not to sell grain to the outfit. They were rebuffed again in the larger city of Provo. They passed through the communities of Springville, Spanish Fork, Payson, Nephi, Buttermilk Fort, and Fillmore, meeting the same refusal at every stop. Finally, at Corn Creek, some Native Americans sold them feed for their cattle. They set off from Corn Creek around August 25 and arrived two days later at the walled city of Parowan, where they would meet up with the Spanish Trail.

Parowan had been built with a Mormon fort against Indian attacks early in the settlement of the territory. But Young had since embraced the Natives as fellow persecuted people who had been driven out of their homelands by the despised U.S. government, and by this time, the Mormons had made peace with them, even baptizing their famous chiefs, Wa-kara and Kanosh.

On Friday, September 4, just before sunset, the Fancher train entered Mountain Meadows, a five-mile-long valley surrounded by piñon-dotted foothills. Opening from a narrow entrance on the east and expanding into an oasis of creeks and cottonwoods, the meadow closed with a bottleneck exit into the rugged Beaver Mountains to the west. The travelers apparently thought the location was safe from Indian attacks, for they did not circle their wagons at night, as they had done throughout the journey.

On Sunday, September 6, the emigrants held a Sabbath service in a big tent they had faithfully transported across the country. Late that night, according to subsequent trial testimony, John D. Lee and his accomplices, some of them Indians, painted their faces and hid in the low hills surrounding the campsite. They took up strategic positions to prevent escapes, controlling access to the meadow from all sides. At dawn on Monday, the emigrants awakened and began their morning routines. Suddenly they heard shots. In the barrage that followed, six or seven men from the wagon train were killed and fifteen more wounded, and the other side suffered an unknown number of casualties. The pioneers had driven the enemy hack, and they dragged their wagons into a circular barricade. Apparently assuming that they had been attacked by Paiutes, they dug a rifle pit while awaiting help from the neighboring Mormons.

The next day seemed to be a standoff, and the emigrants burrowed in further. Each time they ventured to the stream for water, they were turned back by bullets. On the fifth day of the siege, Friday, September 11, Lee and a fellow Danite came into the camp carrying a white flag. They were greeted with cheers. Lee told the party that he had learned of the ambush, hastily recruited Mormons to come to the rescue, and gotten the Paiutes to agree to a truce. "When I entered the corral, I found the emigrants engaged in burying two men of note," Lee would later write. "The men, women and children gathered around me in wild consternation. Some felt that the time of their happy deliverance had come . . . my position was painful, trying and awful, my brain seemed to be on fire." If they relinquished their arms to the Mormons, he told them, they would be escorted safely out of the meadow.

The desperate emigrants agreed. All the children under eight—the age of "innocence," according to Mormon doctrine—were placed in one wagon. The wounded men were placed in a second wagon, and both wagons rolled north out of the camp-site. All the women (some carrying infants) followed, as did all the children over eight. They walked a few hundred feet, smiling and waving, as they caught a glimpse of the militia they thought had come to save them. Then came the men in single file, spaced several feet apart, each accompanied by an armed Mormon.

Suddenly, on a hill overlooking the site, another Danite raised his hand and shouted, "Halt! Do your duty!" At that command, each Mormon shot the man beside him, as others, including Indians, hiding in the embankment ahead, butchered the women and children.

The eighteen surviving children, ranging in age from eighteen months to eight years, were weak from thirst, their skin and clothing smeared with the blood of their parents, brothers, and sisters. The killers spared these few and distributed them to local families. Over the next seventy-five years, some of them would tell the story often, even testifying in detail, but what they had seen always seemed unbelievable. Federal authorities rescued seventeen of them in 1859, two years after they had been captured, and returned them to relatives in Arkansas.

By maneuvering politically with the backstage help of a figure who would be the Mormons' most important defender, Young managed to stave off a federal investigation of the massacre for years. Thomas Leiper Kane, a wealthy Pennsylvanian who had met the Mormons during their exodus from Illinois, was Young's lobbyist and veritable secret agent in Washington both before and after the Civil War. Kane first negotiated personally with General Johnston and ultimately concluded a deal with the Buchanan administration that forestalled any further federal invasion or punishment of past Mormon crimes in return for Young's stepping down as territorial governor.

By 1859, stories about the massacre had been published in

California and in underground Utah papers, covering Major
Carleton's discovery of skeletons, his initial investigation and
report, and the rescue of the children. As the early accounts proliferated, the evidence of Mormon culpability grew, including
eyewitness testimony from older surviving children, who had
watched as white men washed off war paint in a stream, and
reports of the rich spoils dispersed among local farmers or sent
to Salt Lake City. This gathering evidence triggered a new wave
of outrage and anti-Mormon sentiment throughout the country,
but the atrocity was soon eclipsed by the tumult of Lincoln's
election and the outbreak of war.

In the post–Civil War period, the now-aging issue of the
massacre surfaced again, during a renewed push for statehood.
To appease antistatehood forces in Congress demanding some
acknowledgment of and punishment for the incident, John D.
Lee was the single Mountain Meadows culprit arrested. He
went through two trials. At the first, in 1875, the jury of eight
Mormons and four Gentiles predictably deadlocked, with all the
Mormons voting for acquittal. Following a public outcry, Lee
stood trial again the next year. Previously unavailable Mormon
witnesses appeared with vivid testimony that marked him and
absolved all higher church officials. He was convicted by an all-
Mormon jury and ordered executed.

On the cold, windy morning of March 23, 1877, the con-
demned man wore a hat, coat, and muffler to the place of his
execution, not far from the ground where he had given the order
to execute his victims. Overgrazing and torrential floods in 1861
and again in 1873 had ravaged the rich emerald grass, but the
slope and bend of the valley were much the same as when Lee
and his men had ridden in nearly two decades before. Now he
sat patiently on his coffin and waited as a photographer set up
equipment for the official pictures of the scene.

When the camera was ready and the five-man firing squad in

place, anonymous behind covered wagons, Lee rose. "I have been sacrificed in a cowardly, dastardly manner," he said. His accusers hoped that to spare himself in the final moment, he would at last incriminate Young, who government prosecutors believed had ordered him to commit the atrocity. Instead, Lee shook hands with a few men standing nearby and methodically removed his hat, coat, and muffler. Blindfolded, he gave the riflemen a final order: "Center my heart, boys. Don't mangle my body."

At the volley, he fell back silently onto the rough-hewn coffin, his blood spilling into the ground in symbolism all Mormons understood. Two of his sixty-four children, by eighteen wives, took his body to nearby Panguitch, with his temple robes under his corpse. Of the dozens, if not hundreds, of men complicitous in the massacre at Mountain Meadows, Lee was the only one ever brought to justice.

The story seemed to have been laid to rest. The markers at the site remained obscure and hard to reach, the history texts vague and exonerating of the Mormons. Despite all the agitation over the past century and a half, despite the volatility of the issues, and despite the connection with a religion of 11 million adherents, amazingly little has been written on the subject, and the event has been dealt with literarily mainly in fiction and in a handful of nineteenth-century anti-Mormon screeds. The original 1871 edition of Mark Twain's *Roughing It* contained an appendix about the massacre that was deleted from most later editions. A few authors (most notably Sir Arthur Conan Doyle in *A Study in Scarlet*) wrote of the "Avenging Angels" but made no mention of the massacre.

In 1945, historian Fawn Brodie wrote a controversial biography of Joseph Smith, *No Man Knows My History* (for which she was excommunicated), and it encouraged Juanita Brooks to write her benchmark 1950 book, *Mountain Meadows Massacre*. That volume was an original attempt at exposing the massacre

and its cover-up and resulted in the 1961 reinstatement of Lee
into the Mormon Church. (But in 2000, Brooks, a descendant of
one of the participants, was revealed to have admitted to burning
crucial historical documents because "they were just too incrimi-
nating" of the church.) The last critical study of the event was
published in 1976, in a little-known nonfiction book written by a
children's author, William Wise.

> Now descendants of the slain
> and sons and daughters of the slayers
> come, arm in arm, to end the tragic story,
> to share a burial rite, perform a
> ceremony of atonement.
>
> But how to cleanse the stained earth?
> To erase old griefs and grievances?
> To quench long-dying embers of anger?
> To forgive unforgivable acts?
>
> The balm they bring is love,
> the only ointment God offers
> to heal wounds too deep for healing.
>
> —Stewart Udall, great-grandson of John D. Lee.
> Read at the reinterment in 1999.

What happened here that will not die? The Mountain
Meadows Massacre is an American tragedy in a West full of
atrocities. If the bones found in 1999 have been reinterred by
official fiat, and most of the relics of the massacre remain un-
discovered, the valley is still littered with the debris of unsettled
history. For all the reconstructions of the scene, the precise site of
the massacre has never been established. Nor do we know, except
for the first fragments of evidence assembled by the scientists in

1999, exactly how the victims were killed and where more than a hundred bodies were disposed of.

This is an American mystery, and inextricably tied to that mystery is the question of Brigham Young's part. Whatever other motives or circumstances shaped the terrible events of that September week, the extermination of the Fancher train was undeniably an act of religious fanaticism unparalleled by any other event in the country's history. At the new millennium, the tragedy at Mountain Meadows was as hotly debated on the Internet and in e-mailed letters to the editor as it had been by telegraph and post during previous centuries. Today, as before, the conflict centers on the role of the religion's revered Prophet Young, whose reputation is in many ways indistinguishable from the institutional legitimacy of Mormonism. Brooks's history leaves no doubt as to Young's participation in the cover-up, but whether or not he officially ordered the deaths remains uncertain.

As a "Prophet, Priest, and Revelator" of the church, Young is deified and therefore considered not subject to the scrutiny or judgment of other mortals. "There has been no realistic handling of Young by Mormon scholars," says historian Will Bagley (himself a Mormon). "To continue to blame it on the Paiutes is disgraceful." At stake is not only the esteem of the church within its own ranks of 11 million souls and as a $25 billion financial empire but also how it is seen by an outside world with which it has fashioned a respectable truce since overcoming the fears and suspicions of the nineteenth century.

Oddly enough, the most significant new contribution to the literature of the episode is the oldest published record. In the spring of 2000, the western historian R. Kent Fielding compiled and edited all the *Salt Lake Tribune*'s reports on the trials of John D. Lee, a comprehensive collection that presents an unmistakable portrait of Lee as a scapegoat and of Brigham Young as an active and impassioned participant camouflaging his own

role in the massacre. The newspaper's contemporaneous sum-
maries of the trial transcripts show the involvement of dozens
of Mormon leaders—from Philip Klingonsmith to William H.
Dame, Isaac C. Haight, John M. Higbee, and many others—to
have constituted an unbroken chain from church officials to
their Prophet in Salt Lake City. The official concealment and
subterfuge began, according to Lee's later confession, the day
after the massacre: "[The] brethren involved were sworn not to
talk of it among themselves, and each one swore to help kill all
who proved traitors to the Church or the people. . . . It was then
agreed that Brigham Young should be informed of the whole
matter."

Fielding's work, on the heels of a similarly revealing history
of the massacre of Captain Gunnison and his party, establishes
conclusively Brigham Young's role in many depredations of the
era, including Mountain Meadows, albeit most conclusively
after the fact. The transcripts make clear that "the cause of justice
in the Lee trials," as Fielding wrote, "had been manipulated."

Will Bagley takes it further. After a painstaking reevaluation
of original nineteenth-century sources and a fresh examination
of supporting evidence in church documents, he contends that
Young participated in the earliest decisions to slaughter everyone on the train. "He not only engineered the cover-up but gave
orders to the Paiutes prior to the massacre about the distribution
of the wagon train's livestock," Bagley concludes. "Young was
operating with a political purpose. He was in a terribly weak
position with the U.S. government and had a ragtag militia and
a ragtag group of Indians. His only hope against the federal government was to close the overland road to California."

These events occurred at a time in history when instructions
by cautious leaders were almost always oral. But it was also a
time when an extraordinary amount of evidence was committed
to writing. Young rarely met alone with any of his followers, and

church records detailed every meeting with meticulous exactitude. "If the LDS church really wants to 'heal,' it will throw open its archives," a dissident Mormon historian recently said. Such candor seems unlikely, however.

The backhoe incident, as the *Tribune* described it in a probing three-part series in March 2000, was "another sad chapter in the massacre's legacy of bitterness, denial, and suspicion." That series of articles prompted what the *New York Times* described in January 2001 as a "formal dressing-down" of the *Tribune's* publisher by church president Gordon Hinckley and has been cited as a primary reason behind the church's intervention in a convoluted business transaction in which the rambunctious *Tribune* was sold to a company expected to be more congenial to church interests. Founded in 1871 by dissident Mormons who were then excommunicated by Brigham Young, the *Tribune* has been the independent voice of Utah's non-Mormon minority for more than a century. But like the reburied remains, that voice just might be stifled as well.

11

Lakota Noon at the Greasy Grass

GREG MICHNO

Moving Robe dropped the sharp stick she used to dig up prairie turnips, her attention drawn to a dust cloud rising in the east. The twenty-three-year-old daughter of a Hunkpapa Lakota named Crawler had only a few seconds to ponder its meaning. As she stood in the open valley (at the number 1 on the map) on this hot, sultry day, a mounted warrior dashed by, calling out the alarm: Soldiers were coming! Women and children should run to the hills! Moving Robe, however, did nothing of the kind. She dropped her gathered turnips and ran for her tepee. It was June 25, 1876, on the white man's calendar. Elements of Lieutenant Colonel George A. Custer's Seventh Cavalry were rapidly approaching. For his soldiers, whose watches were set on Chicago time, it was about three o'clock. For the Lakota (or Sioux) and Cheyenne Indians, it was high noon.

Back in the village, the news caused havoc. Other women were caught unaware in the middle of their chores. Pretty White Buffalo, the Hunkpapa wife of Spotted Horn Bull, was preparing a buffalo meat stew for her bother and had no thoughts of a fight that day. The thirteen-year-old Oglala Lakota Black Elk was with some other boys, swimming and playing in the waters

Originally published in *Wild West* (June 1996): 52–58, 83–85. Reprinted by permission of Weider History Group.

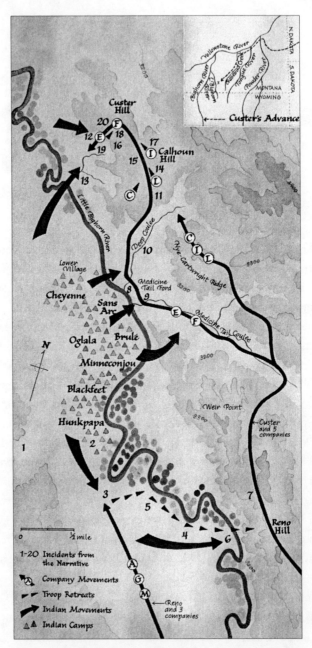

Events of the battle of the Little Bighorn, June 25–26, 1876.

The numbers in parentheses in the text correspond to the numbers on this map.

of the Greasy Grass, when he heard the criers run by with the news. Even the warriors, usually so alert, were caught unprepared. Eagle Elk, twenty-five-year-old nephew of the Oglala warrior Crazy Horse, had been out all night dancing. He was finally on his way home when he heard far-off shooting. The Minneconjou Lakota White Bull, already a famous warrior at twenty-six, was watering his horses north of the village. With a belly full of breakfast, he was about to settle into another long, lazy day when he heard the alarm. He jumped on his fastest horse, a bay mare, and drove the ponies back to camp. The forty-year-old Hunkpapa Rain in the Face was caught with a mouthful of food. "When I was eating my meat, we heard the war cry," Rain said. He dropped the meat and rushed to get ready for battle.

The story was nearly the same throughout the camp, which was on the west side of the river. The Cheyenne Wooden Leg was asleep under a cottonwood by the river. One Bull was in his tepee, combing his hair. Low Dog still slept in his lodge, as did Turtle Rib and Red Feather. Even after the shock wore off, Low Dog thought it was a false alarm. "I did not believe it possible," he declared, "that the whites would attack us, so strong as we were."

There was no trap. There was no preparation. Even in a broad daylight attack, Colonel Custer managed to surprise the Indians in their village.

The soldiers that first attacked were in a battalion commanded by Major Marcus A. Reno. That they caused much confusion in the upper village (the southern end of the Indians' camp [position 2 on the map]) is evident from the predicament of the great Hunkpapa medicine man Sitting Bull. He did not know whether to go out and fight, help rally the warriors, ride his mother to safety, or try to arrange a truce. Sitting Bull grabbed his rawhide shield and *pogamoggan,* a stone war club, and handed them to his nephew, One Bull. "Take my place and go out and meet the soldiers," he ordered. "Try and parley with them."

In the meantime, Sitting Bull's wife, Four Robes, was so frightened that she grabbed one of her infant twins and ran. When she got to the hills, she realized that she had left behind the other baby, a child who came to be known as Abandoned One. This was not the household of a leader who had set a trap for his enemies. Shortly after he sent One Bull out on his mission, Sitting Bull had his gray horse hit by two bullets. "Now my best horse is shot," he called out. "It is like they have shot me. Attack them!"

The warriors needed no further encouragement. Already they flanked the soldiers who had halted and dismounted in the valley south of the Hunkpapa camp. Moving Robe ran back to her lodge, only to be greeted with the news that her young brother Deeds had been killed in the initial charge. "Revenge!" she cried. She hurriedly braided her hair, painted her face crimson, and rushed to get her horse. "I was in mourning," she said. "I was a woman, but I was not afraid." As for One Bull, he found his mission abruptly terminated. When he raised his shield in a peace gesture, it served only to draw more fire. One Bull prayed, "Wakantanka, help me so I do not sin but fight my battle." But the outcome would be settled by bullets, not talk.

As the Indians increased the pressure, the bluecoats fell back and formed a line in the timber near the river, where they were harder to reach. The Indians took casualties. Three Bears and Hawkman went down near the Hunkpapa tepees. The Minneconjou Feather Earring, who got his name from the bright, knee-length plumage he wore at social gatherings, arrived at the fight early, but his brother Dog With Horns was cut down in front of Reno's men. Feather Earring dropped out of the fight to look for a place to hide his brother's body.

Riding next to One Bull, Good Bear Boy was badly wounded (3). One Bull tied a lariat around him and dragged him out of harm's way. When he tried to secure Good Bear Boy to his horse, the pony was hit. One Bull walked them both to the rear and became covered with the blood of Good Bear Boy and the pony. One Bull grimaced when he heard the scraping sounds of his friend's broken bones rubbing together.

There was a brief stalemate. A leader was needed to organize the assault into the timber. Out of the north, another party of warriors arrived, having ridden up from the village. As the teenagers Black Elk and Iron Hawk crept through the woods, they heard the warriors approach. From the distance came the shrill sound of eagle bone whistles. *"Hokahey!"* men began calling. "Crazy Horse is coming."

There was a great yell as Crazy Horse led the assault. But before the Indians could come to grips, the soldiers burst out of the woods, frenziedly spurring their mounts up the valley. Wooden Leg spun his horse around to flee but soon realized that the soldiers were galloping past him in fear. It was grand; the fight had turned into a buffalo chase. Wooden Leg heard the Lakotas calling out to the *wasichu* (white men): "You are only boys. You ought not to be fighting. You should have brought more Crow or Shoshone with you to do your fighting." Wooden Leg rode his pony up to a fleeing trooper and crashed the handle of his elkhorn whip onto the man's head, then seized his carbine and wrenched it from him (4). Finally, he had a good rifle.

One Bull also got back into the chase after dropping off Good Bear Boy. He managed to kill two soldiers on horseback as they fled up the valley. A Two Kettle Lakota named Runs The Enemy noticed a black man (the interpreter Isaiah Dorman) fall from his house as the soldiers ran from the woods. Eagle Elk rode by to see an Indian woman, whose name he thought was Her Eagle Robe, standing over the dark-skinned man, who was begging for his life (5). He heard her call out, "If you did not want to be killed, why did you not stay home where you belong and not come to attack us?"

The running battle continued, and the troops floundered in the river as they frantically made their way to temporary safety on the east bank. Many bluecoats were killed, yet the Indians, too, had suffered. Young Black Moon and Chased By Owls were dead, as were Swift Bear and White Buffalo, the two young brothers of the Hunkpapa leader Crow King.

An Indian woman moved away from the mutilated body of the black man. He had been shot in the knees, his skin stripped off, and his blood drained into a bucket, and an iron picket pin had been driven through his testicles. Years after the battle, Moving Robe stated, "I have not boasted of my conquests." But if she was the Indian woman seen hovering over the black man, she had certainly slaked her thirst for revenge for the death of her brother Deeds.

As the soldiers spilled across the river and up the bluffs, some Indians followed them while others remained in the valley to loot the bodies. Near the riverbank (6), One Bull met up with his uncle Sitting Bull. The medicine man saw blood all over One Bull and said, "Nephew, you are wounded. Go to the women and have your wounds treated." One Bull laughed and explained that the blood was from Good Bear Boy and his pony. He would go back, but first he would go to the hilltop to see whether the soldiers were really defeated. On the bluffs, One Bull received an unpleasant surprise. There were more troops coming from the south, leading pack trains. But worse, there were troops (Custer's five companies) to the north, already between the warriors and the lower village.

Other Indians on the bluffs also saw this new danger. "It looked as if there were thousands of them," Runs The Enemy said. "I thought we would surely be beaten." The Oglala Short Bull was on the bluffs exulting in victory when Crazy Horse rode up. "Too late! You've missed the fight!" Short Bull exclaimed. "Sorry to miss this fight," Crazy Horse said with a laugh. "But there's a good fight coming over the hill." He pointed north, and for the first time Short Bull saw the new threat (7). "I thought there were a million of them," Short Bull said. The Indians all turned their ponies around, leaving the one group of soldiers on what would become known as Reno Hill and heading toward the second group of soldiers. Custer had surprised the Indians not once but twice.

Down in the valley at the fringe of the timber, Black Elk stared at the body of a white soldier. An older warrior rode by and said, "Boy, get off and scalp him." Black Elk nervously slid off his pony's back. He had never done this before. He unsheathed his knife, knelt down, and began to cut. The wasichu squirmed and ground his teeth in pain. He was still alive! Black Elk swallowed hard, finished the cut, and popped off the hair. He raised it high but did not know whether to exult or feel sadness for the life he took. He rode back to his mother to show her his prize.

Indians still in the lower village also became aware of the second group of soldiers advancing on the other side of the river. The Oglala White Cow Bull was with his Cheyenne friends Roan Bear and Bobtail Horse as they stood near the lodge where Esevone, the sacred Buffalo Hat, was kept. They were guarding the tepee during the early action when Bobtail Horse saw more soldiers approaching from a high hill in the east. "They are coming this way!" he cried. "Across the ford! We must stop them!" The three rode toward a ford at the northern end of the village (8), where they met up with the Cheyenne Lame White Man. The latter, older and wiser in the ways of battle, urged caution. The soldiers were too many for them to fight, he said. Bobtail Horse replied, "Uncle, only the earth and Heavens last long. If we four can stop the soldiers from capturing our camp, our lives would be well spent."

The warriors were joined by White Shield, Calf, Two Eagles, He Dog, Eagle Elk, Yellow Nose, and others. They all rode across the river to the east bank. Among the first to charge into the approaching troopers was the Ute-Cheyenne Yellow Nose, closely followed by Contrary Belly and Comes In Sight. A color-bearer rode at Yellow Nose, his guidon poised like a spear. On the top of the flagstaff was a brass ferrule that Yellow Nose mistook for a rifle. With a nimble dodge and a quick lunge, Yellow Nose wrested the "rifle" from the trooper's hands. Then, with a shrill whoop, he held the captured guidon high for all to see (9).

The clash of arms forced the soldiers, who never made it to the river, back up the same high ridge they had come from. More Indians arrived after the repulse of Reno in the south. Crazy Horse was there with his followers, among them Flying Hawk, Fears Nothing, and Red Feather. As the Indians crossed the river in force and streamed up the gulches (10), the soldiers moved north.

In the village, a Cheyenne woman named Antelope ran up to her elder brother, the medicine man Ice. "Let me have a horse," she begged him. Her nephew (Ice's son), eighteen-year-old Noisy Walking, had already gone out to fight. Antelope had no sons of her own, so she felt she had to go out and encourage him by singing strongheart songs. Reluctantly, Ice agreed, and Antelope rode off for the river crossing.

As the soldiers moved downriver (north) along what became known as Nye-Cartwright Ridge and on to Calhoun Hill, the old Hunkpapa warrior Gall was still in the valley, unable to get into the fight. He had missed the Reno action when he went with Iron Cedar to the bluffs to check on the report of a second group of soldiers. He returned to the village to find it abandoned and his family missing. Gall went to find them. He met Sitting Bull and One Bull, who guarded the refugee women and children, but still he could not locate his family. Gall rode back to the village, where he finally found his two wives and children, dead. Killed by the wasichu. Gall grieved. He looked back to the hills where the bluecoats were still fighting his people. "It made my heart bad," he said. "After that I killed all my enemies with the hatchet." At last, Gall rode for the river crossing.

The soldiers spread out on a long, narrow ridge. On the southern end, the pursuing Indians were checked. They could not break the soldiers on the hill, said Runs The Enemy, so they rode north around the defenders' flank, looking for another approach. White Bull joined the charge on the position, but he, too, fell back. Eagle Elk saw an Indian walk dizzily to the rear, his jaw nearly shot off and blood dripping from his mouth. Red Feather's horse was shot from under him, and he had to continue to fight on foot. The Minneconjou Hump charged forward, with the "Hi-yi-yi," the shooting, and the thunder of the horses' hooves almost deafening. Bullets ripped the air, and Hump and his pony went down (11). Almost senseless, Hump examined his wound. A bullet had torn a path from his knee up his leg and out at the hip. He lay in the dirt and watched the strangely serene sky. The charge had failed.

Although the Indians had suffered a temporary setback, they had lost relatively few men, as yet. The fight settled into a long-range contest—for an hour or more, thought Wooden Leg. The Indians crept closer to the soldiers' positions and lofted high-arc arrows down onto the backs and heads of the wasichu and their horses, while the attackers remained in comparative safety behind hill and gully. Although the majority fought at long range, several braves dashed forward to wave blankets to spook the held cavalry horses. Frightened mounts stampeded. Two Minneconjou warriors, Standing Bear and Flying By, caught some horses as they ran toward the river. Eagle Elk managed to run down a bay and a sorrel. Near the soldiers on a hill in the north, Runs The Enemy and about thirty braves rode across the ridge, cut out a number of horses, and ran them to the river. While the horses drank their fill, Bobtail Horse rounded up two grays and drove them back to camp.

A stalemate occurred between the braves and the troopers holding the ridgeline. One company then rode down nearer to the river (12). Wooden Leg, creeping up through a deep ravine, was forced back by their sortie. Antelope saw the troop come down, dismount, and take up a new position. Red Horse saw the Indians fall back—but only temporarily. They stopped and turned, he said, "and the Sioux and the soldiers stood facing each other."

Now was the time. Perhaps stung by Bobtail Horse's earlier words about being overly cautious, Lame White Man rode forward (13). He raised his arm and called out for all to hear. "Come. We can kill all of them." Antelope, still in the area searching for her nephew, Noisy Walking, saw Lame White Man rally the Indians, as did an Arapaho named Waterman. The warriors followed Lame White Man back up the ravine. They struck the exposed troop and forced it to fall back to the hilltop. Many bluecoats fell, but so did many Indians. Red Horse and Wooden Leg said that this assault was the most costly of all that day. Riding through the soldiers, Lame White Man almost reached the ridgetop. Then a bullet knocked him to the ground.

To the east, on the other side of the ridge, White Bull engaged in bravery displays of his own. He rode directly into the surprised troops, circled beyond them, and with bullets kicking up dust all around, dashed back unscathed. He was having a grand time. "I thought I would do it again," White Bull declared. He rode up to Crazy Horse and dared the great Oglala to join him. "*Hokahey*, brother!" cried White Bull. "This life will not last forever!" When he sprang forward again, his reckless courage was infectious, and Crazy Horse and the other Lakota warriors swept forward with him (14).

Red Feather, He Dog, Two Moon, Lone Bear, and others joined in the charge. They cut the ridge in two. White Bull saw one soldier take a bullet and go down. He jumped off his pony, struck the man with his quirt, and grabbed the man's pistol and cartridges. On his horse again, White Bull saw a soldier on a played-out horse. He rushed up, grabbed the soldier by his blue coat, and jerked him off his horse. Again White Bull rode on, this time spying a trooper wielding his carbine. White Bull charged him. The soldier fired and missed, and White Bull struck him with a quirt. Three coups within a few minutes! Then his own pony went down. White Bull stood dazed in the midst of a chaotic battle raging around him.

The disintegration of the line along the three-quarter-mile ridge between Custer Hill and Calhoun Hill led to the collapse of the soldiers' position on Calhoun Hill. Yellow Nose, Contrary Belly, and Comes In Sight made bravery raids up the hill. Yellow Nose had taunted the soldiers three times without effect. Finally, he called out, "Let us charge," and the Indians mounted and followed him. As he rode through the fleeing troopers, Yellow Nose struck them left and right, making good use of his captured guidon. Here, Gall finally got into the action as the mass of warriors swirled up the hill, but the soldiers melted away before them. There was no one left to kill. If Gall got to hatchet anything, it was the flotsam left behind after the tide had swept on. In this battle, he led no one but himself.

Along the ridge (15), the fight degenerated into a second rout, much as during Reno's disorganized retreat from the valley. "It looked like a stampede of buffalo," said Runs The Enemy. The Cheyenne Little Hawk said that the Indians there "chased them like buffalo," as long as the soldiers had their backs toward their pursuers.

White Bull was still in the fight. After Bear Lice rode up and gave him a captured bay pony, White Bull was off. This time he saw a wounded trooper firing a revolver. White Bull circled around and rode down the man from the back side. Again he found another soldier, tall and blond, bluffing the Indians with a rifle. White Bull dove at him. They grabbed each other and fell to the ground, wrestling in the dirt. The soldier was very strong. He punched White Bull in the jaw, grabbed his opponent's long braids in his hands, and pulled their heads together. Then he tried to bite White Bull's nose off. "Hey, hey," White Bull called out. "Come over and help me!" Bear Lice and Crow Boy ran over, but they pummeled White Bull as much as his adversary. Finally, White Bull grabbed the man's revolver out of his hand and struck him with it two, three, four times. He stepped back and fired a bullet into the soldier's head (16). *"Ho hechetu!"* he said. "That was a fight, a hard fight. But it was a glorious battle, I enjoyed it. I was picking up head-feathers right and left that day."

The remaining soldiers ran north to the far end of the ridge, joining the remnants of the Gray Horse Company. They had nowhere else to run. Although these soldiers were cornered, a young Cheyenne named Big Beaver found that they were still dangerous. He crept up the northern knoll and stopped behind a war-bonneted Lakota who poked his head up above the sage-brush to fire. A soldier's bullet crashed square into the middle of the Lakota's forehead. Big Beaver squirmed back downhill toward safer pastures. He was making his way along the gully east of the ridge when he saw a lone soldier make a run for it. Two Cheyenne cut the trooper off, killed him, and left his hair dangling on a branch of sage like a grisly trophy. Big Beaver searched the dead man's pockets, then took his carbine (17). He held it up proudly and admired it. It was the first one he had ever had.

When the soldiers congregated on the hill that would become known as Custer Hill or Last Stand Hill, Two Moon called his followers together for another charge. The attack carried north along the ridge but was deflected by the soldiers' fire. "I could not break the line at the bunch of gray horses," Two Moon said. He wheeled left down the valley, with the soldiers firing as the warriors sped past (18). "The White Horse Troops fought with signal desperation," he declared. "If the others had not given up, but had fought with equal stubbornness . . . Custer would have driven the Indians from the field."

There they were, the last soldiers on the hilltop. They stood and fought well, said Gall, Wooden Leg, Brave Wolf, and Lone Bear. The most stubborn stand of the day was made on Custer Hill, declared Two Eagles. Red Hawk, too, said that it was on Custer Hill that "the soldiers made a desperate fight." Suddenly, in a last forlorn effort, the troopers released their remaining horses, possibly to draw the Indians away in a chase. Standing Bear saw them run, as did Little Hawk. Iron Hawk looked up when he heard the yell, "Now they are going," as the last of Company E's gray horses ran toward the river. But still, there were too many Indians to make the ruse work.

Moments after releasing the horses, several of the remaining troopers abandoned the hill. "Some of the soldiers broke through the Indians and ran for the ravine," said Red Hawk, "but all were killed without getting into it." The Oglala Fears Nothing saw them make a break through a narrow gap in the Indian line, but the warriors ran them down and killed them with war clubs (19). Rain in the Face saw some flee, while another group stayed together at the head of a little ravine, where they fought bravely before they were cut to pieces. Rain had always thought the white men were cowards, but this fight changed his mind. "I had great respect for them after this day," he said.

Standing Bear was directly in the path of the soldiers when they made their run. Enemies mixed together, but there were four or five braves for every soldier. One trooper tried to dodge past Standing Bear, but the Indian managed to crash his revolver onto the soldier's head, then shot him as he fell. Several other soldiers got by Standing Bear and dove into a draw, where they tried to hide in the tall grass. It was hopeless. The warriors converged on them.

Nearby was Iron Hawk, who, at age fourteen, was fighting in his first real battle. When a soldier ran directly at him, he nocked an arrow and stretched his bow to its fullest. The arrow tore right through the man's ribs, and Iron Hawk heard his piercing scream. More soldiers approached. Iron Hawk caught up to one. "These white men wanted it," he said. "They called for it, and I let them have it." He swung his bow like a club and struck the soldier crosswise over the shoulders. Iron Hawk hit him again and again, growling *"Hownh!"* like a bear every time he connected. Even after the bluecoat fell to the ground, Iron Hawk continued to beat him.

White Bull, as always, was in the thick of the action. Two fleeing troopers ran close by, and he drew a bead on one. Down he went, and White Bull ran forward to count another coup—his seventh of the day.

The soldiers had shot their bolt. The warriors closed in on the last of them on the hilltop—men too wounded, too exhausted, or too game to leave their comrades behind. The Brulé Lakota Hollow Horn Bear saw no one run. "They were all brave men," he said. The last fighting was at close quarters, where he was able to wield his war club. In the last rush, amid the chaos of arrows, bullets, dust, and smoke, Turtle Rib's nephew was killed on the hilltop. Nearby, Waterman killed his only soldier. Waterman rushed up and shot him but did not scalp him, he said, "because the Arapaho do not scalp a man with short hair, only long hair."

Runs The Enemy said that the soldiers and Indians were so mixed up, you could not tell one from the other. When the last one was killed, he said, "the smoke rolled up like a mountain above our heads, and the soldiers were piled one on top of another, dead." Wooden Leg compared the scene to what a thousand dogs might have looked like if they were mixed together in a fight. He came upon a big soldier with plump cheeks and a stubby black beard. Suddenly the man rose up on one elbow and frightened some Indians, since he appeared to come back from the dead. Another Lakota jumped forward and shot him through the head (20). "I think he must have been the last man killed in this great battle," said Wooden Leg.

The rattle of bullets subsided to an occasional scattered popping. Suddenly there were no more soldiers to fight. If a man called George Custer died on the field, no Indian knew of it. He was merely another dead, stripped wasichu, one out of many.

Black Elk returned to the scene. Inured to the suffering, a boy who had become a warrior in one day, he took out his bow and drove his last blunt arrow into a wounded man's forehead. Nearby, Black Elk's father and another man were so angry about the terrible wounding of the man's son that they went up to a white man and butchered him. He was plenty fat, said Black Elk, and "the meat looked so good that they felt like eating it."

Wooden Leg walked along the hill and discovered a soldier with enormous side whiskers (Lieutenant W. W. Cooke). "Here is a new kind of scalp," he said, as he skinned off the man's long, light-yellow muttonchops. When Wooden Leg moved downhill, he came upon the body of Lame White Man. The Southern Cheyenne had paid for his pride and courage with a bullet hole through his breast, several stab wounds, and a missing scalp. Evidently, Wooden Leg thought, Lame White Man had been mistaken for one of the soldiers' Indian scouts.

Antelope had given up on finding her nephew when she got word that he was in the deep ravine running down from Custer Hill. Her two-hour search was over. Noisy Walking had been shot and stabbed but was still clinging to life. He was carried back to the village. Later that night, Wooden Leg visited him. "You were very brave," said Wooden Leg. The powerful holy man, so strong in blessing and healing others, could do nothing for his only son. They all kept vigil, but late that night Noisy Walking died.

There was joy in the village after the battle, explained Pretty

White Buffalo, for a great victory had been won. Yet there was sorrow, too, for what wife, mother, or sister gives thought to victory when she finds her own family among the killed? The women, she said, "would not be comforted in knowing that their dead had gone to join the ghosts of the brave."

Too many had gone to the spirit land. As Moving Robe rode back to the village, she thought about her dead little brother. And she thought about the big fight, which she considered a hotly contested battle, not a massacre. Brave men who came to punish the Indians had been met by equally brave warriors, and the soldiers had been defeated. But it was all to no avail. Most of the Indian survivors surrendered within a year of the battle near the Greasy Grass. In the end, Moving Robe realized, the Indians had still lost.

12

T.R. Takes Charge

PAUL ANDREW HUTTON

President William McKinley, roused from a deep sleep by an aide at 2:00 A.M. on February 16, 1898, received terrible news. The battleship *Maine* had exploded in Havana harbor with heavy loss of life. McKinley, who had been gently ministering to the public's war fever for more than a year, was stricken. "The *Maine* blown up," he mumbled over and over to himself. "The *Maine* blown up!" He hated the thought of war to the core of his being. "I have been through one war," said the Civil War veteran. "I have seen the dead piled up, and I do not want to see another." This sentiment was shared by every member of his administration, save one.

As always, Assistant Secretary of the Navy Theodore Roosevelt was up early that morning and working in his office in the Navy Department on Sixteenth Street. "I would give anything if President McKinley would order the fleet to Havana tomorrow," "T.R." wrote to a friend. "This Cuban business ought to stop. The *Maine* was sunk by an act of dirty treachery on the part of the Spaniards, I believe; though we shall never find out definitely, and officially it will go down as an accident."

He was certainly correct about the latter. A naval board of inquiry concluded that the *Maine* had been destroyed by a submarine

---

Originally published in *American History* (August 1998): 30–38, 64–65. Reprinted by permission of Weider History Group.

mine of unknown origin. Predictably, Spain issued a report stating that the cause of the explosion had been internal. Americans who did not work in the White House or on Wall Street thought little of such formal deliberations. They only cared that 260 American sailors were dead, and they wanted a reckoning.

That day of reckoning was at hand, for the rusted, antiquated Spanish Empire had prolonged its existence for far too long. It was not the sinking of the *Maine,* not the rantings of the yellow press, not the jingoistic dreams of American imperialists that brought on the war of 1898—it was the incredible incompetence, myopic shortsightedness, and stunning brutality of the Spanish imperialists in Cuba that made conflict inevitable.

A string of cruel acts in Cuba had enraged Americans for more than a generation. In 1873, five years into a Cuban uprising, a Spanish warship captured the American steamer *Virginius* as it attempted to deliver guns, ammunition, and medical supplies to Cuban patriots. Four rebel leaders aboard the *Virginius* were subsequently shot and decapitated, and their heads were displayed on pikes. Captain Joseph Fry and forty-eight of his crewmen were summarily executed by firing squad. Spain reluctantly released the survivors of the *Virginius* and paid a small indemnity, but the bloody incident was not forgotten in the United States.

In April 1895, the cry of *"Cuba Libre!"* again resonated across the island. Spain responded to this latest revolt by sending General Valeriano Weyler y Nicolau to Cuba. Dubbed "Butcher Weyler" by the New York press, his scorched-earth policy devastated eastern Cuba and led to the deaths of thousands of civilians in concentration camps. The Spanish seemed intent on breaking the Cuban people in a desperate bid to continue the pretense of their position as a world power.

In America, President Grover Cleveland was stridently against intervention. He could take solace as he left office in March 1897 that his successor, William McKinley, held similar views. The business interests in the country adamantly opposed war, as did most of the leading men in Congress. When the Spanish government recalled Weyler and granted more autonomy to Cuba, it seemed that the crisis might pass.

Yet nothing could silence the Cuban cry for freedom. By 1897, Cuban rebels were even appearing nightly in "Buffalo Bill" Cody's Wild West extravaganza as part of his "Congress of Rough Riders of the World." The press exploited every Spanish atrocity, real or imagined, to full effect. The American people fumed with indignation over Cuba, idealizing the insurgents as soulmates of the American revolutionaries of 1776. Their slow-burning anger needed just a spark to explode in rightful wrath. The *Maine* was that spark. Poet Richard Hovey gave them their call—"Ye who remembered the Alamo, Remember the Maine!"—and as it became their byword, action became their creed.

War advocates had their man in the thirty-nine-year-old Roosevelt, who had worked hard for a year to improve the navy. As the days passed, he became nearly frantic over the administration's continuing inactivity. President McKinley, T.R. grumbled to a confidant, "has no more backbone than a chocolate eclair."

Roosevelt, although liked and respected by both McKinley and Secretary of the Navy John Long, found himself increasingly isolated within the administration and the Republican Party. The president would no longer see him, while Long simply humored him. Roosevelt found solace in his correspondence and talks with influential expansionists such as Senator Henry Cabot Lodge, naval officers Alfred Thayer Mahan and George Dewey, and, most important, army captain Leonard Wood.

Wood and Roosevelt had met the previous June, and their jingoistic sensibilities and mutual love of football and vigorous walks led to an instant and warm friendship. A New Englander, Wood was a Harvard graduate like Roosevelt, having received an M.D. in 1884. Bored with private practice, he had gone west,

hiring on as a contract surgeon with the army in Arizona and
winning high praise (and eventually earning the Congressional
Medal of Honor) for his heroic service during the campaign
against the Apache leader Geronimo. Promoted to captain and
assistant surgeon in the regular army in 1891, Wood was transferred to Washington, D.C., four years later.

In the nation's capital, Captain Wood was appointed assistant attending surgeon, giving him medical responsibility and
unlimited access to high-ranking military officers, the secretary
of war, and the president. He became close to President William
McKinley, who placed his faith in Wood's skill and compassion
in treating Mrs. McKinley, who suffered from epilepsy.

When Roosevelt came to Washington in the spring of 1897
as assistant secretary of the navy, he found himself somewhat in
awe of Captain Wood. "It was a pleasure to deal with a man of
high ideals," he wrote, "who scorned everything mean and base,
and who also possessed those robust and hardy qualities of body
and mind, for the lack of which no merely negative virtue can
ever atone." They were, in every way, kindred spirits.

McKinley made a last-ditch effort for peace, demanding
that Spain declare an armistice in Cuba as of April 1, 1898. The
Spanish government hesitated, then finally agreed to end the
fighting on the island and to submit the *Maine* question to ar-
bitration. Only the question of Cuban independence remained.
By then, however, it was too late. On April 11, 1898, McKinley
asked Congress to intervene on behalf of Cuba. On April 19,
the Senate and House of Representatives passed a joint resolution calling for American armed intervention to secure Cuban
independence, while disclaiming any designs on annexing the
island. On April 23, Spain declared war on the United States,
which reciprocated two days later.

McKinley called for 125,000 volunteers to augment the

28,000-man regular army. Young men from every section of the country rallied to his call. They were anxious to prove themselves equal to the task and worthy of their place as Americans. Among the first to volunteer was the man who had perhaps been the leading advocate for war—Theodore Roosevelt.

Everyone was astonished by this act. His wife, Edith, opposed it, as did his best friend, Henry Cabot Lodge. "Theodore Roosevelt," wrote diplomat John Hay, "has left the Navy where he had the chance of his life and has joined a cowboy regiment." Secretary Long also fretted over this act of recklessness but foresaw that the great risk was not without potential reward. "He has lost his head to this folly of deserting the post where he is of the most service and running off to ride a horse and, probably, brush mosquitoes from his neck on the Florida sands," Long confided to his diary, "and yet how absurd this will sound, if by some turn of fortune he should accomplish some great thing and strike a very high mark."

President McKinley twice attempted to change Roosevelt's mind, to no avail. "One of the commonest taunts directed at men like myself is that we are armchair and parlor jingoes who wish to see others do what we only advocate doing," declared Roosevelt. "I care very little for such a taunt, except as it affects my usefulness, but I cannot afford to disregard the fact that my power for good, whatever it may be, would be gone if I didn't try to live up to the doctrines I have tried to preach."

Included in McKinley's call for volunteers had been an appeal for three regiments "to be composed exclusively of frontiersmen possessing special qualifications as horsemen and marksmen." Secretary of War Russell A. Alger offered command of the first such regiment to the administration's only bona fide cowboy, Roosevelt, who had once operated a ranch in Dakota Territory. Roosevelt wisely declined because of his lack of military experience, suggesting that Leonard Wood be named colonel and that he go as second-in-command. Alger agreed.

The First U.S. Regiment of Volunteer Cavalry was to be recruited in the southwestern territories, with 340 men to be raised in New Mexico, 170 in Arizona, 80 in Oklahoma, and 170 from the Indian Territory. Within days of the sinking of the *Maine*, West Point graduate Alexander Brodie, a mining engineer from Prescott, Arizona, along with Phoenix journalist James McClintock and Prescott mayor William "Buckey" O'Neill, had already begun recruiting volunteers.

The first to formally enlist was O'Neill, a frontier legend at age thirty-eight and among the most popular men in Arizona Territory. Born in Ireland, he had gone to Arizona in 1879. He was working as a journalist for the *Tombstone Epitaph* at the time of the O.K. Corral gunfight and soon had his own reputation for gunplay as the hard-riding sheriff of Yavapai County. His nickname came from his passion for faro, or "bucking the tiger" in that frontier game. Dedicated to the cause of Arizona statehood, he was prepared for the greatest wager of his life. "Who would not gamble," he wrote to a friend, "for a new star in the flag?"

Brodie secured an appointment as senior regimental major, with O'Neill and McClintock as company commanders. On May 4, two hundred recruits were gathered in the Prescott plaza. Accompanied by Josephine, a rather ill-tempered young mountain lion given to the troops as a mascot by a local saloon owner, they boarded trains amidst much fanfare and set off for their San Antonio training station.

New Mexico governor Miguel Otero wasted no time in recruiting troops and a remarkable corps of officers. Captain William Llewellyn of Las Cruces had been a federal lawman in Dakota Territory, famed for destroying Doc Middleton's outlaw gang. Captain George Curry, the strapping former sheriff of Lincoln County, had known both Billy the Kid and Pat Garrett, while Captain Maximiliano Luna belonged to one of the most prominent Hispanic families in the territory.

The New Mexico recruits reached San Antonio on May 10, joining the troops from Arizona and 83 men from Oklahoma raised by Captain Robert Huston of Guthrie. A week later, 170 more men arrived from the Indian Territory—including full- or mixed-blood Cherokee, Choctaw, Chickasaw, Pawnee, and Creek Indians. Within days, they were augmented by a remarkable contingent of about 50 well-to-do easterners. These Ivy League friends of Roosevelt's included some of the best athletes and richest young men in America. The westerners initially viewed them with skepticism, and not a little contempt, but were soon won over.

"These men are the best men I have ever seen together," Colonel Wood wrote to his wife, "and will make the finest kind of soldiers." Cowboys and polo players, teamsters and yachtsmen, lawyers and day laborers, lawmen and outlaws, miners and football players, Indians and Indian fighters formed a strange amalgam that forecast, in Roosevelt's eyes, the new American century while harkening back to the old frontier. "Wherever they came from, and whatever their social position," he wrote, "[they] possessed in common the traits of hardihood and a thirst for adventure."

Roosevelt did not arrive in San Antonio until May 15. He had remained in Washington to secure weapons, uniforms, and supplies for the regiment. The press had already dubbed the unit "Roosevelt's Rough Riders"—a name T.R. did not relish, because of its obvious reference to Buffalo Bill's Wild West show—and the men were anxious to see their namesake lieutenant colonel. Many were at first unimpressed with his somewhat comical appearance, but that quickly changed. Lieutenant Tom Hall sized him up immediately: "He is nervous, energetic, virile. He may wear out some day, but he will never rust out."

Rumors abounded that Spanish admiral Pascual Cervera's

Atlantic fleet was headed for either Puerto Rico or Cuba. On May 29, Commodore Winfield Scott Schley's "Flying Squadron" found Cervera moored in the harbor at Santiago de Cuba and set up a blockade. That same Sunday morning, the Rough Riders—1,060 strong, with 1,258 horses and mules—began boarding Southern Pacific Railroad cars for the journey to Tampa, Florida, their jump-off point for Cuba. "In all the world there is not a regiment I would so soon belong to," Roosevelt wrote to the president. "We earnestly hope we will be put in Cuba with the very first troops; the sooner the better."

All was confusion in Tampa. Major General William Rufus Shafter, a Civil War veteran and former Indian fighter, was in command of the Fifth Army Corps. Weighing more than three hundred pounds and afflicted with various ailments that did little to sweeten a notoriously foul temperament, Shafter was totally unfit to lead an expeditionary force into the tropics. In charge of his cavalry was the diminutive Major General Joseph "Fighting Joe" Wheeler, famed Confederate cavalryman and current congressman from Alabama. Ten regular and two volunteer cavalry regiments would be under his command. Despite his age and seeming frailty, Wheeler was as energetic and bold as Shafter was slothlike and cautious. Brigadier Generals J. Ford Kent and Henry Lawton would command infantry divisions. In all, some seventeen thousand men were to embark for Cuba.

Shafter, under intense pressure from Washington to depart for Santiago, did not have the transports necessary to move his entire force. Shafter therefore ordered Wood to dismount his cavalry and to select eight out of his twelve companies for the invasion. Roosevelt and Brodie were selected to command the two squadrons in Cuba.

On June 14, after even more high command bungling and mismanagement, the 578-man Rough Rider contingent finally departed from Tampa Bay aboard the *Yucatan*. "We are just like amateurs at war," correspondent Richard Harding Davis noted acidly.

Amateurs or not, they were off to change the course of history. Colonel Wood noted "that this is the first great expedition our country has ever sent overseas and marks the commencement of a new era in our relations with the world." For the men, however, there was little thought of world politics, just much card playing and even an occasional chorus of the Rough Riders' adopted theme song—"There'll Be a Hot Time in the Old Town Tonight."

Roosevelt, who often shared the ship's railing with Buckey O'Neill, was surprised to find that the two-gun Arizona lawman was also "a visionary, an articulate emotionalist." Under the starlit sky, they contemplated the odds against them, with O'Neill expressing a soaring ambition tempered by a dark fatalism. "He had taken so many chances when death lay on the hazard," T.R. noted, "that he felt the odds now were against him." Some years before, O'Neill had written a short story containing an eerily prescient passage: "Death was the black horse that came some day into every man's camp, and no matter when that day came a brave man should be booted and spurred and ready to ride him out."

The soldiers reached their destination near Santiago, Cuba, in five days; General Shafter, after conferring with Admiral William Sampson and Cuban rebel leader Calixto Garcia, decided to land his troops at Daiquiri and then march inland to Siboney and finally Santiago. Daiquiri was supposedly undefended, with a broad beach and even an old wooden pier built by an American iron company years before. On June 22, the troops began to land. They were fortunate to face no opposition, yet the landing was a fiasco. Because there was no transport for the horses and mules, they were lowered by sling into the water and released, or simply pushed off the ships into the sea to swim ashore. Mercifully, by afternoon the Rough Riders were all ashore, although the landings continued into the night.

Shafter promptly ordered General Lawton to occupy Siboney with his infantry division and Wheeler's dismounted cavalry. Just after dusk on June 23, Wood and Roosevelt entered Siboney. They found Joe Wheeler ("a regular gamecock," as T.R. characterized him) anxious to conduct an armed reconnaissance toward Santiago in hopes of finding the Spanish rear guard. Cuban rebels had spotted enemy troops entrenched a few miles to the north at Las Guasimás.

Wheeler moved out at dawn on the 24th with more than nine hundred men, including all eight Rough Rider companies and four hundred men from the regular First and Tenth regiments. The Cubans estimated the Spanish force ahead at six hundred, but it proved to be three times that number. Moving across unfamiliar terrain against a force of unknown size was dangerous work for seasoned regulars, much less untested volunteers. Wheeler led his regulars down the main road while the Rough Riders traversed a narrow trail to the left. The heat was oppressive in the thick and tangled jungle.

Some three miles from Siboney, a group of Rough Riders led by Captain Allyn Capron and Sergeant Hamilton Fish made contact with the still-unseen enemy. As the bullets of the Spaniards' Mauser rifles whined about them, Capron's men fanned out, briskly returning fire with their .30-caliber Krag-Jorgensen carbines. Wood and Roosevelt had wisely procured these guns for the unit as replacements for the older, black powder Springfield rifles that other volunteers had received. The Rough Rider commanders hurried their men forward, deploying them on both sides of the trail.

Cherokee Rough Rider Tom Isbell drew first blood for the Americans, dropping a Spanish sniper just as he received the first of seven wounds—which he somehow survived. Sergeant Fish and Private Ed Culver were also hit at almost the same time. Fish asked Culver, "You all right?" then slumped over, dead. Captain Capron rushed forward to Fish's body, killing two Spaniards as he advanced before being mortally wounded himself.

Wood calmly led his men forward, taking cover and firing and then advancing again. The Spanish, still well hidden in the jungle, began to melt away before the pressure. Caught up in the excitement of the moment, newspaper correspondent Edward Marshall joined in the combat. The deadly humming of the 7 mm Mauser slugs filled the air, like "a nasty, malicious little noise," wrote Marshall. Within moments, he was wounded by a bullet near his spine. Adjutant Tom Hall, witnessing this from afar, mistook Marshall for Wood and fled to the rear, where he reported the colonel dead and the Rough Riders routed. He was later allowed to quietly resign.

Major Brodie was hit in the arm and went down. Six foot, six Color Sergeant Albert Wright was grazed three times. Captain James McClintock took a bullet in the leg and also fell. Still the Rough Riders advanced, with Roosevelt taking command of Brodie's squadron as well as his own. O'Neill's volunteers joined up with a unit of regulars, and the Spanish began to pull back. With a whoop, Captain Robert Huston's troops opened fire on a group of panic-stricken, fleeing Spaniards. "Don't shoot at re-treating men," Wood angrily shouted. He ordered the men forward to occupy a deserted, ramshackle building. Black troopers of the Ninth Cavalry moved up to reinforce the Rough Riders, but the battle was over.

Roosevelt walked the corpse-littered field with Buckey O'Neill. The Rough Riders had lost eight killed and thirty-one wounded. "Colonel," O'Neill asked, "isn't it Whitman who said of the vultures that 'they pluck the eyes of princes and tear the flesh of kings?'" Roosevelt, still a bit stunned by the scene, could not recall but later remembered it to be Ezekial: "Ye shall eat the flesh of the mighty and drink the blood of the princes of the earth."

Generals Shafter and Lawton were angry with Wheeler for bringing on an engagement—or walking into an ambush, as many of the regular officers thought. Ambush or not, the Rough Riders had fought their way through, driving a superior force of entrenched infantry from a vital strategic point on the road to Santiago. For six days, Shafter kept his men encamped along that road while more supplies and troops came ashore and the road up from the beach was improved.

Already men were dropping in great numbers with fevers; General Wheeler was among them. Brigadier General Samuel Sumner took temporary command of the cavalry, with Wood taking over the second brigade. Roosevelt became colonel of the Rough Riders. Shafter, himself ill, needed to act quickly before sickness further reduced his army.

From El Pozo, a commanding hill about five miles east of Santiago, Shafter could easily see the Spanish entrenchments on the San Juan Heights, about a mile and a half away and rising some 125 feet above the valley. A blockhouse stood on the highest of these crests—San Juan Hill—while to its right lay another hill topped with ranch buildings and several old sugar cane cauldrons. It was promptly dubbed Kettle Hill. Between the two heights was a small valley with a pond. Roughly four miles to the north was the Spanish strongpoint of El Caney. Between El Pozo and the San Juan Heights flowed the San Juan River.

Shafter decided to attack on July 1. General Lawton's Second Infantry Division would assault El Caney. Following Lawton's success, a force of roughly eight thousand men was to charge the San Juan Heights. Shafter had apparently learned little since the Civil War, when it took a good soldier at least twenty seconds to load and fire his single-shot rifled musket. The entrenched

Spaniards could fire eight shots from their 7 mm Mausers in the same amount of time. If Major General Arsenio Linares y Pombo's units had any automatic weapons, the American frontal assault would turn into a bloodbath.

Roosevelt, whose contempt for Shafter was growing by the minute, was astonished at the vagueness of the general's orders. "No reconnaissance had been made," he grumbled, "and the exact position and strength of the Spaniards were not known." Astride his horse, Little Texas, Roosevelt led the Rough Riders forward late on the afternoon of June 30 onto the increasingly congested trail leading to El Pozo. The heat, as always, was intense, so he had cast off his jacket in favor of a dark blue shirt, khaki pants, and a polka-dot bandanna around his neck. A similar bandanna floated from his crumpled campaign hat much like a knight's plume. He carried a pistol retrieved from the *Maine* on his hip. Four hours later, he halted to encamp for the long, sleepless night before the battle.

At 8:00 A.M. on Friday, July 1, 1898, Captain George Grimes's battery opened fire on the San Juan Heights. For nearly an hour, he dueled with the Spanish artillery. Enemy fire killed one Rough Rider, wounded four others, and brought down Wood's horse. Shrapnel grazed Roosevelt's wrist. Shafter finally ordered the cavalry to ford the San Juan River, moving to the right in hopes of meeting up with Lawton. Lawton, however, was having a hard time of it at El Caney, where five hundred tenacious Spaniards were putting up a brave defense. Roosevelt got his men across the river and within an hour had them positioned along a sunken trail to the left of Kettle Hill. Spanish sniper fire was as intense as the suffocating heat, however, and the men were quickly pinned down. Volleys came at regular intervals from the Spanish entrenchments just a few hundred yards away.

Quickly recognizing his position as untenable, Roosevelt turned to his orderly, Harvard man William Saunders, only to find Saunders stretched in the grass, near death from heat prostration. Roosevelt called to another private, ordering him back up the trail to ask the first general officer he found for permission to charge. As the trooper saluted, a bullet struck his throat and he fell dead into Roosevelt's arms.

Not far away, Buckey O'Neill was strolling along the line, smoking a cigarette and ignoring the hail of bullets. His prone men kept begging him to get down, but he laughingly refused, declaring at one point that "the Spanish bullet isn't made that will kill me." Moments later, a bullet drove through his mouth and out the back of his head. Roosevelt was devastated, believing O'Neill's death to be the "most serious loss that I or the regiment could have suffered."

An officer suddenly galloped up, breathlessly ordering Roosevelt to support the regulars in their assault on the hills. Instantly mounting Little Texas, Roosevelt galloped up and down shouting orders to his officers and cheering on the men. They needed no encouragement. William Pollock, a Pawnee artist from Guthrie, gave out a chilling war whoop, and soon all the men were shouting and rushing forward.

As they advanced into the tall grass, the adrenaline-charged troops came upon the position of the Ninth Cavalry. Captain Henry Barber was holding his men in position, for he had no orders to advance. "Then let my men through, sir!" demanded Roosevelt. He led them on, and the black troopers of the Ninth joined the charge, orders or not. Two Ninth cavalrymen tore down a wire fence in their path, and Roosevelt galloped forward, waving his hat and yelling "Charge!"

The whole line surged forward, as the men of the regular cavalry regiments—the First, Third, Sixth, and Tenth—rushed Kettle Hill alongside the Ninth Cavalry and the Rough Riders. Lieutenant John J. Pershing of the Tenth—whose service with black troops earned him the nickname "Blackjack"—remembered that charge as a moment of unification: "White regiments, black regiments, Regulars and Rough Riders, representing the young manhood of the North and South, fought shoulder to shoulder, unmindful of race or color . . . mindful only of their common duty as Americans."

Atop El Pozo, an assortment of officers, foreign observers, and journalists watched in amazement. The foreigners were as one in condemning the folly of the charge. "It is gallant, but very foolish," said one officer. Melancholy *New York World* reporter Stephen Crane was lost in the glory of it all. "Yes, they were going up the hill, up the hill," Crane wrote. "It was the best moment of anybody's life."

It was certainly the best moment of Colonel Theodore Roosevelt's life. He was the only man on horseback, but his life seemed charmed. "No one who saw Roosevelt take that ride expected him to finish it alive," wrote correspondent Richard Harding Davis. "He wore on his sombrero a blue polka-dot handkerchief, *á la* Havelock, which, as he advanced, floated out straight behind his head, like a guidon." Like Crane, Davis was overcome by the sheer emotion of the charge. "Roosevelt, mounted high on horseback, and charging the rifle-pits at a gallop and quite alone, made you feel that you would like to cheer," he declared.

Forty yards from the summit, a wire fence stopped Little Texas. Roosevelt dismounted and with his new orderly, Arizona miner Henry Bardshar, jumped the fence and blazed away at the Spanish troops above them. Bardshar killed two Spaniards directly in front of them. Other Rough Riders crowded forward, firing their Krags and taking cover behind the huge sugar cauldrons near the summit. New Mexico troopers planted their guidons on the summit as the defenders fled.

From Kettle Hill, Roosevelt could see General Jacob Kent's First Infantry Division moving painfully up San Juan Hill. At the same time, the Rough Riders came under both artillery and volley fire. Suddenly, they heard a drumming sound and a cry went up that the Spaniards had machine guns. Roosevelt, however, recognized the sound. "It's the Gatlings, men, our Gatlings!" he exclaimed. The troops cheered as Lieutenant John Parker's battery of rapid-fire Gatling guns raked the Spanish trenches on San Juan Hill.

With the enemy pinned down, now was the time to act. Roosevelt impetuously rushed forward, leaping a wire fence and heading toward San Juan Hill to support the infantry. Suddenly he realized that he had only five men with him, and within moments two of them were hit. Leaving his surviving comrades behind, he angrily backtracked to the crest of Kettle Hill. "We didn't hear you!" the Rough Riders exclaimed sheepishly. "We didn't see you go. Lead on. We'll follow." And off they went.

They rapidly crossed the little valley, splashing through the pond and up the hill toward the Spanish trenches. Roosevelt and Bardshar were in the lead when two Spaniards jumped up and fired directly at them. Roosevelt returned fire, killing one of them. The enemy was in full retreat as Roosevelt's men overran the trenches and pushed over the crest of San Juan Hill. Suddenly they found themselves overlooking the city of Santiago. As Roosevelt and his exhausted men stood there, a staff officer came up, ordering a halt. The men were to entrench and hold the ridge at all costs. Roosevelt found that he had but 339 men still fit for service.

Shafter, far to the rear, was characteristically unsure of the outcome. He had lost more than 220 men killed and 1,000 wounded since daybreak and actually contemplated retreating from the exposed San Juan Heights. Little did he realize how fortunate he had been that General Linares had committed but 1,200 men to defend the Spanish positions. Roosevelt was simply disgusted with his commander. "Not since the campaign of Crassus against the Parthians has there been so criminally incompetent a general as Shafter," he wrote to his friend Lodge. "The battle simply fought itself."

Two days after the battle, Admiral Cervera's small squadron challenged the American fleet under Commodore Schley and Admiral William T. Sampson and was promptly wiped out. Santiago then surrendered to General Shafter on July 17. On August 12, the humiliated Spaniards agreed to an armistice that secured the freedom of Cuba and transferred Puerto Rico, Guam, and the Philippines to the United States. The Spanish-American War was over.

Soon after the battle of July 1, Theodore Roosevelt posed with his Rough Riders atop the crest of San Juan Hill. Volunteers and regulars—Hispanic Americans, Native Americans, African Americans, and Anglo-Americans—stared grimly yet proudly at the camera. They did not yet know it, but on that bloody hillside they had not only helped liberate Cuba but also had moved to heal their own country's sectional wounds and made their nation into a world power. Roosevelt had led them, as he soon would the whole nation, into the new century. San Juan Hill was a moment of momentous transition—for the world would never be the same again.

Note

1. See Michael Haydock, "This Means War," *American History* (January–February 1998): 42–50, 62–63.

Western Heritage
Magazine Article Award Winners
1961–2010

1961   "The Old Chisholm Trail," by W. Bruce Bell,
Kiwanis Magazine

1962   "The Look of the Last Frontier," by Mari Sandoz,
American Heritage

1963   "The Prairie Schooner Got Them There," by George R. Stewart,
American Heritage

1964   "Nine Years among the Indians," by Herman Lehmann,
Frontier Times

1965   "Titans of Western Art," by J. Frank Dobie,
The American Scene

1966   "How Lost Was Zebulon Pike," by Donald Dean Jackson,
American Heritage

1967   "The Red Man's Last Struggle," by Jack Guinn,
Empire Magazine, Denver Post

1968   "The Snows of Rimrock Ridge," by Carolyn Woirhaye,
The Farm Quarterly

1969   "W. R. Leigh: The Artist's Studio Collection,"
by Donnie D. Good, *The American Scene*

1970   "Bennett Howell's Cow Country," by May Howell Dobson,
Frontier Times

1971   "Cattle, Guns and Cowboys," by James Edsall Serven,
Arizona Highways

1972   "Echoes of the Little Big Horn," by David Humphreys Miller,
        American Heritage

1973   "Horses of the West," by James Edsall Serven,
        Arizona Highways

1974   "40 Years Gatherins," by Spike Van Cleve,
        The Dude Rancher

1975   "George Humphreys, Half Century with 6666,"
        by James R. Jennings, *Quarter Horse Journal*

1976   "The Pioneer Woman: Image in Bronze," by Patricia Janis Broder,
        American Art Review

1977   No award given

1978   "Where the Cowboys Hunkered Down," by John L. Sinclair,
        New Mexico Magazine

1979   "The Farther Continent of James Clyman," by Richard Rhodes,
        American Heritage

1980   "Glory Days in Medora," text by David McCullough,
        photographs by Tomas Sennett, *GEO Magazine*

1981   "The Last Empire," by William Broyles, Jr.,
        Texas Monthly

1982   "Buffalo Bill and the Enduring West," by Alice J. Hall,
        National Geographic

1983   "Saga of an American Ranch," by Patricia Nell Warren,
        Reader's Digest

1984   "Eight Decades a Cowboy," by Tom Blasingame,
        The Quarter Horse Journal

1985   "Showdown at Hollywood Park," by Max Evans,
        Southern Horseman Magazine

1986   "Santa Rita del Cobre," by John L. Sinclair,
        New Mexico Magazine

1987   "The Remodeling of Geronimo," by C. L. Sonnichsen,
        Arizona Highways

1988   "Fairs, Expositions, and the Changing Image of Southwestern
        Indians, 1876–1904," by Robert A. Trennert,
        New Mexico Historical Review

1989   "Blizzard," by E. N. Coons, *American Heritage*

1990   "Powder River Country: The Movies, the Wars,
        and the Teapot Dome," by Oakley Hall,
        American Heritage

1991   "Yellowstone Kelly," by Jerry Keenan,
        Montana The Magazine of Western History

1992   "Strange and Benevolent Monsters," by Kathryn Marshall,
        American Way Magazine

1993   "Western Art Museums: A Question of Style or Content,"
        by Peter H. Hassrick,
        Montana The Magazine of Western History

1994   "Charlie's Hidden Agenda: Realism and Nostalgia in
        C. M. Russell's Stories about Indians," by Raphael Cristy,
        Montana The Magazine of Western History

1995   "The Twilight of the Texas Rangers," by Robert Draper,
        Texas Monthly

1996   "Showdown at the Hollywood Corral:
        Wyatt Earp and the Movies," by Paul Andrew Hutton,
        Montana The Magazine of Western History

1997   "Lakota Noon at the Greasy Grass," by Greg Michno,
        Wild West

1998   "When the Buffalo Roamed," by Dan Flores,
        Wild West

1999   "T.R. Takes Charge," by Paul Andrew Hutton,
        American History

2000   "Halloween Hermit," by Lou Dean, *Guideposts*

2001   "The Gillette Brothers," by Renee Kientz, *Houston Chronicle*

2002 "What Happened at Mountain Meadows?" by Sally Denton, *American Heritage*

2003 "Tales of the Texas Rangers," by Robert M. Utley, *American Heritage*

2004 "The Water Crisis Continues," by Paul A. Canada, *The Paint Horse Journal*

2005 "'It Was but a Small Affair': The Battle of the Alamo," by Paul Andrew Hutton, *Wild West*

2006 "Tragedy at Red Cloud Agency: The Surrender, Confinement, and Death of Crazy Horse," by Jeffrey V. Pearson, *Montana The Magazine of Western History*

2007 "Six Days Ablaze," by John R. Erickson, *American Cowboy*

2008 "Silver Screen Desperado: Billy the Kid in the Movies," by Paul Andrew Hutton, *New Mexico Historical Review*

2009 "Bringing Home All the Pretty Horses: The Horse Trade in the Early American West, 1775–1825," by Dan Flores, *Montana The Magazine of Western History*

2010 "My Heart Now Has Become Changed to Softer Feelings: A Northern Cheyenne Woman and Her Family Remember the Long Journey Home," by John H. Monnett, *Montana The Magazine of Western History*

About the Authors

William Broyles, Jr., a native Texan who graduated from Rice University before earning an M.A. from Oxford in 1968, served as the first editor of *Texas Monthly* magazine in 1972. The success of *Texas Monthly* led Broyles to a stint as editor of *Newsweek* from 1982 until 1984, when he turned his attention to television, creating the critically acclaimed series *China Beach* in 1998 and scripting the miniseries *J.F.K.: Reckless Youth* in 1993. He was soon writing feature films for Ron Howard, and with the commercial and critical success of *Apollo 13* (1993) and *Cast Away* (2000), he achieved an enviable reputation as a top Hollywood screenwriter. Films such as *Planet of the Apes* (2001), *Unfaithful* (2002), and *The Polar Express* (2004) followed. A decorated Vietnam War veteran, Broyles also authored the classic *Brothers in Arms: A Journey from War to Peace* in 1984. He lives in Santa Fe.

Raphael Cristy received a bachelor's degree in literature from Stanford University, an M.A. in history from the University of Montana, and a Ph.D. in history from the University of New Mexico. He is widely known for his one-man show "Charlie Russell's Yarns," which he has performed at numerous venues including the Northern Appalachian Storytelling Festival, the Elko Cowboy Poetry Gathering, Michael Martin Murphey's WESTFEST, and Australia's Festival of Sydney. He is the author of *Charles M. Russell: The Storyteller's Art* (2004). He lives in Albuquerque.

Sally Denton, born and raised in Nevada, is one of America's most noted investigative journalists. She has been a Guggenheim Fellow, a Woodrow Wilson Scholar, and a Hoover Institute Media Fellow. Her early best-selling works were investigative exposés such as *The Bluegrass Conspiracy* (2001) and (with Roger Morris) *The Money and the Power: The Making of Las Vegas and Its Hold on America* (2002), but her love of western history led her to write *American Massacre: The Tragedy at Mountain Meadows, September 1857* (2004), *Faith and Betrayal: A Pioneer Woman's Passage in the American West* (2006), and *Passion and Principle: John and Jessie Frémont* (2007). A two-time winner of the Wrangler Award, she now makes her home in Santa Fe.

Dan Flores, who holds the A. B. Hammond Chair at the University of Montana, is one of America's premier environmental historians. He has authored eight books, most recently *Horizontal Yellow: Nature and History in the Near Southwest* (1999), *The Natural West* (2001), and *Visions of the Big Sky: Painting and Photography in the Northern Rocky Mountain West* (2010). He has won numerous honors, including the Ray Allen Billington Award from the Western History Association as well as two Wrangler Awards. He lives in Montana's Bitterroot Valley.

Oakley Hall, who died in 2008 at age eighty-seven, was a novelist best remembered for his historical westerns. His Wyatt Earp–inspired novel *Warlock* (1958) was a finalist for the Pulitzer Prize and was adapted by Edward Dmytryk into a cult-classic film starring Henry Fonda and Richard Widmark. Hall's 1963 novel, *The Downhill Racers,* was made into a 1969 film starring Robert Redford. Other noted westerns included *The Bad Lands* (1978),

The Coming of the Kid (1985), and *Apaches* (1986). Hall directed the writing program at the University of California, Irvine, for nearly twenty years.

Paul Andrew Hutton is Distinguished Professor of American History at the University of New Mexico and Executive Director of the Western Writers of America. He is the author or editor of nine books, including the prize-winning *Phil Sheridan and His Army*. He is a frequent on-air commentator for television programs on the History Channel, A&E, PBS, and other networks and is the author of a dozen documentaries. From 2002 to 2004, he served as President of the Western Writers of America. Among his numerous writing awards are the Evans Biography Prize, the Billington Prize from the Organization of American Historians, four Spur Awards from the Western Writers of America, and six Wrangler Awards from the National Cowboy & Western Heritage Museum.

Gregory Michno, a Michigan native and a graduate of Michigan State University, received his M.A. in history from the University of Northern Colorado. A prolific author, he is a noted expert on both World War II and the American West. Among his numerous publications are *Lakota Noon: The Indian Narrative of Custer's Defeat* (1977), *USS* Pampanito: *Killer-Angel* (2000), *Encyclopedia of Indian Wars: Western Battles and Skirmishes, 1850–1890* (2003), *Battle at Sand Creek: The Military Perspective* (2004), and *The Mystery of E Troop: Custer's Gray Horse Company at the Little Bighorn* (2009). He lives in Longmont, Colorado, with his wife, Susan, who has co-authored several books with him.

Jeffrey Pearson, a native Hoosier who received his bachelor's from Indiana University, earned his doctorate in history from the University of New Mexico, where he focused on early America and the U.S. West. He is especially interested in the history of westward expansion, the frontier army, and the nineteenth-century Indian Wars. Among his other publications are "Nelson A. Miles, Crazy Horse, and the Battle of Wolf Mountains" (*Montana The Magazine of Western History*, 2001), which won the Burlingame-Toole Award from the Montana Historical Society, and "Philip St. George Cooke" (in *Soldiers West: Biographies from the Military Frontier*, edited by Paul Andrew Hutton and Durwood Ball, 2009). From 2008 to 2010, he taught history at Texas A&M University–Commerce. He currently lives in Dallas, Texas.

C. L. (Charles Leland) Sonnichsen, who died in 1991 at age ninety, was a titan of American letters. After receiving his bachelor's from the University of Minnesota in 1924, he went on to earn a doctorate in English literature from Harvard in 1931. He spent his entire academic career at the Texas College of Mines and Metallurgy (later renamed University of Texas, El Paso), rising from Associate Professor to Dean of the graduate school before retiring in 1972. He then moved to Tucson, where he edited the *Journal of Arizona History* for five years. In El Paso he became fascinated with the folklore, history, and literature of the Southwest, embarking on a writing career that produced such classics as *Billy King's Tombstone: The Private Life of an Arizona Boom Town* (1942), *Roy Bean: Law West of the Pecos* (1943), *I'll Die before I'll Run: The Story of the Great Feuds of Texas* (1951), *Ten Texas Feuds* (1957), *The Mescalero Apaches* (1958), and *From Hopalong to Hud: Thoughts on Western Fiction* (1978). He served as President of the Western Writers of America, the Texas Folklore Society, the Western Literature Association, and the Western History Association. Both the WWA and the WHA honored him with a lifetime achievement award. He also received the Bowdoin Prize from Harvard University, as well as a WWA Spur Award and two Wrangler Awards.

Robert M. Utley, the author of eighteen books, is the leading western historian of the past quarter century. A former Chief Historian for the National Park Service, he received back-to-back Wrangler Awards for his books *High Noon in Lincoln: Violence on the Western Frontier* (1987) and *Cavalier in Buckskin: George Armstrong Custer and the Western Military Frontier* (1988), as well as the Western History Association Caughey Prize and a Western Writers of America Spur Award for *The Lance and the Shield: The Life and Times of Sitting Bull* (1993). Among his other important publications are *The Last Days of the Sioux Nation* (1963), *Frontier Regulars* (1973), *The Indian Frontier of the American West, 1846–1890* (1984), *Billy the Kid: A Short and Violent Life* (1989), *A Life Wild and Perilous: Mountain Men and the Paths to the Pacific* (1997), and his two-volume history of the Texas Rangers, *Lone Star Justice* (2002) and *Lone Star Lawmen* (2007). The latter won him a second WWA Spur Award. His memoir, *Custer and Me: A Historian's Memoir,* was published in 2004. He now lives in Scottsdale, Arizona, with his historian wife, Melody Webb.

CPSIA information can be obtained at www.ICGtesting.com
Printed in the USA
LVOW080040210112

264932LV00001BA/2/P